The Background to the Novels

MARGARET TILLETT

London

OXFORD UNIVERSITY PRESS

NEW YORK   TORONTO

1971

Oxford University Press, Ely House, London W.1

GLASGOW NEW YORK TORONTO MELBOURNE WELLINGTON
CAPE TOWN SALISBURY IBADAN NAIROBI DAR ES SALAAM LUSAKA ADDIS ABABA
BOMBAY CALCUTTA MADRAS KARACHI LAHORE DACCA
KUALA LUMPUR SINGAPORE HONG KONG TOKYO

SBN 19 212549 4

Printed in Great Britain by
Hazell Watson & Viney Ltd, Aylesbury, Bucks

Contents

Introduction

Henri Beyle, who did not become Stendhal until 1817, when he was thirty-four, lived constantly with a poignant sense of the swift passing of time. His ambition to become the greatest writer of comedies since Molière remained unfulfilled; he published nothing until he was over thirty, and no work of fiction until past forty; but the journal, letters, notes, essays, and commentaries on his reading that he wrote during his youth contain many anticipations of future fame. They, and his later published travel journals and autobiographical works, are full of dates, those of the Revolutionary calendar giving place to the traditional ones of later regimes; he recorded not only years and months, but often days of the week and hours of the day. Born in the late eighteenth century, and hardly acquainted with the nineteenth, he was already looking ahead to the twentieth, and continued to believe that this was the one when his works would be appreciated. Like his Julien Sorel who, having just joined his regiment as a lieutenant, was already calculating the course of action necessary for becoming Commander-in-Chief at thirty,[1] Henri Beyle in his youth had in mind precise dates in the future at which certain literary triumphs must be achieved. But his conviction that he must write for the twentieth century may also be associated with a marginal note dated 'Ier avril 1823', in a copy of *Lettres persanes;* on a reference in Letter 34 to 'les sentiments de la vertu, que l'on tient de la Nature', he comments 'Bêtise', and elaborates: 'Je n'ai pas l'erreur de ce grand homme, donc je suis plus sage que lui. Pas du tout. Mon siècle est plus sage que le sien. Voyons si je suis supérieur aux préjugés de mon siècle.'[2] The remark is typical of him, displaying as it does an impatient and impulsive first reaction, followed by reflection, a movement towards generosity and common sense, and a note of self-deprecation.

The influence of Montesquieu upon him was considerable. He

---

1. *Le Rouge et le Noir*, ch. 35, vol. ii.
2. *Mélanges intimes et Marginalia*, vol. ii, p. 154. (See bibliography.)

first read *De l'Esprit des Lois* in 1803. The lively and humane intelligence in the work, the skill with which Montesquieu leads the reader to formulate in his mind an urgent question to which the answer is indefinitely delayed, the teasing irony and dry humour —all these decisively influenced Stendhal's manner of thought and expression. In his chapter 'Du droit de conquête', (Book 10, Chapter 3) Montesquieu stresses the advances made by his own times over those of the Romans: 'Il faut rendre ici hommage à nos temps modernes, à leur raison présente, à la religion d'aujourd'hui, à notre philosophie, à nos moeurs.' Stendhal, following this, is optimistically convinced of the constant progress of society, and looks to the future for greater political maturity, and for more enlightened readers. His appreciation of the advances achieved in his own times did not prevent his being bitterly critical of them. He expected our century to be wiser than his own. Since hypocrisy, cant, and affectation were what he constantly attacked in the nineteenth century, he hoped perhaps that the spread of education and political sophistication would make the generations of the future wiser than his own just as his generation was, in his opinion, wiser than Montesquieu's. Certainly he made no concessions to the literary fashions of his times—his irony gives sharp edges to Romantic vocabulary—and he was in any case appreciated as a travel-writer and journalist rather than for the works which are now famous. And there is no doubt that he was right to look forward to the twentieth century, for his works are probably valued more now than at any time since he wrote them. His nineteenth-century heroes and heroines express still, with poignancy, the fears, doubts, and ecstasies of the young. And his works as a whole express, with equal poignancy, the dilemma of ageing liberals, trapped between turgid conservatism on one side and retrograde anarchy on the other. Much critical attention has been devoted to the young heroes of Stendhal. But perhaps the most important feature of his work is the dialogue between youth and maturity, a dialogue without rancour, composed by a man amusedly accepting the inevitable continuing presence in himself of a bewildered and angry child, and aware that this very acceptance is perhaps, paradoxically, a sign of maturity. Accepting, too, the precariousness, and often the dullness, of mature attitudes, and the transience of joy, but able to write, at the age of fifty-two, 'Je passerais dans d'horribles douleurs, les cinq, dix, vingt ou trente ans qui me restent à vivre qu'en mourant je ne dirais pas: Je ne veux pas recommencer',[3] so intense had been his experience of the brief moments of visionary joy in his life.

He thought that he had made little progress in the self-knowledge which seemed to him to be an essential preliminary to that 'connaissance du coeur humain' for which he strove. 'Je vais avoir cinquante ans, il serait bien temps de me connaître. Qu'ai-je été, que suis-je, en vérité je serais bien embarrassé de le dire.'[4] And one comes to realize that impermanence is his element; he proceeds in his exploration by a series of precarious holds, hanging on grimly to each dogmatic statement with the consciousness of perilous uncertainty below. Each triumph of reason over emotion is fleeting, and must be battled for again and again. Thought is a tangled skein to be laboriously teased out into some workable strands (there is no better illustration of this than the record of Julien Sorel's thinking in the prison scenes of Le Rouge et le Noir). The capacity to experience aesthetic pleasures is at the mercy of physiological frailties and cannot be commanded at will. 'N'avoir que vingt-quatre heures à passer dans une maussade petite ville, et, pendant ce temps, ne pas trouver une once de sensibilité pour le genre de beauté qui vous y a fait venir! Je suis très sujet à ce malheur.'[5] But his own restless avidity for change, which reflects that of our times, is balanced by the assurance of a changeless 'world elsewhere' of indestructible beauty.

Unique avantage of Dom[inique]

Pour tout bonheur Dom[inique] a une petite lorgnette d'un pouce de diamètre ouvrant dans un monde sublime. La bonne musique rend beaucoup plus claire la vue de ce monde. Deux heures d'ennui poli chez Ancilla plonge ce monde dans le néant.[6]

The persistence of a profound faith in the ideal, in the face of a close acquaintance with the disillusioning forms of everyday reality, is of course a distinguishing mark of the Romantic, and must be constantly associated with Stendhal.

3. Vie de Henry Brulard, Pléiade, Oeuvres intimes, ch. 47, p. 428.
4. Ibid., ch. 1, p. 38.   5. Rome, Naples et Florence, vol. i, p. 177.
6. Mélanges intimes et Marginalia, vol. ii, pp. 108–9.

In *Mémoires d'un touriste* he says: 'Je n'ai rien vu d'aussi semblable que le paysage du bac de la Vilaine et l'Ecosse désolée, triste,
puritaine, fanatique, telle que je me la figurais avant de l'avoir vue.
Et j'aime mieux l'image que la réalité; cette plate réalité, toute
dégoûtante d'amour exclusif pour l'argent et l'avancement, n'a
pu chez moi détruire l'image poétique.'[7] A development of this
point of view can be found in *Promenades dans Rome*:

Celle de nos compagnes de voyage qui comprend Mozart me disait ce
soir: 'La première vue de Saint-Pierre m'a troublée, mais ne m'a point
fait plaisir, bien loin de là. Il m'a fallu défaire l'image toute différente
de la réalité que mon imagination m'avait tracée, puis voir et com-
prendre Saint-Pierre tel qu'il est. Ensuite je n'admirais point ce monu-
ment; toutes mes émotions étaient encore pour ce Saint-Pierre que je
m'étais figuré d'après vos récits avant d'arriver à Rome. Je commence
à peine, après un an, à oublier cette ancienne inclination, et à me
complaire dans l'idée de Saint-Pierre tel qu'il est.' Le *cicérone* devait
bien se garder de troubler par aucun avis ce beau travail de l'âme.[8]

But 'that which exists in the imagination is alone imperishable'.
And perhaps the imaginary Saint Peter's never quite vanished
from the mind which had cherished it. Yet the 'beau travail de
l'âme', leading to the triumph of the firm outlines of a real
structure over the ones created from emotion and reverie is
calculated to appeal to the prevailing temper of our time, so
concerned to establish truths without surrendering the pleasures
of imagination or even those of recognized prejudices. Stendhal
was an atheist, a materialist not inclined to waste time in meta-
physical speculation, full of faith in the power of reason and
science, a competent and practical government official (it is
excellent to see this aspect of his talent stressed by Professor
del Litto in the preface to the last volume of the Pléiade edition
of the Correspondence) yet restless, avid for experience and
change. He seems to qualify for that supreme accolade of the
late twentieth century, to be judged capable of communicating
with us, to be 'on our wavelength'. But he was nevertheless a
nineteenth-century bourgeois, educated in the traditions and
tastes of the eighteenth century, taking for granted familiarity

7. *Mémoires d'un touriste*, vol. ii, pp. 3–4.
8. *Promenades dans Rome*, vol. iii, p. 155.

with the languages and history of the classical world. Though it may be inevitable that we should see his times in the light of our own, it is also essential to remember Montesquieu's comment: 'Transporter dans les siècles reculés toutes les idées du siècle où l'on vit, c'est des sources de l'erreur celle qui est la plus féconde.'[9] And Stendhal is nearer to the eighteenth century, in spirit as well as in time, than to our own.

But there is little chance of any writer's being able to capture attention in our times unless he has looked hard at violence and cruelty and acknowledged the presence in the world of pervasive evil. Like so many other artists of his time, a time of cataclysmic revolution and war, Stendhal was drawn to confront the nightmare aspects of human life. But he did so as an enforced discipline, not with relish; in his 'Voyage dans le Midi' we find 'Dans les romans ou drames que j'admire ou que je relis, je saute les scènes odieuses; je voudrais pouvoir oublier le laid de la vie.'[10] But he was too honest to pretend to do so. He does not dwell upon horrors, and the works in which he set out to explore the darker aspects of human experience are mainly unfinished—brief fragments, sketches of characters and outlines of incidents, certain sombre anecdotes, an occasional turn towards the grotesque or the obscene, an occasional venture into the grimacing forest of symbols. In *Lamiel* he forced himself to exploit a dark vein. 'Dominique aura-t-il assez d'esprit pour avilir comme il faut Sansfin?'[11] He could draw on long-held resentments and anger for this work, on the darker side of his memory; he had after all had the courage to present, in *Souvenirs d'égotisme*, a most unflattering picture of himself at a time of misfortune. But the interesting thing is that, drawing on this uncongenial source for *Lamiel*, it seems as though he makes the human lineaments of his characters fade out, to be replaced by depersonalized embodiments of attitudes, abstractions, consciousnesses reacting to situations. These characters are not human as are those of *Le Rouge et le Noir* and *La Chartreuse de Parme*. On the whole *Lamiel* is in advance of its times—it was later that the first moving away from represen-

---

9. *De l'Esprit des Lois*, ch. 14, bk. 30.

10. 'Voyage dans le Midi', *Mémoires d'un touriste*, vol. iii, p. 146.

11. *Lamiel* (Plan, 6 mars 1841). *Romans et Nouvelles*, Pléiade, vol. ii, p. 1037.

tational portraits in literature began. Stendhal had the courage
to experiment in defiance of his own inclinations; this is why all
the unfinished fragments of writing are interesting.[12] But all the
works that he completed, make plain that for him the record of
vice, cruelty, or any other aspect of evil is justified only if it is
also a record of the human capacity to oppose and transcend it.
What Stendhal has to say is mainly concerned with love and
courage, and with the unique individuality of human beings. His
passionate interest in a number of human concerns—art, politics,
economics, social theories—and in the behaviour of man in society,
may perhaps have lost something of its practical value for the
twentieth century because at least two of our major preoccupations, the destructive inventions of science, and the pressures of
over-population, were hardly known in his time. But it is possible
to regard as the most important aspect of all his work, fictional
and non-fictional, the presentation of the kind of character he
called the *âme généreuse*, and the difficulties and triumphs of this
character in life—and this may prove to be eternally interesting.

Paradoxically, considering the vast amount that has been written
about Stendhal in the twentieth century, and the admirable quality
of much of the writing, it becomes difficult to form a whole
impression of him as a writer. He seems an essential collaborator
in other people's *chasse au bonheur* as they pursue the study of their
own particular interests. Thus Stendhal and the history of the
Restoration, the Risorgimento, the July Monarchy; Stendhal the
art critic, Stendhal the journalist; Stendhal the traveller, the political
economist, the civil servant, the opera-goer and musicologist;
Stendhal and Italy, England, Germany; Stendhal the psycho-
analyst's case-history; we have a vast exhibition all devoted to
portraits of one man. He is a writer for any age in which the
difficulty of living is acutely and widely felt. The problems con-
fronted by all social classes in adapting to change, the quest for
precarious maturity, the energy and rebelliousness of youth, the
absurdities and turpitudes of certain middle-aged attitudes as well
of the Left as of the Right, and the rather bitter wisdom of others
—above all the need for each individual to find his own formula

12. This is made apparent in Crouzet's edition: *Stendhal: Romans abandonnés.*
(Collection Jalard—Bibliothèque 10/18, 1968.)

for happiness and to be reconciled to savouring that happiness in brief moments, not permanently—these are aspects of Stendhal's preoccupations which are also those of most human societies. The novels, of course, form the most remarkable expression of these preoccupations; their characters are the imperishable figures in the foreground of a great painting. Are his other works—apart from the autobiographical ones which can be ranked with the novels—really interesting in their own right, or does one force oneself to find them interesting because of the novels? *Histoire de la peinture en Italie, Rome, Naples et Florence, De l'Amour, Promenades dans Rome, Mémoires d'un touriste* and the others—Stendhalians will recognize that the mere recalling of the titles creates a background landscape for the characters, which is vast, beautiful, and an indispensable part of the picture. These works record more directly than the novels his own experience and reflections on life. They help to make clear what he has to say about the mysterious complexities of human darkness and light, about the unique individuality that constantly defies attempts to explain and classify; and they help him to achieve a certain beauty of form and style that is most difficult to analyse, but which gives life and endurance to his work. A passionate interest in and sympathy for his fellow human beings irradiates his writing—the art, music, literature that he loves are above all for him a triumph of human achievement. But he never pretended that his 'étude du coeur humain' was anything but the most difficult and the most unending of studies, demanding the collaboration of all the reader's experience. J.-P. Sartre, in the first chapter of *Qu'est-ce que la littérature?* writes, shortly after a reference to *Armance*, 'il faut que le lecteur invente tout dans un perpétuel dépassement de la chose écrite. Sans doute l'auteur le guide; mais il ne fait que le guider; les jalons qu'il a posés sont séparés par du vide, il faut les rejoindre, il faut aller au-delà d'eux. . . .' And 'Ainsi la lecture est-elle un exercice de générosité. . . .' He is here describing exactly Stendhal's ideal readers, so frequently invoked by him as the *Happy Few;* those among the *âmes généreuses* for whom reading was a way of willing collaboration with the author. Like the artists in Baudelaire's 'Les Phares', he signals to other ages, illuminating the *âmes généreuses* of his own times, as the writers and artists he most admired had done for earlier times, and as he knew others would do in times to come. In trying to trace the fortunes of Stendhal's *âmes généreuses* through his work, I have concentrated mainly on works of non-fiction which were written, it seems, in response to certain critical experiences in the writer's own life. Seven works of non-fiction, as well as literary and political pamphlets and articles, precede the great fictional and autobiographical works. These earlier works are a precious record of experience, and I shall try to examine certain of them in connection with the problems encountered by the *âme généreuse*. But first it is necessary to attempt to explain the meaning of this term as Stendhal uses it.

1 The *âme généreuse*

When, in 1803, Henri Beyle was living in Paris, reading and writing and preparing for his chosen career as a great playwright, having resigned his commission in the army, (to the annoyance of his cousin Pierre Daru, to whom he owed all his appointments in the army and in the higher ranks of the administrative service during the Empire) he started writing a play called 'Les Deux Hommes'. One of the main characters, Charles Valbelle, is an idealized self-portrait ('je me désignerai dans le cours de ce récit sous le nom de Charles'),[1] and in a letter to his friend Louis Crozet, he wrote 'Charles . . . c'est-à-dire . . . moi-même.'[2] Charles is intended to prove the superiority of 'l'éducation philosophe' over 'l'éducation dévote', and in fact represents Stendhal's idea of the 'republican character'. A discussion about Charles between his mother and uncle indicates the kind of character that in 1803 Stendhal admired and wished to resemble. It is obvious from his notes that he had drawn considerably on his reading, to create it; but also on his own experience, as another important observation shows:

Dans Charles j'ai à peindre cette première impression que le monde, vu imparfaitement, fait sur une âme neuve, ardente, et voyant tout en bien. Il sent cependant les grandes masses du mal, et les déteste franchement; dans cette partie, Charles se rapproche du Misanthrope, mais ce qui l'en différencie assez c'est qu'il ne doit pas avoir la moindre teinte d'humeur. Cet enthousiasme de vertu et de bonheur, la chose la plus touchante qui existe.[3]

Between this, written when he was twenty, and the last idealized self-portrait, Count Mosca in *La Chartreuse de Parme*, drawn when he was fifty-five, the character of the *âme généreuse* is gradually elaborated in the whole of his work, in the non-fictional work as well as in the novels. For the characters in the novels have little time for the long meditations on literature and art that for Stendhal

1. *Théâtre*, vol. ii, p. 64.
2. *Correspondance* (7 juin 1804). Pléiade, vol. i, p. 99.
3. *Théâtre*, vol. ii, p. 82.

were inseparable from the cultivation of the sensibility of the *âme généreuse*. Without the arts, the essential character would of course remain, but in some sense etiolated. The time-span of the novels is relatively brief and occupied with action and discussion of affairs of the moment; the arts provide an aura, a kind of tissue of *correspondances*, surrounding the lives of the characters.

'Les Deux Hommes' remained unfinished and Stendhal's notes and comments are infinitely more interesting than the few scraps of the play itself that were written. Much more important was 'Letellier', begun in 1803 and not finally abandoned until 1830. He was obsessed with this satirical work, started when his passionate admiration for Bonaparte had temporarily succumbed to such betrayals as the Concordat, and the growing personal power of the First Consul. The title of the work, though he usually referred to it as 'Letellier', was constantly changing; he took the manuscript with him to Grenoble, Marseilles, Moscow, Milan, Naples, and London, never advancing in it, always returning to the starting-point. How could he adapt it and keep it topical throughout the Consulate, the Empire, the defeat and invasion of France, the early Restoration, the 1830 Revolution, and the beginning of the July Monarchy? For as he conceived it, its success would have depended on topicality. The story of Stendhal and 'Letellier' is perhaps more amusing than any comedy he himself could have devised. But what is interesting in this abortive work is the gradual emergence of an *âme généreuse*, called first Vardes, then Chapelle, who was to be the adversary of the hero Letellier, the *âme commune* and *antiphilosophe*, who, envious and pusillanimous, 'haît profondément tout ce qui est grand'.[4] Of great interest too is the way in which the characters gradually become more interesting themselves than the idea they were meant to illustrate.

'Letellier' too was abandoned at last. But it is not only in the plans for plays that the notion of the groups into which he was always to divide human beings, appears. In a letter to his sister Pauline, written on 19 April 1805, he proclaims:

Les hommes que nous rencontrerons, dans le voyage de la vie que nous commençons, seront ou, comme nous, âmes ardentes, ou entièrement froids et secs, ou entre deux. Le nombre des âmes ardentes est infiniment

4. *Théâtre*, vol. iii, p. 159.

petit, et il est très aisé de s'y méprendre. Nous sommes les amis nés de ces grandes âmes, nous sommes dépositaires de leur bonheur, comme elles du nôtre. Il suffit de se connaître pour s'aimer à jamais; nous pourrons avoir les plus grands torts avec elles, elles avec nous, nous finirons toujours par être rejetés dans les bras l'un de l'autre, les secs nous sont trop insupportables.[5]

This may not be particularly original or profound; it is nevertheless the basis of all the subtle and profound knowledge of character revealed in Stendhal's later work.

The *âme généreuse*, then, at first, is Stendhal as he believed himself to be, and as he thought those dearest to him to be. So far his idea of this character is simply the age-old one of the upholder of freedom, justice, magnanimity, and devotion to beauty—the *preux chevalier* and all the other legendary forms of the character, brought up to date by the addition of *la vertu républicaine*. Temperament, reading, and observation—in that order—were responsible for his preoccupation with it. And it is important to remember that the period of Stendhal's childhood and early youth was that of the Revolutionary years. In this connection, one of the most illuminating works must certainly be Pierre Trahard's *La Sensibilité révolutionnaire* (1789–94). It is obvious that Stendhal's education and reading were exactly similar to those of the Revolutionary leaders; his sensibility was that of his times. 'Le sentiment existe; on ne se contente pas de l'éprouver, on l'analyse, on en fait un objet d'étude, on cherche ses origines dans la sensation.'[6] And again, on the early Revolutionary deputies and their parliamentary sessions ' vie agitée, tumultueuse, tragique, dont il faudrait reconstituer le mouvement pour bien juger des hommes à qui jamais le calme, la tranquillité d'esprit et le repos ne sont assurés. Presque toujours les Assemblées délibèrent dans la tempête, sous la menace, au son du tocsin et du canon d'alarme.'[7] Stendhal must have picked up the vibrations of this passionate epoch. His whole work is pervaded by its fervour, in middle age he recalls it with nostalgia and with regret for the inevitable fall of temperature and loss of idealism.

But perhaps a starting-point for the specifically Stendhalian

5. *Correspondance*, vol. i, p. 194.
6. Op. cit., p. 33.   7. Op. cit., p. 58.

conception of the *âme généreuse* is to be found in *Filosofia Nova*, that ambitiously titled collection of notes which also belongs to the revolutionary years.

La majeure partie des hommes ont la folie de croire qu'ils ont éprouvé tout ce qu'on peut sentir. Par conséquent, si un homme qui n'a éprouvé que 5/10 d'amour voit une pièce où le poète en ait montré dans ses personnages 6/10, intérieurement il le trouvera hors de nature, parce qu'il prend sa propre nature pour celle de l'homme en général. C'est la majorité des hommes qui ont imposé les noms. Ils n'ont pu en donner à ce qui n'était jamais tombé sous un de leurs cinq sens et à ce que n'avait jamais éprouvé leur âme.

Donc plus on devient passionné plus la langue vous manque.[8]

This ruthless observation introduces the idea that the *âmes généreuses* may be distinguished from the rest not by upright conduct, or intellectual power, or success, or any easily observed superiority, but by their capacity for intensity and range of feeling, and strength of imaginative sympathy. They are an élite, they are privileged, but not by birth, wealth, or intellectual brilliance; they belong to no class or faction; some may seek power, others remain contentedly obscure. What they all possess is the sensibility which gives them access to a range of experiences outside the scope of less favoured human beings. Stendhal applied a similar standard of judgement on other occasions to his friends and acquaintances:

Jugement littéraire

Κλαρα [Mérimée] touche supérieurement 8 touches de son piano (le *fear of death*, la vengeance, etc.) mais il n'en touche que 8, et naturellement doit être mère poule envers les petits canards pour qui en touche librement 24.

7 janvier 1830[9]

Since moral aspiration is natural to the *âmes généreuses*, they are frequently dissatisfied with themselves and frustrated by their own limitations. For the state of impermanence and transience which is central to Stendhal's view of human life and activity extends to these characters too; they must constantly battle against the *âme commune* who inhabits them. One may have the capacity to be an

---

8. *Pensées. Filosofia Nova*, vol. ii, pp. 123.
9. *Mélanges intimes et Marginalia*, vol. ii, pp. 102–3.

âme généreuse – it is impossible to be one all the time. This seems to me to be the core of Stendhal's view of character. One of the sad facts of the encounter of the *âme généreuse* with the world is that it cannot avoid contamination by the world. In *De l'Amour* Stendhal says: 'Les émotions les plus généreuses et les plus nobles sont paralysées par le contact de ce qu'il y a de plus bas dans les produits de la civilisation.'[10] Paralysed, not destroyed; but their strength may remain impaired. And constant effort, watchfulness, and action against the promptings of the *âme commune* are necessary. There must be from time to time a slackening of tension, a slipping back into apathy or vacuity. Stendhal stresses this constantly, as for example in the very short Chapter 15 of *De l'Amour*, beginning: 'L'on rencontre, au milieu de la passion la plus violente et la plus contrariée, des moments où l'on croit tout à coup de ne plus aimer; c'est comme une source d'eau douce au milieu de la mer. . . .'[11] This is illustrated particularly well in *Lucien Leuwen*, when Lucien is astonished to find that he seems to have stopped loving Madame de Chasteller. 'Mais tout ce détail de beautés et d'avantages ne faisait rien pour l'amour de Leuwen; il ne renaissait point. Il se parlait de Mme de Chasteller comme un connaisseur se parle d'une belle statue qu'il veut vendre.'[12] In such a mood, art can be a distraction, but nothing more. Lucien stops at a small Gothic chapel 'que les habitants admiraient avec des transports d'artiste depuis trois ans qu'ils avaient lu dans une revue de Paris que c'était une belle chose.'[13] He has taken little account of it before; now he finds pleasure in examining it, and in looking at the small carvings of saints' heads and of animals 'il était étonné à la fois de ce qu'il sentait, et de ce qu'il ne sentait plus.' [14] Of the same order is the failure to react to some beautiful scene or work of art. Having gone to Bologna to visit the art galleries, Stendhal finds himself in the state so well described by Coleridge in a mood of dejection looking at the night sky, the moon, clouds, and stars: 'I see them all, so excellently fair, // I see, *not feel*, how beautiful they are!' This 'wan and heartless mood' is the penalty to be paid for the ability at other times to experience joy. It is something of

10. *De l'Amour*, ch. 38, vol. i, p. 190.   11. Ibid., ch. 15, vol. i, p. 67.
12. *Lucien Leuwen*, ch.25, vol. ii, p. 313. (See Bibliography. Chapter numbers vary slightly in different editions of this work.)   13. Ibid., ch. 24, p. 306.   14. Ibid.

which the writers of the Romantic period seem to have been particularly aware; for example Shelley in 'Rarely, rarely comest thou,//Spirit of delight . . .'; and, in 'Lines written among the Euganean Hills', the other side of the failure of sensibility, the moments of respite in periods of grief or misery. The forms of expression of the Romantic years seem exaggerated to us, perhaps, but we are living in the backwash of the Romantic period and have evolved other exaggerations of our own.

The young heroes of Stendhal reflect only part—though of course a vitally important part—of the *âme généreuse*. Stendhal in middle-age had certain characteristics that none of them possess —humour, which like M. Leuwen *père* he frequently directed against himself; and a small measure of resignation to the difficulty of being alive. It was clear to him that part of the *chasse au bonheur* could lie in temporarily forsaking the pursuit of the ideal, realizing one's limitations, allowing oneself the relief of being the plain, stout, practical talker for effect, the enjoyer of 'les espèces subalternes d'amour',[15] as he put it; Valéry's commercial traveller.[16] No one can have realized more clearly than he—though the knowledge, implied rather than stated, is illustrated through the more extreme characters, Julien Sorel, Sansfin,—that to break down the distinction between good and evil, to abolish traditional moral absolutes, is to remove one of the richest and darkest of human pleasures, that of deliberately choosing sin. Most of Stendhal's characters, and certainly he himself, understood the fierce pleasure of being at some time less than themselves. Julien Sorel, just after receiving from Mathilde de la Mole a letter declaring her love for him, stifles an impulse of gratitude and affection for Monsieur de la Mole, and maintains his 'triste rôle de plébéien révolté': 'Que je suis bon, se dit-il; moi, plébéien, avoir pitié d'une famille de ce rang. . . .'[17] He becomes again a clever, suspicious, vindictive little upstart as he plans how to cope with this development in his adventure. 'Il faut en convenir, le regard de Julien était atroce, sa physionomie hideuse; elle respirait le crime sans alliage. C'était l'homme malheureux en guerre avec toute la société.'[18] Because

15. *De l'Amour*, ch. 49, vol. ii, p. 28.
16. Valéry, Preface to *Lucien Leuwen*, vol. i, p. xlix.
17. *Le Rouge et le Noir*, ch. 13, vol. ii, p. 165.   18. Ibid., p. 169.

he feels constantly in danger, he has the idea of sending to his friend Fouqué, for safe keeping, the original letters from Mathilde and an account of his own position in the de la Mole household. These chapters from Chapter 13 onwards in volume two, must surely be among the most brilliant that Stendhal ever wrote; touching, amusing, and wise. The important fact is that Julien cannot get into the skin of his part. Here he is reflecting on his situation, surrounded, as he mistakenly believes, by mortal enemies plotting against his life:

J'eusse été tué dans les jardins de M. de Rênal qu'il n'y avait point de déshonneur pour moi. Facilement on eût rendu ma mort inexplicable. Ici, quels récits abominables ne va-t-on pas faire dans les salons de l'hôtel de Chaulnes . . . partout enfin. Je serai un monstre dans la postérité.

Pendant deux ou trois ans, reprit-il en riant, et se moquant de soi. Mais cette idée l'anéantissait. Et moi, où pourra-t-on me justifier? En supposant que Fouqué imprime mon pamphlet posthume, ce ne sera qu'une infamie de plus. Quoi! je suis reçu dans une maison, et pour prix de l'hospitalité que j'y reçois, des bontés dont on m'y accable, j'imprime un pamphlet sur ce qui s'y passe! j'attaque l'honneur des femmes! Ah! mille fois plutôt, soyons dupes.[19]

One of the most important aspects of the *âme généreuse*, and one that can on occasion create difficulties in that it may prevent him from taking the hard attitude that his immediate interest may require, is his imaginative sympathy for others. Among innumerable examples of this, there is a very striking one at the end of Chapter 10 of *Lucien Leuwen* when one realizes that Lucien, who so far has appeared spoilt and vain, has this imagination. He looks at the plain daughters of the Comte de Serpierre, sitting with their sewing round one lamp ('cette année-là, l'huile était chère'); their meekness and vulnerability strike him. 'On dirait, pensa Lucien, qu'elles demandent pardon de n'être pas jolies.'[20] After this he never fails to treat them with consideration. Similarly, with the young provincial aristocrats, most of whom have given up their army careers out of loyalty to the exiled Charles X, and are leading impoverished and futile existences filled only by the social life of gossip and intrigue, and vain hopes for the return of the Bourbon branch; they regard Lucien and his entry into their exclusive

19. Ibid., ch. 15, vol. ii, p. 188.   20. *Lucien Leuwen*, vol. i, p. 195.

society with suspicion and jealousy, and will eventually become his enemies. But, 'C'est que son âme noble avait au fond un respect infini pour la situation malheureuse de tous ces pauvres jeunes gens qui l'entouraient.'[21]

And again Julien in the seminary:

Après avoir été comme suffoqué dans les premiers temps par le senti-ment du mépris, Julien finit par éprouver de la pitié: il était arrivé souvent aux pères de la plupart de ses camarades de rentrer le soir dans l'hiver à leur chaumière, et de n'y trouver ni pain, ni châtaignes, ni pommes de terre. Qu'y a-t-il donc d'étonnant, se disait Julien, si l'homme heureux, à leurs yeux, est d'abord celui qui vient de bien dîner, et ensuite celui qui possède un bon habit! Mes camarades ont une vocation ferme, c'est-à-dire qu'ils voient dans l'état ecclésiastique une longue continuation de ce bonheur: bien dîner et avoir un habit chaud en hiver.[22]

And the inability to continue to hate a rival is a characteristic of several of the heroines, perhaps the most striking example being Madame de Chasteller. Reflecting on the charm and wit of Madame d'Hocquincourt, she looks at herself in her mirror: 'elle conclut qu'elle était décidément laide, et en aima davantage Leuwen du bon goût qu'il avait de lui préférer Mme d'Hocquincourt.'[23]

In *Promenades dans Rome*, Stendhal himself reflects at the time of the death of the Pope Leon XII: 'Un pauvre vieillard seul, sans famille, abandonné dans son lit aux soins de personnes qui hier le flattaient bassement, et qui aujourd'hui l'exècrent et désirent ouvertement sa mort, présente une image trop laide pour moi. On m'a plaisanté sur ma sensibilité. . . .'[24]

The imagination of the *âme généreuse* is of the kind that enables him to have insight into other lives. This insight works against hatred. And the next step, from this imaginative insight, is the generous action.

Dans presque tous les événements de la vie, une âme généreuse voit la possibilité d'une action dont l'âme commune n'a pas même l'idée. A l'instant même où la possibilité de cette action devient visible à l'âme généreuse, il est de son intérêt de la faire.

21. Ibid., ch. 17, vol. i, p. 286 ('Le Chasseur Vert'), and vol. ii, p. 227.
22. *Le Rouge et le Noir*, ch. 26, vol. i, pp. 313–14.
23. *Lucien Leuwen*, ch. 34, vol. iii, p. 101.   24. Vol. iii, p. 239.

Si elle n'exécutait pas cette action qui vient de lui apparaître, elle se mépriserait soi-même; elle serait malheureuse. On a des devoirs suivant la portée de son esprit. Le principe d'Helvétius est vrai même dans les exaltations les plus folles de l'amour. . . .[25]

This idea may perhaps be considered as the corner-stone of all Stendhal's presentations of character. Everything is there: the superior sensibility of the *âme généreuse* which enables him to see what the generous action would be, the fact that this action is a means of achieving happiness, and is therefore self-interest. No particular praise is deserved; the *âme généreuse* can no more avoid committing the *action généreuse* than the acorn can avoid growing into an oak and not a weed. Stendhal returns again and again to the same idea:

L'homme n'est pas libre de ne pas faire ce qui lui fait plus de plaisir que toutes les autres actions possibles.

Helvétius a eu parfaitement raison lorsqu'il a établi que le principe d'utilité ou l'*intérêt* était le guide unique de toutes les actions de l'homme . . . M. de Loizerolles marchant à la mort pour sauver son fils, obéit au principe de l'intérêt. Faire autrement eût été, pour cette âme héroïque, une insigne lâcheté, qu'elle ne se fût jamais pardonnée; avoir cette idée sublime crée à l'instant un devoir.[26]

This principle is constantly illustrated in the novels, and even more frequently, perhaps, in the non-fictional works. Generosity, it is suggested, is a matter of instinct, almost a self-indulgence— a form of vanity, one way like any other of pursuing the search for happiness. Stendhal's ironical turn of mind may well have brought him near, on occasion, to seeing the generous action as a form of egoism; but his common sense would at least have accepted that it can have practical uses. Four hungry *âmes communes* in retreat from a battlefield could not but welcome the presence of the quixotic *âme généreuse* whose 'interest' is to take the smallest piece of bread, or give away his last drop of water. The *âme commune* may be saved by the *âme généreuse*, and survive to speak cynically of him. But Stendhal also understood a certain 'douce volupté' to be found in simultaneously laughing at the *âmes*

25. *De l'Amour* (Fragments divers, 91), vol. ii, p. 172.
26. Ibid., vol. i, p. 31, and *Correspondance* (13 novembre 1820), vol. i, pp. 1044–5.

généreuses and their world and feeling a total affinity with them: 'quand Octave se trouvait avec les ennemies de mademoiselle de Zohiloff, il était le premier à convenir de ses défauts. . . .' He listens to malicious remarks, and 'Pendant que sa malignité en jouissait, il se livrait en silence et avec délices à un petit mouvement d'admiration passionnée.'[27] The sensibility of the *âme généreuse* gives rise to a complexity of feeling which makes the search for truth increasingly difficult. Self-knowledge, so constantly advocated by Stendhal, is presented not only as difficult, or even impossible, but when achieved suddenly and violently, as possibly mortal. This is perhaps an interpretation of that epigraph in *Le Rouge et le Noir*, 'La vérité, l'âpre vérité'. Though it appears more likely that the reference was to a political and social truth, the truth about the society of his times learnt by Julien Sorel in his four years of ambitious progress through this society and expressed by him in his speech at his trial, it is also possible that this *âpre vérité* is the truth that he learns about his own character and the profound forces which lead him to make his attempt on the life of Madame de Rênal—the truth which he glimpses about the nature of love and the reason for the vanity of his wordly triumphs, the impossibility of surviving uncorrupted by the corruption through which he has passed—an *âpre vérité* indeed, with which he cannot live. For the young heroes of Stendhal express an unwillingness to compromise, a tragic sense of life that for him belongs to youth. In this sense they represent the greatest of the symbols he uses; their deaths, the inevitable passing of youth, and the fading of its generous fervour. As the two brothers sing in *Cymbeline* (which Stendhal knew so well and which was perhaps one of the strongest of the literary influences upon him), finding a form of words that translates a knowledge beyond their experience: 'All lovers young, all lovers must//Consign to thee, and come to dust.' Each of the young heroes, or heroines, reaches a moment at which it becomes necessary to abandon the game, throwing away what looks like a winning hand. Octave de Malivert, Julien Sorel, Fabrice del Dongo, Hélène de Campiréali, Lamiel, take an immediate or an ultimately sure way to death; Lucien Leuwen, whose story remained unfinished, has already

27. *Armance*, ch. 5, pp. 65, 66.

renounced his life of success in the social and political world of
Paris when he exclaims: 'Il est drôle de sacrifier son coeur à
l'ambition et pourtant de n'être pas ambitieux.'[28] Fabrice, at
twenty-nine, is the oldest of them. For each of them reality at a
certain moment conflicts too sharply with a vision or aspiration,
or, like Fabrice, they are mortally wounded by some irreparable
loss. Possible recovery and future triumphs do not interest them.
Their successor, Anouilh's Antigone, speaks for them all: 'Je suis
là pour dire non et pour mourir.' Their emotions of course reflect
Stendhal's own; but in making the connection between a writer
and his characters, one vital fact is often, strangely, overlooked—
that the creator of enduring characters is, as they are not, an artist.
And moreover, in Stendhal's case, one for whom all other forms
of art besides his own are passionately interesting and indeed an
indispensable part of life. Thus, while his novels are concerned
with the reasons for the deaths of his young heroes, his works
of non-fiction are concerned with his own reasons for survival.
It quickly becomes apparent that his interest in other arts is an
aspect of interest in his own; looking at paintings, listening to
music, watching actors or dancers, Stendhal is always a writer,
with an ideal reader in mind. His adult ambitions lay mainly in
the field of administration—he would have liked a prefecture—
but he never imagined that any official occupation would prevent
him from writing. At the beginning of the most successful period
of his career, he wrote to his sister: 'Je comptais pour cet hiver
faire de mes occupations officielles la broderie de ma vie. Le fond
aurait été employé à quelques études approfondies relatives à la
connaissance de l'homme. . . .'[29] And so it always was; but this
did not prevent him from carrying out his official duties com-
petently and even with a certain zeal. Yet another aspect of the
âme généreuse is that he accepts participation in the social life of
his time; he must prove to himself that he can make his way in
a society which may seem uncongenial, that he can succeed in
it by playing the roles imposed by its standards and values, before
he considers that he has a right to despise it. He must convince
himself that his contempt for it is not a cover for incompetence,

28. *Lucien Leuwen*, ch. 53, vol. iv, p. 164.
29. *Correspondance* (9 oct. 1810), vol. i, p. 591.

weakness or misunderstanding on his part. Stendhal's grievance against the society of the Restoration and the July Monarchy was that it was not possible for the *âme généreuse* to succeed in it if he expressed his true enthusiasms and allegiances. Courage, idealism self-sacrifice for a great cause, seemed out of fashion. The expression of left-wing sympathies could endanger a career. The intelligence, energy, and pride of the *âme généreuse* make him wish to succeed in the society he happens to be living in. Stendhal is not alone in referring, as he does in the preface to *Armance*, to 'le siècle qui finit en 1789 et celui qui commença vers 1815'.[30] The apocalyptic years between were those of his childhood and youth, his formative years. The liberal ideals of the early Revolution and the betrayal of those ideals by the individuals and classes who rose to power later because of them, their betrayal by Stendhal himself in his pursuit of material success under later regimes, are reflected in all his mature work. The combination of natural rebelliousness, family circumstances, precocious intelligence, and the events of the times, made of him, as he said, a passionate Republican at the age of nine. This republicanism he later renounced, but the concern for justice and liberty remained. The Revolutionary years, and particularly the Italian campaign, were for him a heroic age, the meeting point of liberal France and liberal Italy, nostalgically recalled at the beginning of *La Chartreuse de Parme*. In the *Vie de Henry Brulard* he looks back at these years and tries to classify them according to what they contributed to his experience:

Enfance et première éducation, de 1786 à 1800	15 ans
Service militaire de 1800 à 1803	3 ans
Seconde éducation, amours ridicules	
Vie rue d'Angivilliers. Enfin beau séjour à Marseille avec Mélanie, de 1803 à 1805	2 ans
Retour à Paris, fin de l'éducation	1 an
Service sous Napoléon, de 1806 à la fin de 1814 (d'octobre 1806 à l'abdication en 1814)	7½ ans[31]

These were years of intense experience, effort and struggle, in which his outlook on life and his main interests were formed. He

---

30. *Armance*, Avant-propos, p. 5.
31. *Vie de Henry Brulard*, ch. 2, p. 54. He omits the date of his birth, 23 January 1783, and extends his military service by two years.

was conscious, as he says in *Henry Brulard*, of having experienced more in one day than many men in a lifetime. There are abundant records of his development in this time, apart from the retrospective view given in *Henry Brulard*. From 1800 to 1806 not only his journal and letters, but also his notebooks, the *Filosofia Nova*, and his drafts of plays, make a commentary on his daily life and thought. His nostalgia for the penurious years of study and writing in Paris began early. On Christmas Day 1810, at the height of his career in the service of Napoleon, he wrote to his sister '. . . j'ai senti le regret de ne plus vivre au milieu de ces idées nobles, fortes et tendres qui m'occupaient sans cesse lorsque, logé rue d'Angivilliers, en face de la belle colonnade du Louvre, et n'ayant souvent pas six francs dans ma poche, je passais des soirées entières à contempler des étoiles brillantes se couchant derrière le fronton du Louvre. . . .'[32] That this was not entirely a Chateaubrianesque selective recollection of the past, his letters to his sister Pauline and to his friend Edouard Mounier in the year 1803 demonstrate. His main preoccupation as far as Pauline was concerned, was to educate her as befitted the *âme généreuse* that he imagined her to be. His journal for 1803 opens with an imposing list of the works he planned to write. The prose ones were to be a history of Bonaparte, a history of the French Revolution, and a history of the great men who had lived during the Revolution. 'Commencer ces trois ouvrages à 35 ans, dans quinze ans d'ici,' he concludes.

As one reads his autobiographical works, his journal, notebooks, and letters, it soon appears that he was one for whom characters from the real and imagined past—Tancred and Clorinda, Julie and Saint-Preux, Don Quixote, the heroes of Plutarch—were as living and important to him as his own contemporaries. The literary origins of Stendhal's *âme généreuse* are very numerous and of great importance; I have not investigated them here because they have already been the subject of so much critical work. Stendhal was an omnivorous reader from an early age; everything that he read and enjoyed contributed something to the formation of his own genius. One might perhaps say that the reading of Corneille was decisive for his conception of character. To take only one example, Sévère's exclamation in Act I scene 2 of *Polyeucte*: 'Puisse

32. *Correspondance*, vol. i, p. 601.

le juste Ciel, content de ma ruine,//Combler d'heur et de jours Polyeucte et Pauline!' combines both the essential imaginative insight and the resulting generosity of thought and action. (It is interesting that Gide's *Porte Etroite*, which owes so much to *Armance*, contains more overtones of Corneille than *Armance* itself.) Stendhal's reading was so much a part of his experience that as he looked back from middle age, he recognized the difficulty of disentangling real events and scenes from those in books. By calling the hero of his autobiography Henry Brulard, he was recognizing the fact that the child seen through the eyes of the mature man is always to some extent a fictitious character. His childhood was spent in the power of people whose temperaments were incompatible with his own, in that they seemed to lack gaiety, humour, and breadth of mind; even in the older people he preferred, his grandfather and great-aunt, one senses a certain dogmatism, a certain rigidity of attitude, whereas for Henri Beyle the possibility of constant change and escape, even from his own opinions and standpoints, as well as from his physical environment, was essential. In *Lucien Leuwen* he rejects the too commonly held Romantic view of the strengthening and ennobling power of suffering, in favour of the more realistic view: 'Rien ne rend méchant comme le malheur.'[33] He himself later admitted the exaggeration of his dislike for his father, his aunt Séraphie, and his tutor the abbé Raillane. But like many unhappy children, if they are fortunate enough to be able to do so, he escaped into books. The impression of lack of companionship, of intense moral solitude, endured by the child Henry Brulard is a disturbing one—it explains the restlessness, the rebelliousness, the love of argument for its own sake, the dread of boredom, in his later years, and also the passion for action, travel, engagement in the life of his times. When reading *Henry Brulard* or such studies of Beyle's youth as Arbelet's *La Jeunesse de Stendhal*, one has a painful impression of a creature enclosed in too small a cage or held on too short a leash. Because of his home, because his family were Royalists and devoted Catholics, he identified himself with the Revolutionary struggle against injustice and tyranny, and with all those characters in his reading who had been involved in this struggle. Certainly, he later became aware that self-sacrifice

33. *Lucien Leuwen*, ch. 42, vol. iii, p. 222.

for political principles was not the particular form of Helvétian self-interest that fitted his own *chasse au bonheur*. But he remained a fervent respecter of the right of each man to achieve by individual endeavour the highest development of which his nature was capable. The tyrants who stood in the way of this right were absolute monarchy, organized religion, the inevitable currently powerful group, the masses with no imagination. The quest for liberty for himself and others was a lifelong preoccupation, and he had no illusions about its difficulty.

For the child Henry Brulard, the quest had begun with hatred—hatred of the relatives who imposed unjust restrictions upon him, and of the authorities approved of by them. In *Filosofia Nova*, after noting 'Toute haine est un grand mal', he observes, 'La haine des tyrans a été ma plus forte passion après l'amour de la gloire.'[34] This hatred could however be considered as an altruistic sentiment, a Revolutionary principle, and therefore worthy of the *âme généreuse*. But the hatred against which he warned the reader in the preface to *Lucien Leuwen*—'Adieu, ami lecteur; songez à ne pas passer votre vie à haïr et à avoir peur'[35]—was class or party hatred, meanly adapted to meaner times, a sign of pusillanimity and a mark of the *âme basse*. But by that time 'liberal' had become a party label, no longer a synonym of 'generous', 'magnanimous', 'freedom-loving'. It was the 'liberals' of the Restoration period who now formed the *juste-milieu* government engaged in the 'guerre aux tronçons de choux' against the workers, and who incurred the bitter scorn of Lucien's companion Coffe, the man who could not afford the luxury of living according to his principles: 'Si j'avais trois cents francs de rente seulement, je ne servirais pas le ministère qui retient des milliers de pauvres diables dans les horribles cachots du Mont-Saint-Michel et de Clairvaux.'[36] This was the government of which Stendhal himself was a servant at the time. Certainly, the idea of political imprisonment was for him an affront to the dignity and humanity of any age, and the protest against it may be regarded as one of his major themes. The liberals of his generation must have had engraved upon their

34. *Pensées. Filosofia Nova*, vol. ii, p. 159.
35. *Lucien Leuwen*, Letter to the reader, preceding ch. 1, vol. ii, p. 2.
36. Ibid., ch. 48, vol. iv, p. 27.

hearts two clauses in particular from the 1789 Declaration of Rights: the tenth, 'Nul ne doit être inquiété pour ses opinions, même religieuses, pourvu que leur manifestation ne trouble pas l'ordre public établi par la Loi', and the eleventh, 'La libre communication des pensées et des opinions est un des droits les plus précieux de l'homme, tout citoyen peut donc parler, écrire, imprimer librement, sauf à répondre de l'abus de cette liberté dans les cas déterminés par la Loi.' But though his presentation of the political emotions—they can hardly be called theories—of his young heroes is more often than not ironical or even sarcastic, his conception of the *âme généreuse* is inseparable from his own response to the political developments of his times. The 'liberalism' of Stendhal is no easier to define than any other form of liberalism. But in trying to understand what he meant when he referred to himself as a 'liberal' and to other people as 'Jacobins', it is essential to try to cut oneself free from the various twentieth century interpretations of the words. It is necessary to attach great importance to the statement made by Stendhal at various times after the publication of Destutt de Tracy's *Commentaire sur 'De l'Esprit des lois' de Montesquieu*, that the book represented his 'credo politique'. In fact, as I shall suggest in a later chapter, this work and Constant's *De l'Esprit de conquête et de l'usurpation* . . . were probably instrumental in helping Stendhal, at a period of crisis in his life, to clarify his political views once and for all. An ideal of liberalism, and a contempt for betrayals of this ideal by those who used the name, like hermit crabs scuttling into an empty shell from which the original life has departed, stayed with him all his life. But Montesquieu would already have impressed upon Stendhal that the natural egoism of the man is in perpetual conflict with the altruism desirable in the citizen, and Stendhal was by temperament more '*homme*' than '*citoyen*'. Though his deep concern for the welfare of individuals, the respect for their lives and their search for happiness, their freedom, their right to justice, suggest an association with the traditional concerns of the Left, he was aware, as were all those who had lived through the Revolution, that tyranny was Hydra-headed, and the instinct to survive and prosper, whatever the current regime, very strong. Between the ardent good-citizenship of Charles in 'Les Deux Hommes' and the cynical egoism of Sansfin in *Lamiel* there is a gulf of disillusion as much with self as with events. He became content to love and sympathize with those who were active and self-sacrificing in the causes he admired, and constantly reaffirmed his admiration for the heroic times of his youth. But the self-absorption of the most energetic heroes and heroines of the *Chroniques italiennes*, and of Gina Sanseverina, of Julien Sorel, of Lamiel—the willingness to destroy, be ruthless, be totally indifferent to civic responsibilities, is ultimately what absorbs him most.

> Let Rome in Tiber melt, and the wide arch
> Of the ranged empire fall; here is my space.
> Kingdoms are clay . . . .

As an artist, he takes to its extreme limits the search for individual liberty, in a rejection of inherited beliefs and prohibitions. The ideal of self-sacrifice for the good of the community was one which, in common with the 1789 revolutionaries reared on Plutarch, he admired and respected all his life, and his works of non-fiction are full of references to characters in history and legend who fulfil this ideal. The passage from the altruistic 'vertu' of the anecdotes in the earlier works to the instinctive egoism of the main characters in the novels, is made by way of Helvétius' observations on the self-interest of the *âme généreuse*, and also by way of Henri Beyle's realization of the absolute disinclination to self-sacrifice in his own character.

Society is necessary—'On peut tout acquérir dans la solitude, hormis du caractère'[37]—as an aid to self-knowledge, and for the pleasure that success brings to the man of talent. Solitude too is necessary, to take stock of the past, plan for the future, and draw refreshment from 'la rêverie tendre'. But most necessary of all, for the fulfilment of the *âme généreuse*, is love—the ideal, enduring relationship, the *amour-passion*, described in *De l'Amour*. The idea of this owes much to the medieval tradition of courtly love, much to Dante, much to Stendhal's realization that human beings need an object of devotion beyond themselves, and preferably unattainable. The decisive moments in the lives of all his main characters,

---

37. *De l'Amour* (Fragments divers, 1), vol. ii, p. 141.

when they reject their own successes and with these the values of the society in which they have triumphed, are always the result of love. The *amour-passion* can be experienced only by the *âme généreuse*; it is of all his experiences the one which sets him apart, the most totally inaccessible to the *âme commune*. It is possible to maintain that the genius of Stendhal lies more in his studies of relationships than in his pictures of individuals, and that the presentation of Lucien and Madame de Chasteller in the first volume of *Lucien Leuwen* is unsurpassed in his other works. This was the relationship that most clearly reflected the sorrows and ecstasies of his own love for Métilde Dembowski, and it is the character of Madame de Chasteller that reveals perhaps more than any other an interesting aspect of his way of developing a relationship. This is that words spoken by a character either in soliloquy or in conversation are not necessarily connected logically with an existing situation or recorded sequence of events, but reveal the working of the character's mind; thus Madame de Chasteller's exaggerated fear of having compromised herself in Lucien's eyes refers not to any real event, but to the intensity of her preoccupation with him and the affront to her pride that her realization of this has created. The proud and independent natures of the *âmes généreuses* tend to complicate all their relationships, but for Stendhal the development of understanding and sensibility, in all fields of experience, is incomplete without the relationship created by what he calls 'le véritable amour'. In this connection Salviati, in *De l'Amour*, is an important witness:

Comme la réformation de Luther, à la fin du moyen âge, ébranlant la société jusque dans ses fondements, renouvela et reconstitua le monde sur des bases raisonnables, ainsi un caractère généreux est renouvelé et retrempé par l'amour.

Ce n'est qu'alors qu'il dépouille tous les enfantillages de la vie; sans cette révolution, il eût toujours eu je ne sais quoi d'empesé et de théâtral. Ce n'est que depuis que j'aime que j'ai appris à avoir de la grandeur dans le caractère, tant notre éducation d'école militaire est ridicule.

Quoique me conduisant bien, j'étais un enfant à la cour de Napoléon et à Moscou. Je faisais mon devoir; mais j'ignorais cette simplicité héroique, fruit d'un sacrifice entier et de bonne foi. Il n'y a qu'un an,

par exemple, que mon coeur comprend la simplicité des Romains de
Tite-Live. Autrefois je les trouvais froids, comparés à nos brillants
colonels. Ce qu'ils faisaient pour leur Rome, je le trouve dans mon
coeur pour Léonore. . . .[38]

Salviati realizes that his love for Léonore has transformed, permanently, his view of the world, and that though his love is not
returned and he will be separated from her, and though the
pressures of society, and his outward behaviour, remain the same,
nothing will have the power to destroy her effect upon his life.
For him, she is a messenger from the *monde sublime*, confirming
and strengthening his belief in its existence.

Among the names of real and fictitious characters mentioned
throughout Stendhal's writings as examples of *âmes généreuses*,
that of Charles James Fox recurs. It is doubtful that Stendhal knew
more of Fox than his reputation as a 'friend of Liberty'; (though he
refers to him thus in *L'Italie en 1818*: 'Combien de fois le sublime
Fox . . . n'est-il pas sorti de la Chambre des communes au milieu
des huées de ce peuple qu'il venait de défendre, non seulement aux
dépens de sa fortune pécuniaire, mais même de sa réputation? Il
a passé sa généreuse vie à protester contre deux guerres qui ont
triplé le prix de la subsistance du peuple anglais.')[39] Yet in many
ways Fox's letters reveal a personality that might be considered
the prototype of the *âme généreuse* as Stendhal conceived it. The
tendency to seek extremes of experience; the imaginative sympathy for others; the passionate enthusiasms and deep love of
literature and the arts; the strong sense of duty balanced by
periods of nonchalance and withdrawal to the delights of 'la rêverie
tendre'; the capacity for 'le véritable amour'; all the distinguishing
marks are there, as the following extracts from letters which were
written in 1794 by Fox to his dearly loved nephew Lord Holland,
show:

However, in these bad times, here am I with Liz, enjoying the fine
weather, the beauty and (not its least beauty) the idleness of this place
[St. Anne's Hill] as much as if these horrors were not going on. When
one has done all one can, as I think I have, to prevent mischief, one has

38. *De l'Amour*, ch. 31, vol. i, p. 151.
39. *Rome, Naples et Florence*, vol. ii, p. 582.

a right I think to forget its existence if one is happily situated, so as
not to be within its reach; and indeed I could not name any time of
my life when I was happier than I am now, but I do not believe I should
be so, if I had acted otherwise than I have done. This is quite such
weather as you would like, warm enough to sit under a tree, and do
nothing all day, or as Ariosto says:

> All'ombra de' poggetti
> Legger d'antichi gli amorosi detti[40]

Here I am perfectly happy. Idleness, fine weather, Ariosto, a little
Spanish, and the constant company of a person whom I love, I think,
more and more every day and every hour, make me as happy as I am
capable of being, and much more so than I could hope to be if politics
took a different turn. Though the death of Robespierre took place on
the 28th of last month, we have yet no regular account of it here. I own
I think it is a very good event in one view, that it will serve to destroy
an opinion which was gaining ground, that extreme severity and
cruelty are the means of safety and success to those who practise them.[41]

    . . . our tastes are certainly not very like in painting, for to doubt
about Correggio, seems to me just as if a man were to doubt about
Homer, or Shakespeare, or Ariosto. . . .[42] . . . The weather delicious,
and the place looking beautiful beyond description, and the nightingales
singing, and Mrs. A. as happy as the day is long; all which circumstances
enable me to bear public calamities with wonderful philosophy: but
yet I cannot help thinking now and then of the dreadful state of things
in Europe, and the real danger which exists, in my opinion, of the total
extinction of liberty, and possibly of civilization too, if this war is to
go on upon the principles which are held out. . . .[43]

The affinities are obvious, not least that of the unquiet intelligence ranging over the European political scene even while the
heart rejoices in its own *chasse au bonheur* amid the pleasures of
love, beautiful scenes, and the fine arts. One evening in August
1802, Fox visited the Théâtre Français to see *Phèdre*, with Mlle
Duchesnois in the title role; he was acclaimed by the audience,
which may well at that time have included Stendhal, then living
in Paris, and visiting the theatre practically every evening. Fox's

---

40. *Memorials and Correspondence of Charles James Fox*, ed. Lord John Russell,
1853, vol. iii, p. 78.
41. Ibid. (18 August 1794), p. 81.   42. Ibid. (5 Oct. 1794), p. 86.
43. Ibid. (25 April 1794), pp. 71–2.

devoted secretary John Trotter remarks in his *Memoirs* 'the most profound attention, the liveliest sensibility' in the audience, and 'a just and honorable sympathy with every noble and grand sentiment. . . .'[44]

Nothing is more difficult than to attempt to write briefly about the *âme généreuse*, and I am aware that no reader of Stendhal is likely to be satisfied with this chapter. But I think it may be true to say that it was he who created for the literature of the post-Revolutionary period a democratized form of the *homme d'honneur* of the *ancien régime;* a human being both *homme* and *citoyen*, valuing love and courage, a member of an intensely self-critical élite to be found in all walks of life, in all nationalities, crossing the social, political, and racial barriers that time has accumulated to separate human beings. All Stendhal's characters individually, and all his works on art, music, and society, contribute different features to the composite portrait of the *âme généreuse* that emerges from his work as a whole. There is often a point of danger in the youth of an *âme généreuse*, for impatience with human limitations, and the attraction of death for an ideal, are strong. How and why survival is possible is perhaps more evident in the works of non-fiction than in the novels.

The Revolutionary years were for Stendhal above all others the period of the *âme généreuse*. Certain of his earliest published works, to be discussed in the next chapter, show how each of his passionate interests, in the period immediately following these years, is made to serve his record of the lively sensibility of the *âme généreuse* struggling with the problems of its times.

44. J. B. Trotter, *Memoirs of the Latter Years of the Right Hon. Charles James Fox*, London, 1811, p. 202.

O *19me Siècle*.

2 Prospero's Dukedom

Stendhal was able to give to each of his works of non-fiction, even when he had borrowed heavily from other writers for its substance, its peculiar atmosphere and intense individuality; thus, thinking of *Mémoires d'un touriste*, it is not the facts recorded that one remembers, but the solitary traveller, and rain falling heavily at dusk in small provincial towns. The works that he wrote during or immediately after his Italian years—*Histoire de la peinture en Italie, Rome, Naples et Florence, De l'Amour*—he probably considered for a long time to be his most important, though at the time of *La Chartreuse* he must, even without Balzac's generous praise, have realized that this was the height of his achievement and the indestructible shrine of his ideals. The work of the years 1816–21 was to help him to understand his own position, that of a man whom cataclysmic events had forced to rethink his beliefs, to formulate decisively his attitude to liberalism, to Napoleon, to art, and to determine what was essential for his personal *chasse au bonheur*.

Looking back later on the end of the Empire, Stendhal described, in *La Chartreuse*, Fabrice del Dongo making his way from the field of Waterloo to his own country. 'Pendant les quinze jours que Fabrice passa dans une auberge d'Amiens . . . les alliés envahissaient la France, et Fabrice devint comme un autre homme, tant il fit de réflexions profondes sur les choses qui venaient de lui arriver.'[1] Henri Beyle in 1814 was thirty-one, more disillusioned than Fabrice was ever to be, and disillusioned above all with himself. His letters and journals in this year of disasters national and personal, reveal a bitterness of self-knowledge almost too great to be borne, a state reflected later in such characters as Julien Sorel and Hélène de Campiréali, both of whom preferred to die rather than live with it. Beyle survived; his resilience, curiosity and vitality ensured this. But the letters and journal of that year suggest that he had been tried to the limit by his experience of the Napoleonic wars.

His disenchantment with the army had followed closely upon

1. *La Chartreuse de Parme*, ch. 5, vol. i, p. 144.

his first experience of army life, in fact very closely upon the heroic episode of the crossing of the Alps by Bonaparte and the Army of Italy, his own crossing into Italy in the wake of the reserves, and the five months of sublime happiness in Milan in 1800. On sick leave from the end of December 1801, he resigned his commission in the following year, having seen little if any active service. He seems to have turned his back completely on this life; in any case, the war was over for the time being, the preliminaries to the Peace of Amiens having been negotiated in October 1801. He became entirely absorbed in the preparation for becoming the greatest comic playwright since Molière. For four years, until October 1806, he was occupied by reading, writing, studying the arts of the theatre, formulating ambitious projects for fame and fortune, and falling in love. It was not through any desire of his own, but rather through the pressures exerted by his family, that he renounced this life for service in the commissariat of the army, under the protection of his cousin Pierre Daru. From this time onwards, he travelled widely in Europe, following the campaigns of the Emperor. He saw the results of the war at very close quarters, though his duties were non-combatant. No one knows at what point the heroic image of the soldier died in his mind. Of his heroes, Lucien Leuwen probably reflects most faithfully his disenchantment—the pettiness of garrison life, the company of *âmes communes*, the lack of opportunity for heroism. Lucien 's'était toujours figuré mourir sur le gazon, la tête appuyée contre un arbre, comme Bayard';[2] there is a reference to 'l'Empire et sa servilité', and the exclamation 'Heureux les héros morts avant 1804!'[3] But Lucien's meditations on war, in the second chapter of the novel, undoubtedly reflect those of Stendhal himself: 'une fois la nation en colère et amoureuse de la gloire, adieu la liberté; le journaliste qui élèvera des doutes sur le bulletin de la dernière bataille sera traité comme un conspirateur, comme l'allié de l'ennemi. Encore une fois nous serons distraits de la liberté par l'amour de la gloire. . . .'[4] In all his writings it is clear that his enthusiasm was for a conception

---

2. *Lucien Leuwen*, ch. 44, vol. iii, p. 244.
3. Ibid., ch. 3, vol. i, p. 39, ('Le Chasseur Vert').
4. Ibid., ch. 2, vol. ii, p. 14.

of liberty that experience showed to be an impossible ideal—the
liberty of the Declaration of Rights, together with the fraternity
and equality of all *âmes généreuses*, fighting for that liberty against
all tyrants. The young Republic, the young general of the Army
of Italy, in fact the short period before the first assumption of
dictatorial power by Bonaparte, was the one to which Stendhal
constantly looked back in imagination, endowing it with the
moral nobility and revolutionary fervour that he needed to believe
in. It is constantly to men and women of this period that he refers
as examples of *âmes généreuses*—Madame Roland, Fox, Lafayette—
associating with the heroes of this period those of Republican
Rome. In fact, like all his educated contemporaries, he seemed
to live in constant imaginative association with the heroes of
Plutarch's *Lives*. Constantly referred to by writers and orators,
their examples of physical courage, heroic self-sacrifice for the
general good, and deep love of country, inspired the Republicans
of France and the young Bonaparte. The Empire, on the contrary,
increasingly came to represent for Stendhal the triumph of self-
seeking, the futility of carnage, the absurdities of court life. Yet
he was happy to reach, in the years 1810–12, a position of eminence
in this society, happy in successfully acting the role of the competent servant of the Empire. 'Il faut jouer et mépriser la comédie!'[5]
Undoubtedly he both despised and enjoyed the society of those
times, discovering in himself an ambition for money and position,
a need for a certain ease in life, for the sake of which he was
willing to set aside his deepest beliefs. He was not prepared to
accept poverty and obscurity under the despised Bourbons, and
in 1814 desperately sought for a situation in the new regime that
should confirm his importance and permit a lavish social life. No
wonder that his Julien Sorel, Leuwen, Mosca are made in his
image, cherishing position, success, social acceptance, yet always
keeping the '*arrière-boutique*' to which they retire to contemplate
their store of liberal ideals—the '*arrière-boutique*',[6] whose windows
give on to a sublime world of the imagination.

5. *Correspondance* (3 juin 1807), vol. i, p. 352.
6. The passage in Montaigne's *De la Solitude* which contains this expression,
and indeed Montaigne's *Essays* as a whole, obviously contributed much to the
conception of the *âme généreuse*.

The year 1814 marked the failure of his hopes of a brilliant position in Restoration society. Perhaps because he wrote comparatively little about his experiences of the war, not much attention seems to have been given to the extreme physical and moral ravages of the empire campaigns upon Stendhal. The retreat from Moscow alone was surely enough to mark for life anyone who survived it. The fact that he is supposed to have invented some tales about it for the benefit of Byron seems singularly unimportant compared with the fact that he actually experienced it and was, as usual, reticent about these experiences. He left Paris on 23 July 1812 with 'deux énormes portefeuilles et cinquante paquets particuliers, entre autres, une lettre que S.M. l'Impératrice vient de me remettre en me recommandant de la porter vite à l'Empereur'.[7] His luggage included the manuscript of his *Histoire de la peinture en Italie*, which was subsequently lost. His journal contains only two entries about the retreat from Moscow; they are mainly concerned with the exodus from the burning city, they are factual, objective, almost dry. He is perfectly honest about his hope that his resourceful conduct may attract some reward: 'Je ne regretterais pas de telles journées quand elles se renouvelleraient cent fois, si elles me conduisaient à avoir *in my dear Italy* un emploi du même rang que celui que j'ai à Paris. . . .',[8] and he stresses, in terms that were later to be familiar, his need for solitude in order to appreciate a beautiful or grandiose sight. 'C'était un grand spectacle, mais il aurait fallu être seul pour la voir ou entouré de gens d'esprit. Voilà la triste condition qui a gâté pour moi la campagne de Russie, c'est de l'avoir faite avec des gens qui auraient rapetissé le Colisée et la mer de Naples.'[9] The letters of the year 1813 are more explicit than the journal: '. . . un voyage charmant; trois ou quatre fois par jour, je passais de l'extrême ennui au plaisir extrême. Il faut avouer que ces plaisirs n'étaient pas délicats. Un des plus vifs, par exemple, a été de trouver un soir quelques pommes de terre à manger sans sel, avec du pain de munition moisi. . . .'[10] But even so, there are few

7. *Correspondance*, vol. i, pp. 652–3.
8. *Journal* (28 août 1812), Pléiade, *Oeuvres, intimes*, p. 1224.
9. Ibid. (14/15 septembre 1812), p. 1229.
10. *Correspondance* (7 novembre 1812), vol. i, p. 680.

indications of the appalling hardships endured; only an occasional suggestion. 'Moi, je me suis sauvé à force de résolution; j'ai souvent vu de près le manque total de forces et la mort.'[11]

Immediately on his return to Paris he took up his old pursuits, but with complete lack of heart. A sensation of deathly cold seemed to paralyse his mind. He was evidently preoccupied with this incapacity for feeling. 'Cet état de mort morale est-il un effet nécessaire d'une lutte de six mois avec le dégoût, le malaise et le danger?'[12] In Paris, there was talk of the nominations to prefectures; his greatest wish was to be given one of the Italian departments, or, even better, the position of *intendant de la couronne* at Rome or Florence. No reward of any kind for his services during the Russian campaign was forthcoming, nor was any time for recuperation of health and spirits allowed—in April 1813 he was sent to Prussia and appointed *intendant* of Sagan. Then a breakdown in health forced him to take some leave; he spent a short time in Italy, renewed his love affair with Angela Pietragrua, and worked again at the *Histoire de la peinture*. At this time it is particularly in his letters to his friend Félix Faure that the clearest indications of a carefully controlled but acute sensibility appear. Of his work in Germany 'ce travail n'occupe pas toute ma force; si je n'ai quelque douce pensée à chantonner entre mes dents, en faisant mes lettres officielles, je suis un animal flambé.'[13] But once in Milan he expressed in his journal his relief at returning to Italy 'je songeais que mes voyages en Italie me rendent plus original, plus *moi-même*. J'apprends à chercher le bonheur avec plus d'intelligence.'[14]

No sooner had he returned to France than he was involved in organizing the defence of the Grenoble region against the Allied forces. The abdication of Napoleon once again placed his career and future in jeopardy. In fact, some reading between the lines is necessary in the recital of the events of these years, 1811–14, to imagine the immense strain, and indeed the complete nervous exhaustion, in which he must have lived. His journal and letters

11. Ibid. (28 décembre 1812), p. 689.
12. *Journal* (13 mars 1813), p. 1239.
13. *Correspondance* (16 juillet 1813), vol. i, p. 701.
14. *Journal* (7 sept. 1813), p. 1272.

reveal the persistence with which he attempted to retain a hold
on his intellectual and social interests and pursuits, and to maintain
the complicated and delicate structure of his life intact. One can
only wonder at the remarkable mental balance and physical
resilience that enabled him to get through these years without
disaster. Probably the short return to Italy in September 1813
provided an indispensable relief; at last under the date 11 September is the entry in the journal 'sono felice'.[15] But he admitted
that the intensity of the happiness was less than formerly. Reading
his journal for this period, one realizes the power that renewed
pleasure and interest had to revive his physical strength; presumably a convalescent, he seems to have led a singularly demanding
life, reading, writing, opera-going, love-making, and standing in
the street talking with friends till one in the morning. That his
love for Angela Pietragrua, though absorbing, was not an *amour-
passion* as he later defined it, is apparent from the journal; but it
provided him with the desired dramatic emotions of ecstasy and
despair.

The journal of 1814 covers briefly his mission to Grenoble, his
return to Paris, and the early days of his arrival in Italy; and his
letters for the year complete and explain the journal. The letters
written when he was *aide* to the Comte de Saint-Vallier give
a running account of the defence of the Dauphiné against the
advancing Allies. It also appears that though sick leave was
requested for Beyle on 30 January, he was not released until the
second week in March. The last letter written during this period
of service was a report on the atrocities committed by the occupying forces of 'Croates, Kalmoucks et autres barbares'.[16] From
Paris his letters to his sister mention briefly the Allied assault on
Paris. The abdication of Napoleon meant the probable loss of
his position as 'auditeur', and he comments 'trente mille nobles
qui ne savent rien faire affluent par toutes les diligences pour tout
demander'.[17] His main preoccupation now was his own situation;
the Beugnots, his only support, were attempting to get him
nominated to a post in Italy. 'Vivre ici dans une demi-misère
m'est impossible aujourd'hui, lié comme je suis, presque seulement

15. *Journal*, p. 1274.   16. *Correspondance* (10 mars 1814), vol. i, p. 762.
17. Ibid. (15 avril 1814), vol. i, p. 767.

avec des gens riches.'[18] The letters of May and June are of the
greatest interest, recording his accesses of despair and renewal of
hope, his desperate financial situation, his gratitude to those of
his powerfully placed friends who were trying to help him. But
the most interesting of all are the official letters to members of
the new government. In what state of mind did he write, in a
letter to the Comte de Blacas, begging for his name to be retained
in the Almanach Royal as Honorary Inspector of the Crown
Furniture: 'Je ne tiens nullement aux appointements; l'honneur
de servir le Roi me suffit'?[19] He had no dependents; it was a
question of deciding what was essential to his own life and happiness. The answer was money and social standing. The 'arrière-
boutique' in which the liberal principles of the âme généreuse were
stored away seems at this period to have been a long way back
from the façade, and it is not surprising to find H. F. Imbert in his
valuable work *Les Métamorphoses de la liberté, ou Stendhal devant
la restauration et le risorgimento*, saying 'J'avoue aimer fort peu ce
Stendhal 1814'.[20] The fact is, however, that Stendhal's experience
during this year is the key to his whole work. Whether at this
time he realized it or not, he was a writer and an artist; his instinct,
fortunately, was to take the action that would preserve this most
essential aspect of his life. To focus attention too exclusively on
his political views is to falsify the picture. Disturbing as it may
be to find him in his letters of solicitation at this period referring
to Napoleon as 'l'usurpateur' and 'Buonaparte', and protesting
his constant devotion to the cause of the Bourbons, it is this that
enables him to understand, and later to present in his characters,
the element of self-betrayal so frequently to be found in the lives
of talented and ambitious men. At this point the young hero dies;
the artist survives to make of bitter experience the core of his
art. Stendhal was not in the habit of revealing, either in his letters
or in his journal, his deepest thoughts. What his thoughts about
himself, about politics and current events were, at the time, when,
poor, disappointed, humiliated even, he left Paris for Italy, one
can only deduce from occasional comments: 'On se connaît et

18. Ibid. (7 mai 1814), vol. i, p. 769.
19. *Correspondance* (23 mai 1814), vol. i, p. 772.
20. p. 608.

on ne se change pas, mais il faut se connaître'.[21] 'Ainsi il faut se brûler
la cervelle tout de suite, ou chercher à vivre comme je pourrai'.[22]
Having chosen the second alternative he sought distraction from
his troubles in the composition of the *Lettres sur Haydn*,[23] the
first of his adaptations of other men's works. He was writing it in
Paris as a distraction from his suspense about his future career,
and it is difficult to see it as having any but this therapeutic value.
The transforming genius of Stendhal is not yet sufficiently established; and it seems unreasonable to regard the Italian author[24]
of the original letters as less than completely justified in resenting
this adaptation of his work for the French market. After all, his
obscure plagiarist was not yet 'Stendhal'; there was no reason
why he should have felt himself honoured to provide the frame,
the materials, and the pattern for this small-scale tapestry. Beyle
remained impenitent—his letter to the editor of the *Constitutionnel*,
defending his 'brother's' work, is witty, inventive, and impudent.[25]
The question is why he should have continued to regard the work
with affection and wish it to be reissued unchanged in later years.
First, in the desperate hope of making money by it; secondly,
perhaps, because it was a memorial to his ability to work at and
become absorbed in a subject totally unrelated to his most urgent
preoccupations, and in the middle of turbulent events in which
he was intimately concerned; and also because the farcical aspects
of life appealed to him, and he already had the un-Romantic
trait of seeing the comic side of his own personality and circumstances. His choice of a pen-name—Louis-Alexandre-César
Bombet—does not suggest any great seriousness on his part, and
I must admit to finding this the least interesting of his works and
to having tried in vain to share the interest it arouses in other critics.
Infinitely more interesting, though possibly not more important,
are his efforts to come to terms with changed circumstances.

21. *Journal* (4 juillet 1814), p. 1292.
22. *Correspondance* (28 avril 1814), vol. i, p. 768.
23. The full title is: *Lettres écrites de Vienne en Autriche sur le célèbre compositeur Jh.
Haydn, suivies d'une Vie de Mozart et de considérations sur Métastase.*
24. G. Carpani. For a detailed account of the circumstances of the composition
of the Haydn letters, as of all Stendhal's writings, see H. Martineau: *L'Oeuvre
de Stendhal.*
25. *Correspondance* (26 sept. 1816), vol. i, pp. 816–18.

He reread Destutt de Tracy, his life-line and defence against self-pity. His love for mathematics, for formulae and neat categorizing, remained constant and vitally important all his life;[26] they were his shield against the terrors of the Romantic imagination. 'Je vois que nos malheurs, nos désappointements, viennent presque toujours de désirs contradictoires. En raisonnant juste, d'après Tracy, je vais à la chasse du contradictoire qui peut se trouver encore dans mon coeur.'[27] His need to reflect coldly on his position, and determine a course of action, is evident, as a marginal note of 20 October 1814, in *Histoire de la peinture* shows: 'il n'y a d'espoir assuré que beaucoup de mouvement physique, et de s'imposer la loi de faire quelque chose de difficile.'[28] His need for work—at least five or six hours a day—is stressed too in the journal at this time. The sorting out of his ideas on politics, which was to be an important activity during his years in Italy, had already begun. He was a liberal, a former servant of Napoleon, and as such his position in Milan under the Austrian occupying authorities was delicate. One must be grateful to Georges Blin for his defence of Stendhal's use of pen-names, and for his justification of what has seemed to many critics an absurd preoccupation on Stendhal's part with police spies and censorship.[29] Presumably any of our contemporaries who have been in danger of arrest for their political views will understand exactly how he felt. 'A vrai dire il était fatigué d'héroïsme', like Julien Sorel towards the end of his story. To recognize in himself a civil servant desperately anxious to keep his post, and willing to bow to the Bourbons in order to do so; the bitter disappointment of having received from the Emperor no reward for his services, after surviving, creditably if not heroically, the retreat from Moscow; anxieties over money; health seriously impaired; all these he had endured and was still enduring when he reached Italy. His journal at times contradicts his letters: 'Je suis blasé sur Paris, nullement en colère (je dis ceci pour le Beyle de 1820). J'étais bien dégoûté du métier

26. 'Ma cohabitation passionnée avec les mathématiques m'a laissé un amour fou pour les bonnes *définitions* sans lesquelles il n'y a que des à peu près.' *Brulard*, ch. 37, p. 359.
27. *Correspondance* (28 octobre 1814), vol. i, p. 791.
28. *Mélanges intimes et Marginalia* (20 oct. 1814), vol. i, p. 328.
29. G. Blin. *Stendhal et les problèmes de la personnalité*, pp. 238 ff.

d'auditeur et de la bêtise insolente des puissants. Rome, Rome est ma patrie, je brûle de partir.'[30] He was thirty-two, and his circumstances must have given him little cause for faith and hope. The whole of the year 1815 was spent in Italy, and almost uninterruptedly in Milan. His letters reveal an increasing anxiety over his financial situation, and great bitterness towards his father to whom he attributed his poverty; yet the journal of that year shows the same unquenchable interest in people and events. But the Hundred Days, and Waterloo, the exile to St. Helena, the second Restoration, went on while he was absorbed in love, finance, opera-going, and sight-seeing, having himself abdicated, as it were, from his former life. The great Napoleonic saga and his involvement in it had ended, as far as he was concerned, in 1814. In Venice, 'J'ai lu au café Florian les malheurs et l'avilissement de la France, je veux dire l'entrée du roi et ses premiers actes',[31] he wrote on 25 July 1815. By this time he had come to a firm conclusion, that the most desirable regime for France was that of the constitutional monarchy. 'La France ne sera jamais heureuse que gouvernée par un souverain illégitime, c'est-à-dire qui tienne sa place de la constitution.'[32] It was at this point that he would have supported the accession of the Duc d'Orléans (Louis-Philippe, son of Philippe Egalité), anticipating the arguments of the Liberal doctrinaires in Louis-Philippe's favour in 1830, when the 'citizen king' actually began his reign. The early Revolutionary idea of King and Constitution quickly supplanted that of the Republic. In July 1815 he had the idea of a poem: 'Idée d'un poème didactique sur les Constitutions pour expliquer aux peuples la constitution anglaise, sujet unique . . .',[33] which fortunately he did not waste time in attempting to write. But this marks a renewal of the seriousness and enthusiasm with which he had written the notes for his early attempts at plays. He now held one of his major themes—his conviction that 'les deux chambres' must be the goal of every politically mature nation, but *only* of the politically mature. In *Rome, Naples et Florence en 1817* he would examine the reasons why he considered Italy not to be ready for 'les deux chambres', and it is to this work that one

30. *Journal* (4 juillet 1814), p. 1293.   31. Ibid., p. 1308.
32. *Journal* (25 juillet 1815), p. 1309.   33. Ibid. (17 juillet 1815), p. 1305.

must look for the explanation of Mosca's role in *La Chartreuse*.
And the last entry in his journal for 1815 reads: 'Dans le siècle
dernier, on était en avant de l'opinion commune en médisant de
saint Paul; dans celui-ci on méritera le titre de philosophe en
faisant voir l'utilité de la non-légitimité des S[ouverains], et qu'hors
de la constitution anglaise, il n'y a point de salut.'[34]

All this biographical detail from his journal and letters is intended
to show how he gained his own bitter experience of the difficulties
confronting the *âme généreuse* in life; how he was forced to understand that his own case was that of a left-wing idealist who is also
an egoist and a hedonist, unwilling to sacrifice well-being for his
ideals, but full of generous admiration for those rare beings in
whom action and ideal move in harmony. By this time a life of
varied experience, observation, omnivorous reading, and constant
reflection had provided him with the material for his study of
the human heart. In the Milan years he drew out from this chaotic
mass of emotional, political, aesthetic experiences the principles
on which his work was henceforward to be firmly based. He still
considered that his destiny was to be, eventually, a playwright—
'Letellier' was still on the stocks—but at the same time it is already
obvious from certain earlier writings that his approach to character
was that of a novelist. He had, in any case, been occupied since
1811 in writing a work of vital importance in his development as
a writer: *Histoire de la peinture en Italie*. His most important
achievement in the Milan years was undoubtedly the slow and
laborious formation of an individual style. With very few original
ideas, he has as an artist complete originality. The habit acquired
in childhood of concealing his most cherished enthusiasms to
protect them from unsympathetic discovery, persisted throughout
his life and affected his writing, with the result that 'la sorcellerie
évocatrice' was almost forced upon him and that his whole work
is enlivened by it. This art he learnt in a hard school, in Milan he
brought it near to perfection.

34. Ibid. (23 aout 1815), p. 1313. His enthusiasm for the English Constitution
did not last long. See the section entitled 'Angleterre' in the notes for *L'Italie en
1818. Rome, Naples et Florence*, vol. ii, p. 576. Also L. Jansse: *Stendhal et la constitution anglaise*. Stendhal Club: 15 juillet 1967, pp. 327–48. M. Jansse describes
Stendhal's political thought as 'lucide, exigeante et avertie'. The adjectives seem
excellently chosen.

The difficult and interesting problem is how to convey the importance of the *Histoire de la peinture en Italie*, particularly since it is almost entirely composed of translations or adaptations of the work of other writers. It has been the subject of much scholarly research; Paul Arbelet's critical edition in the Champion series, and his *L'Histoire de la peinture en Italie et les plagiats de Stendhal*, are indispensable for a fair judgement of the work. Jean Prévost's chapter in *La Création chez Stendhal*, and H.-F. Imbert's in *Les Métamorphoses de la liberté*, are particularly valuable. The *Histoire de la peinture* is compiled from the works of practically every known eighteenth-century writer on art, every traveller in Italy—the list is very long and includes Lanzi, Vasari, the abbé Dubos, the Président de Brosses. To an unfriendly eye Stendhal might here appear as a kind of industrious Bouvard or Pécuchet in the 'aesthetics' period of those two collaborators; a man without an original idea, an autodidact attempting to profit from his own compulsive passion for note-taking, a 'library cormorant', and also a thieving magpie. Even if one defensively seizes upon an idea which is asserted by Arbelet to be Stendhal's own, someone is sure to produce triumphantly a page reference in Goethe or Madame de Staël. But the first idea of the book was that of a translation: 'I have thought to translate Lanzi,—he has 1,900 pages, —and to make of that 2 vol. of 450.' [35] In fact he translated not only Lanzi but many other works, more or less accurately, adding comments of his own, quoting in a footnote a line of poetry or prose suggested by what he has just read. He takes his reader with him in his discoveries. The best prelude to the *Histoire de la peinture* is the journal of his two months in Italy in 1811; much of this journal is occupied with an account of his relations with Angela Pietragrua, whom he then met again after nine years; but there are many illuminating comments on his reactions to art, music, and scenery. For example, he finds that 'Tous ces grands peintres des trois écoles d'Italie ont manqué d'expression,' [36] and any expressiveness found in them by travellers exists only in the latters' imagination. He is unimpressed by a picture of Tancred and Herminia; in Herminia he finds 'pas l'ombre, je ne dis pas

35. *Journal*, 'Voyage en Italie 1811', ch. 77, p. 1210.
36. *Journal*, 'Voyage en Italie 1811', ch. 42, p. 1168.

de cette nuance divine exprimée par le Tasse, de ce coeur combattu d'Herminie entre l'amour et la pudeur, mais pas l'ombre d'émotion'.[37] It is precisely 'cette nuance divine' that he later strove for in his heroines, Mme de Rênal, Clélia, Mme de Chasteller, Hélène de Campiréali. In fact he looked at pictures with the eye of a potential novelist; the fact that he considered plays from the same point of view also becomes apparent at this time.

Writing to Crozet in 1816, to explain why he intended to leave the *Histoire* unfinished (he completed only the first two volumes) he says 'Par hasard, en 1811, je devins amoureux de la c[omte]sse S[imonetta] [Angela Pietragrua] et de l'Italie. J'ai parlé d'amour à ce beau pays en faisant la grande ébauche, en douze vol[umes], perdue à Molodetchno.'[38] He then recalls how, in 1814 and 1815, he rewrote the work as a distraction from misfortunes of various kinds. What he had to discover was how to create a style that would convey emotion without affectation and over-emphasis; he does it by making a direct, almost brusque informality of approach contrast with a kind of controlled rhetoric that became one of his greatest assets. The strength of the underlying feeling creates a structure of overtones. The despairs and disappointments dissolve; the strong emotion is all turned into passionate interest and joy. There is no need to be taken in by Stendhal's frequent protestations that to attempt to describe happiness was to destroy it; he never described it, he recreated it; no writer could ever claim with more justification: 'Je sais l'art d'évoquer les minutes heureuses. . . .' His *Histoire de la peinture* already has examples of this magical aspect of his art, later to reach its height in the last pages of *Henry Brulard* and in certain chapters of *La Chartreuse de Parme*.

The best way to enjoy the *Histoire de la peinture* seems to be to accept that it owes a great deal to other writers, and that Stendhal's choice of authorities to borrow from indicates not only the extent of his reading and the depth of his interest in his subject, but also his feeling of inadequacy. It was a way of escaping from 'Letellier'; before grappling again with that elusive work he needed to know what he believed about all the subjects that were important to him.

37. Ibid., ch. 43, p. 1169.
38. *Correspondance* (30 sept. 1816), vol. i, p. 824.

The *Histoire* was a way of finding out. And one of the many delights of the book is to see how characters and situations of the great novels can already be glimpsed, just beyond the circle of light in which he was working. For example, Chapter 119, on the modern ideal of beauty, is important less because of the aesthetic views it expresses than because it is an exact description of Gina Sanseverina:

Si l'on avait à recomposer le beau idéal, on prendrait les avantages suivants:

1. Un esprit extrêmement vif.
2. Beaucoup de grâces dans les traits.
3. L'oeil étincelant, non pas du feu sombre des passions, mais du feu de la saillie. L'expression la plus vive des mouvements de l'âme est dans l'oeil, qui échappe à la sculpture. Les yeux modernes seraient donc fort grands.
4. Beaucoup de gaîeté.
5. Un fonds de sensibilité.
6. Une taille svelte, et surtout l'air agile de la jeunesse.[39]

But we had better begin with the long Introduction, written between 14 August 1814 and 30 January 1815. When Stendhal himself wrote a notice of the book for the Paris Monthly Review on its reissue in 1823, he described this Introduction in the following terms: 'une introduction de 80 à 90 pages, qui présente une esquisse vivante et frappante de l'énergie féroce des barbares nordiques qui conquirent la France et l'Italie aux premiers siècles de notre ère, et un tableau magistral des moeurs, des coutumes et des passions dominantes des habitants de l'Italie à la naissance des beaux-arts.'[40] This is a fair enough judgement. The vigour and vehemence of the style comes from a genuine passion for the subject. The Introduction of *Histoire de la peinture* must be seen in its context; it is a fervent expression, among many in the late eighteenth and early nineteenth centuries, of European liberalism, a hymn to Freedom and Joy, at a period when passion and eloquence were more admired than common sense. The following sentence is typical. 'C'est en Italie que ce phénomène éclate dans toute sa splendeur. Quiconque aura le courage d'étudier l'histoire

39. *Histoire de la peinture en Italie*, ch. 119, vol. ii, p. 117.
40. *Courrier anglais*, vol. i, p. 369.

des nombreuses républiques qui en ce pays cherchèrent la liberté, à l'aurore de la civilisation renaissante, admirera le génie de ces hommes, qui se trompèrent sans doute, mais dans la recherche la plus noble qu'il soit donné à l'esprit humain de tenter.'[41] But the continuation of Stendhal's paragraph reveals precisely the quality that many readers have found in his work: the harmonious union of fine sensibility with reason and lucidity. Freedom, for him, is necessarily linked to forms of government. He knew well enough the wild and anarchical side of his own naturally head-strong and rebellious character, with its ardent imagination, and the necessary discipline provided by lucid analysis and the calm working out of problems. So 'Elle a été découverte depuis, cette forme heureuse de gouvernement; mais les hommes qui arrachèrent à l'autorité royale la constitution d'Angleterre étaient, j'ose le dire, fort inférieurs en talents, en énergie et en véritable originalité aux trente ou quarante tyrans que le Dante a mis dans son enfer, et qui vivaient en même temps que lui vers l'an 1300.'[42] This marks the introduction of the idea, to become familiar in Stendhal's work, that enviably stable and just government is always accompanied by the possibility of flatness and boredom. 'Chose singulière! L'époque brillante de l'Italie finit au moment où les petits tyrans sanguinaires furent remplacés par des monarques modérés.'[43]

His taste for breaking up his commentary by anecdotes, itself characteristic of the eighteenth century, comes quickly into play. He introduces his stories with typical nonchalance. 'Prenons au hasard un recueil d'anecdotes du 16e siècle. Je dis indifféremment dans tout ceci le quinzième siècle ou le seizième; les chefs d'oeuvre de la peinture sont du commencement du seizième siècle, où tout le monde était encore gouverné par les habitudes du quinz-ième.'[44] In these anecdotes he approaches what he loves best in literature, the circumstances and facts which throw strange light on the depth of the human heart. And he passes rapidly from past to present, frequently leaving it to the reader to make the connec-tion. 'Côme (de Médicis) fut distrait par le mélange de courage et de finesse dont il avait besoin pour avilir des coeurs brulants

---

41. *Histoire de la peinture en Italie*, vol. i, p. 11.
42. Ibid.
43. Ibid., vol. i, p. 16 n.   44. Ibid., p. 16.

encore pour la liberté.'[45] His summary of the governments of
Florence, Venice, Rome, and Naples contains an attack on the
Papal government, always to be a subject of interest to him. In
Rome, 'au milieu de tant de grands souvenirs, à la vue des ruines
de ce Colisée, qui inspirent une mélancolie si sublime, et remuent
même les coeurs les plus froids, rien n'encourage les rêves d'une
imagination jeune et ardente.'[46] The whole of this Byronic lament
is original and deeply felt; it is the climax of the main point of his
Introduction, which is the relationship between art and the politics
of the society in which it appears. Art in Italy will be great again,
says Stendhal, 'lorsque les quinze millions d'Italiens réunis sous
une constitution libérale estimeront ce qu'ils ne connaissent pas,
et mépriseront ce qu'ils adorent.'[47]

Soon after this there begins the attack on religion and its influence that runs like the fire of the *mortaretti* at Grianta in *La Chartreuse* through the whole book. The equivalent of the saint for
the Greeks was Theseus, saviour of Athens; in contrast to whom
Stendhal mentions St. Simeon Stylites, whose self-martyrdom
seems to him the height of uselessness and the antithesis of virtue
in the Republican sense. For the atheist Stendhal the Catholic
church, its ministers, its teaching, and most of its works, is constantly a target for sarcastic comment. But not of bitter hostility.
His thought on changing attitudes to religion is best summed up
in Chapter 15: 'ces vagues religieuses et antireligieuses, se succédant
tous les dix ans, en s'affaiblissant sans cesse, finiront par se perdre
dans l'ennui naturel au sujet.'[48]

The question of Stendhal's opinions on religion are of permanent interest. In *Henry Brulard* he traces back to his childhood
his hatred of priests and contempt for organized religion. His
extremely guarded and sceptical attitude to religious faith is well
expressed in the course of his review for the *London Magazine*, in
November 1824, of Benjamin Constant's *De la Religion*: 'Tous
les hommes bien constitués ont de l'imagination. A la fin de
chaque déluge, de chaque tremblement de terre, ou même simplement après un coup de tonnerre, cette imagination révèle aux
peuples l'existence des dieux. C'est là ce que M. Constant appelle

45. Ibid., p. 18.   46. Ibid., p. 43.   47. Ibid., p. 44.
48. Ibid., p. 108.

le sentiment religieux.'[49] He is severe to Constant: 'ce mauvais livre, ce triste acte d'hypocrisie. . . .'[50] though he had greatly admired earlier works of his.

But another point of view is expressed in a letter to Sainte-Beuve, written on 21 December 1834: 'je crois qu'il y a un *God*: il est méchant et malfaisant. Je serai bien étonné, après ma mort, si je le trouve, et s'il m'accorde la parole je lui en dirai de belles.'[51] This may appear petulant and even childish, but it is at least uncompromising. He maintains an extremely matter-of-fact attitude to the human need for the transcendental. Though he respected religious faith in others, if it appeared simple and sincere, what seemed to exasperate him most was the apparent absurdity of asking human beings to base their lives on faith in the irrational when they are so constituted that their whole existence and survival depend on their capacity for rational and logical thought. He could not be called a violent enemy of religion—his indifference was too great for that—but he continued to regard the Church and most of its ministers as a reactionary temporal power founded upon hypocrisy. He gave full play in his works to the current Restoration view of the political intrigues of the Jesuit *Congréga-tion* and its spies. He created the reprehensible characters of the abbés Frilair and Castanède; but he balanced the picture by creating also the excellent abbés Chélan, Pirard, and Blanès. But on the whole religious faith, as he sees it for example in *L'Abbesse de Castro* or *La Chartreuse*, is at best half-pagan superstition and at worst a cover for dishonest scheming for advancement. In all the solitary hours of meditation spent by his characters, only a few are devoted to reflection about religion; the most famous are those of Julien Sorel in prison. But when Julien hears that Madame de Rênal is still alive: 'Dans ce moment suprême il était croyant. Qu'importent les hypocrisies des prêtres? peuvent-elles ôter quelque chose à la vérité et à la sublimité de l'idée de Dieu?'[52], are the questions those of Julien or of Stendhal himself? In any case it is the *idea* of God which is seen as true and sublime—an idea conceived by the human mind, and not necessarily divinely revealed.

49. *Courrier anglais*, vol. iv, p. 26.   50. Ibid., p. 27.
51. *Correspondance*, vol. ii, p. 762.
52. *Le Rouge et le Noir*, ch. 36, vol. ii, p. 394.

Stendhal had no interest in creeds. Fixed opinions—even occasionally his own—dogmatism, fanaticism, aroused his irony and impatience. He preferred on the whole the possibility of surprise to certainty. But he was able in his finest pages to give expression to moods of contemplative ecstasy. Beautiful and valuable as these pages may be, they are not sufficient grounds for attributing to him aspirations towards religious faith. Speculations about the existence of God he regarded as a waste of time: 'Quelle folie de discuter ces grands problèmes! . . . J'oublie de vivre et d'aimer, quand il me reste si peu de jours à vivre. . . .'[53]

As the Introduction of the *Histoire de la peinture* proceeds, it becomes clear that the 'energy' he so much admired is the capacity for passionate feeling. So in the Italy of the *cinquecento*, it is the *love* of art that works so many miracles. 'Il aima avec passion cet art bienfaiteur qui embellit de plaisirs faciles les temps prospères de la vie, et qui, dans les jours de tristesse, est comme un refuge ouvert aux coeurs infortunés.'[54] This is how he himself considered all art at that time; it was the attitude of his generation. When he later realized that 'le métier de l'animal est d'écrire un roman dans un grenier',[55] he proceeded quite unpretentiously to exercise a skill that was the result of about thirty-five years of hard work that he had enjoyed. There was never any suggestion of converting the garret into the shrine of Apollo or a high priest's tabernacle. Romantic traits Stendhal certainly had, but solemnity was not one of them, particularly where he himself was concerned.

Towards the end of the Introduction, there is a section called 'Considérations générales', in which some of his main points are stressed. The social conditions which ensured the flourishing of art, in a century which possessed 'la partie principale du goût, celle qui peut les suppléer toutes, et qu'aucune ne peut remplacer, je veux dire *la faculté de recevoir par la peinture les plaisirs les plus vifs*'[56] is one of these principal considerations, and was to remain so throughout his work. Another was 'les liaisons d'idées qui font les trois quarts du charme des beaux arts';[57] this would create

53. Ibid., ch. 44, p. 473.
54. *Histoire de la peinture en Italie*, vol. i, p. 48.
55. *Correspondance* (5 nov. 1832), vol. ii, p. 487.
56. *Histoire de la peinture*, vol. i, p. 48.   57. Ibid., p. 49.

some of the richest effects in his own art. The notion of relative ideas of beauty, changing taste, is again a principal and much-used theme in all his work from this time onwards. In the last pages he develops *con brio* the theme that painting will always be mediocre under absolute monarchies because of the habits of servility that they engender, their repression of originality and encouragement of conformity. Stendhal's only experience of absolutism so far had been gained during the Empire; he despised the dynastic ambitions of Napoleon and frequently refers to the servility of the Emperor's entourage. He concludes his Introduction with a reference to 'notre glorieuse Révolution' which has had the merit of practically extinguishing absolute monarchy in Europe. The political and religious views expressed in this book and in *Rome, Naples et Florence*, in works published in that year 1817 so vividly characterized by Victor Hugo in *Les Misérables*, seem highly imprudent. Any footnotes disavowing rebellious intent on the part of the author are usually so impudently ironical in tone that it is no wonder that at this period Stendhal acquired among the powerful reactionaries of Europe the reputation of a dangerous Liberal. His views are always more openly expressed in the works intended for publication than in his journal or letters. He had always used whimsical pseudonyms in signing his letters; he published the *Histoire de la peinture* under the initials M.B.A.A.; 'Monsieur Beyle Ancien Auditeur' or 'Monsieur B. A. Aubertin'; in any case Stendhal refers to the *Histoire* as 'M. Aubertin' in a letter to Mareste in 1818.[58] Just as he had also called it 'Mocenigo' when he was writing it, and as he referred to *Rome, Naples et Florence en 1817* as 'Stendhal'.

The attempt to select from the rich material of the *Histoire* what is particularly interesting for the study of Stendhal as a writer is a difficult one; there is so much that reflects this many-sided genius. But a good deal of important comment is to be found in his footnotes to the text, and I should be inclined to choose two of these, and the chapter on Ghirlandajo. The first

---

58. *Correspondance* (25 janvier), vol. i, p. 890. He signs a letter with this name in September 1818 (vol. i, p. 939). See too B. Pincherle, *In Margine all' Histoire de la peinture*. (*In Compagnia di Stendhal*, pp. 29–47.) Also in *Stendhal Club*, 15 April 1959.

of the footnotes is in Chapter 6, on art in thirteenth-century Siena:

Comme dans ce siècle Sienne était libre, du moins par les sentiments, ses artistes méritent d'être nommés immédiatement après ceux de Florence. Les savants diront: 'Voilà bien l'esprit de système et la manie de tout voir dans la liberté.' Mais les philosophes savent que l'esprit humain est une plante fort délicate que l'on ne peut arrêter dans une de ses branches sans la faire périr.[59]

It is not of course that there is anything startlingly original in the idea itself, but that it is fundamental to the whole of Stendhal's work, and particularly to the non-fictional works. He constantly tries to show, in individuals and in societies, the close inter-relationships of all their interests and activities, so that each of his books, whatever its title, reflects on a multitude of other concerns. Love, art, politics, religion, education, literature, music, social attitudes, each work is concerned with all of these, and with Stendhal's own passionate and lively interest in past and present, unchecked by misfortune, unquenchable. The ceaseless pre-occupation with liberty in society is matched by the constant evidence of his aesthetic independence; critical, often caustic, unwilling to accept without question, he takes what his fastidious taste approves of in what the works he is consulting have to offer, and in *Histoire de la peinture* one can follow the gradual elabora-tion of his own aesthetic, and see the future novelist appearing before he himself realized what his own future was to be. In this connection, another footnote, the one on *Cymbeline*, in Chapter 101, is particularly important. It was written in 1811, in collabora-tion with Crozet, who had, however, very little part in the actual composition of it. Using both the Malone edition of the plays, and the Letourneur translation, Stendhal embarks on a highly interesting analysis of *Cymbeline*; but he writes of it as though it were a novel or one of his 'chroniques italiennes'. To my mind this note is one of the most important early indications of how he was later to construct his novels; his ideas on the creation of character, the significance of plot, his adaptation of the Shake-spearean soliloquy in the form of the interior monologue, his

59. *Histoire de la peinture en Italie*, vol. i, pp. 74–5n.

willingness to manhandle historical facts for the purposes of art,
his acceptance of fantasy and melodrama, his use of historical
time, all are indicated here, and above all the poetic sensibility
which make him respond to the play and defend it against the
judgements of reason and common sense. It is also interesting to
see what at this point he failed to appreciate in the character of
Imogen, and to look ahead to the novels to see how he later
appreciated the finer shades of her personality and situation. The
profundities and oddities of the play undoubtedly made a deep
impression on him, and its characters and situations, comedy and
tragedy, became woven into the fabric of his art.[60]

This analysis of *Cymbeline* now seems far more interesting than
the considerations on the different temperaments in the chapters
on the *beau idéal*, in which Stendhal borrowed so much from
Cabanis and the abbé Dubos. Similarly, in the chapter called
'Ghirlandajo et la perspective aérienne', it is not now the question
of Stendhal's representation of the artist, or of the accuracy of his
translation of Lanzi or Vasari, that matters, so much as what the
chapter tells us about the sensibility of Stendhal as an artist.
Arbelet notes in his edition that Stendhal has falsified a passage
from Raphael Mengs: 'Ainsi la petite phrase de Mengs [on linear
perspective] transformée par l'imagination déformante de Beyle,
va devenir la source unique de tout le chapitre.'[61] But this is not
the point. It is the content and style of the following passage
which are important:

La magie des lointains, cette partie de la peinture qui attache les
imaginations tendres, est peut-être la principale cause de sa supériorité
sur la sculpture. Par là elle se rapproche de la musique, elle engage
l'imagination à finir ses tableaux; et si, dans le premier abord, nous
sommes plus frappés par les figures du premier plan, c'est des objets dont
les détails sont à moitié cachés par l'air que nous nous souvenons avec
plus de charme; ils ont pris dans notre pensée une teinte céleste.

Le Poussin, par ses paysages, jette l'âme dans la rêverie; elle se croit
transportée dans ces lointains si nobles, et y trouver ce bonheur qui

---

60. For fuller information about this footnote, see P. Arbelet, *L'Histoire de la
peinture en Italie et les plagiats de Stendhal;* and *V. del Litto: La Vie intellectuelle de
Stendhal. Genèse et évolution de ses idées (1802–1821).*

61. *Histoire de la peinture en Italie,* vol. i, pp. 340–1.

nous fuit dans la réalité. Tel est le sentiment dont le Corrège a tiré ses beautés.

And the note at the end of this passage is equally important, beginning, 'Tel est notre misère. Ce sont les âmes les plus faites pour ce bonheur tendre et sublime qu'il semble fuir avec le plus de constance. Les premiers plans sont pour elle la prosaïque réalité', and which ends, 'Les sentiments divins ne peuvent exister ici-bas qu'autant qu'ils durent peu.'[62] One of the few occasions in the book when he allows a personal note of melancholy to appear. But it is precisely 'la magie des lointains' that he learnt to create in his own works, so that however clearly the characters in the foreground are defined, infinite distances open up beyond them. His love of this shadowy world of rêverie is as much as anything responsible for his refusal to finish so many of his works. The characters too wander off into the 'lointains si nobles', and both author and reader are left to silent conjecture.

The parts of the *Histoire de la peinture en Italie* that attracted the most attention were Book 3, the life of Leonardo da Vinci, and Book 7, so greatly admired by Delacroix, the life of Michelangelo. Both artists are portrayed as Stendhalian characters, *âmes généreuses*. The consecrating words soon appear in the Leonardo chapter, 'âme tendre, et que la contemplation de la beauté menait à l'attendrissement'. Stendhal suggests a picture that Leonardo might have painted; a scene from *Gerusalemme Liberata:* 'Angélique trouvant Médor sur le champ de bataille'. The last chapter of the book on Michelangelo, 'Le goût pour Michel-Ange renaîtra', traces the change in taste from the beginning of art to the age of 'une politesse cérémonieuse', hostile to enthusiasm and strong emotion; then he forecasts the renaissance of the desire for strong emotion, and its reflection in art. In concluding, he associates art closely with politics once again. The whole of this chapter, as Arbelet points out, is taken from an article in the *Edinburgh Review*; but again it is a footnote which gives Stendhal's own point of view, and in another footnote he acknowledges his debt to the review. The sentence 'C'est donc par une peinture exacte et enflammée du coeur humain que le dix-neuvième siècle se

62. Ibid., ch. 28, pp. 152–3. See too J.-P. Richard, *Littérature et sensation*, pp. 83–4.

distinguera de tout ce qui l'a précédé', taken from the review, has this note:

Le dix-neuvième siècle portera les gens de génie au rôle de Fox ou de Bolivar; ceux qui se consacreront aux arts, il les portera à une peinture froide. Mais une peinture froide n'est pas de la peinture. Ceux qui échapperont à ces deux écueils marcheront dans le sens du chapitre.

En 1817, j'aimerais parbleu bien mieux être un Fox qu'un Raphael.[63]

One might say, in fact, that he makes no secret at all of his borrowings, and even that it may never have occurred to him that the 'Happy Few' for whom the book was written would fail to realize that it was a translation and adaptation simply enlivened by his own reflections and judgements. Here, for example, the point of view expressed in the footnote goes against that of the rest of the chapter.

The whole of the *Histoire de la peinture en Italie* is devoted to showing the impossibility of separating human activities into compartments; the artist must be involved in the life of his times, and passionately involved. For all his profound love of the arts, Stendhal cannot conceive, at this point, of a life devoted exclusively to them. The Romantic conception of the Artist is completely alien to him. His letters to Louis Crozet in 1816, when he was rewriting his chapters, and dispatching them to Crozet with exhortations to get on with criticizing the content and style, making any necessary corrections, arranging for the printing, correcting the proofs, and so on, give the impression of feverish haste, irritability, and impatience, and suggest that the main consideration was to promote the sale of the book as quickly as possible and make money by it. There is an excellent account of the preparation of the book, and of the help given by Crozet and other friends, in Henri Martineau's *L'Oeuvre de Stendhal*.[64] The whole enterprise was enough to fill any serious and dedicated literary artist with scorn. Yet all the surface chatter and agitation dies away, leaving the book with its warmth, humour, and emotion unspoiled. Beyle's personality and way of life seem often to have been a means of protecting what he most valued, even from his friends; a fortification to defend his art. Sooner or later

63. Ibid., ch. 184, vol. ii, p. 327.
64. See note 24, page 29; and Bibliography.

one has to consider Proust's strictures on the method of Sainte-Beuve; that the critic's preoccupation with the daily life of the writer ignores the fact that 'un livre est le produit d'un autre *moi* que celui que nous manifestons dans nos habitudes, dans la société, dans nos vices.'[65] Yet, unless one knows something of the life of the writer, it is impossible to appreciate fully how this other 'moi' used and transformed the experience of the man who was the friend of Crozet and Mareste. But at the end of 1817 in a letter to Adolphe de Mareste he admits,

Je me suis trouvé, à la chute de mes grandeurs, rempli d'orgueil, mais d'un orgueil tenace, que jeûnes et prières n'ont pu chasser. Cet orgueil se sent fait pour être préfet ou député. Le métier d'aut[eu]r lui semble avilissant ou, pour mieux dire, *avili*. J'écris pour me désennuyer le matin; j'écris ce que je pense, *moi*, et non pas ce qu'*on* pense; le tout en attendant que le *Moniteur* m'apprenne que je suis appelé à la préfecture de N., place que je refuserais avec horreur, tant que je me verrais le collègue de MM. Montlivaut, etc., etc., etc. . . .[66]

It is as though the passionate commitment of the artist to his 'monde sublime' can best be experienced not in opposition to but in delightful juxtaposition with the practical mundane considerations of administrative duties.

His first years in Italy were marked by personal unhappiness, indifferent health, financial worries, and disappointed hopes; there was also considerable moral isolation. It was not until the end of June 1816, while he was still preparing the *Histoire de la peinture en Italie*, that the change in his fortunes took place which enabled him to write later to Crozet: 'Un hasard le plus heureux du monde vient de me donner la connaissance *of* quatre ou cinq *Englishmen of the first rank and understanding*. Ils m'ont illuminé, et le jour où ils m'ont donné les moyens de lire *the Edin[burgh] Review* sera une grande époque pour l'histoire de mon esprit. . . .'[67] His meeting with Ludovico di Breme and through him with Liberal society in Milan was indeed a turning-point; it provided him with the new ideas and enthusiasms which he always needed, and, in the *Edinburgh Review*, with a kind of indispensable digest

65. *Contre Sainte-Beuve*, ch. 8, 'La méthode de Sainte-Beuve'.
66. *Correspondance* (1 décembre 1817), vol. i, p. 881.
67. Ibid. (28 septembre 1816), p. 819.

from which he borrowed zestfully for his next works. It also formed a prelude to what he later described as *The Greatest Event of his Life*:[68] his meeting with Métilde Dembowski and his first experience of '*l'amour-passion*'.

Published one month after the *Histoire de la peinture en Italie*, in mid-August 1817, *Rome, Naples et Florence en 1817* is a journal of experiences partly real, partly imaginary; the natural habitat of 'l'animal' seems to be a box at La Scala in Milan, and he leaves it for occasional excursions into other parts of Italy. But whereas the *Histoire de la peinture* had been drafted in 1811, and then rewritten in the light of later events, *Rome, Naples et Florence en 1817* is the work of that year, spontaneous, lively, shrewd, impulsive, flashing with humour. This is where M. de Stendhal, cavalry officer, first makes his appearance. It should be emphasized immediately that this character was always, for Henri Beyle, slightly fictitious; he refers to him in a detached way in notes and letters. For example, in the margin of a copy of the book, 'Le 4 fevrier 1817. J'étais à Pouzzoles. Donc, j'a vu Naples en même temps que M. de Stendhal que je trouve très menteur. C'est un libéral-Jacobin.'[69] In a letter to Mareste, 'Delaunay a-t-il vendu les Stendhal? Combien cela a-t-il produit?'[70] Referring to an article in the *Edinburgh Review* on 'l'esprit d'observation qui, sans s'en douter, *ne songe plus aux rangs*. Violà Stendhal tout pur, et il volerait cela s'il en avait l'occasion.'[71] Whether or not Beyle himself was at Naples when he said Stendhal was, or whether he really met Byron or Rossini, matters very little; the point is that these are the places likely to have been visited and the people to have been met in Italy at this time by a traveller with the intellectual interests and social position of M. de Stendhal. From the opening sentence: 'J'ouvre la lettre qui m'accorde un congé . . .' and his departure post-haste for Milan and La Scala, the book is the record of months of voluptuous pursuit of the enjoyment of all that Italy had to offer in the early nineteenth century, and also it is an astute comment on the Italian social and political scene. His habit of borrowing paragraphs from other writings being now

68. *Mélanges intimes et Marginalia*, vol. ii, p. 41.   69. Ibid., pp. 23–4.
70. *Correspondance* (30 avril 1820), vol. i, p. 1037.
71. *Correspondance* (19 avril 1820), p. 1020.

firmly established, it is always possible that in recent editions a
note on some lively and amusing anecdote or observation may
record that he took it from the *Edinburgh Review*. But, as usual,
he made no secret of his borrowings, even mentioning them in
a letter in which he mildly protested to the editor of the journal
about the use, in a review of *Rome, Naples et Florence en 1817*, of
the word 'flippant'.[72] It is the wrong word, certainly; lively,
spontaneous, even jaunty as the manner is at times, there is an
undercurrent of deep seriousness that no delicate irony or
humour can conceal. Jean Prévost gives this book great importance
in Stendhal's literary development, referring to it as the 'Premier
ouvrage de Stendhal dont la substance soit personnelle. . . .'[73]
One might say that the substance of the *Histoire*, too, has been
transformed into something personal by the exercise of a style
already forged; and that this book simply provides another
example of this phenomenon. It is also an example of how every
subject may be made to lead into politics. Already in this work,
more strongly marked than in the *Histoire* because of the greater
freedom conferred by the subject, appears the collaboration
between several Stendhals: the artist, the psychologist, the student
of drama, the competent administrator, the visionary, and the
observer interested in the politics of his own and other times.
The artist is the most important. His work survives because he
found the words to communicate the strength of his feeling, and
because of the vitality and conviction, rather than the originality
of his opinions. What he manages to do is to express something
that he rightly saw as widespread in his own times and as likely
to be so in ours; the dilemma of the liberal idealist. It is because he
refuses to separate human activities into compartments, that he so
constantly demonstrates that '*l'homme*' and '*le citoyen*' are the same
person. After all, it is Salviati's love of Léonore which enables him
to understand the nature of republicanism! Insofar as his own love
for Métilde Dembowski enabled him to understand the nature
of idealistic liberalism, it could be said that the whole of his
subsequent work was concerned with her liberalism, a one-sided
conversation in which heart and intellect worked together, love

72. Ibid. (10 avril 1818), p. 902.
73. Prévost, *La Création chez Stendhal*, p. 148.

and irony together. But this anticipates. He had not yet met her when he published *Rome, Naples et Florence en 1817*; it is interesting to see the position at which he had arrived by this date.

This record of a traveller of great sensibility, humanity, and intelligence, with one of the greatest capacities for enjoyment that can be imagined, is also the record of a love for Italy deep enough to risk his taking a detached, critical view of Italian people, manners, and politics. His preface is important:

On verra la progression naturelle des sentiments de l'auteur. D'abord il veut s'occuper de musique: la musique est la peinture des passions. Il voit les moeurs des Italiens; de là il passe aux gouvernements qui font naître les moeurs; de là à l'influence d'un homme [Napoléon] sur l'Italie. Telle est la malheureuse étoile de notre siècle, l'auteur ne voulait que s'amuser, et son tableau finit par se noircir des tristes teintes de la politique.[74]

The last sentence is a typically casual and negative statement of what is in fact deliberate and positive. It is in line with the title, which neglects the fact that much of the book is concerned with Milan; and with the fact that a book so ostensibly concerned with Italy should also be about France. The great problems confronting the French at the beginning of the Restoration lie behind every page of *Rome, Naples et Florence en 1817*, Stendhal, much as he loved Italy, was quintessentially French; in many ways his 'Italy' is an anti-France, a kind of *repoussoir*.

It is particularly interesting now to read the letter from Mareste, written in December 1817, in which he criticized *Rome, Naples et Florence* very severely indeed. Mareste was after all in a position which is impossible now for any critic of Stendhal—that of not being able to look ahead to the novels. The most serious charge he makes is that the book lacks truth, and that it is simply a record of the prejudices and preconceived ideas of his friend Henri Beyle. Then comes the famous reference to snobbery: 'La *ducomanie* de Stendhal est aussi par trop bouffonne. Il n'est question que de Marquis, de Comtes, de Princes, de Comtesses et toute cette gentilhommerie, mise en oeuvre à tout propos, à toutes pages,

74. *Rome, Naples et Florence*, vol. ii, pp. 119–20. (The title of the Cercle du Bibliophile edition omits any date, and prints first the 1826 version. The text of *Rome, Naples et Florence en 1817* appears in the second volume of this edition, which is used for all page references.)

est sans motifs *plausibles*.'[75] In his reply on 3 January 1818 Stendhal defended his views with great good-humour, including a comment on the vanity of young Frenchmen: 'Paraître est toujours plus pour eux qu'être' And also 'Quant à la *ducomanie* de Stendhal, outre qu'elle est fort naturelle chez un homme d'une si haute naissance, un beau jour, pour *n'être pas* reconnu, il a *multiplié* par la quantité . . . *comtes et marquis*, toutes les initiales citées.'[76] He goes on to stress the great wealth of the Italian nobility, and that only they entertain. His defence seems perfectly justified.

The detailed study of Stendhal's presentation of Italian politics may safely be left to the expert attention of H.-F. Imbert.[77] But the text of *Rome, Naples et Florence en 1817* makes perfectly clear the nature of certain political convictions which were by that time fairly established for Stendhal. They may be summarized, in Stendhalian fashion, as follows:

1. The conviction that the Revolution was still in progress, and would continue at least until the end of the century.

2. The conviction that the constitutional monarchy and the two-house parliament is the most desirable and enlightened form of government; that Italy was not yet ready for it; and that France was in process of discovering, through its reaction to the Charter, whether it was ready for it or not.

3. That one of the most interesting problems of the Restoration period was the dilemma of those generous spirits, statesmen and ordinary citizens alike, who were intellectually aware of the need to move forward into the nineteenth century, while emotionally attached to habits of thought and to individuals of the eighteenth. The extreme difficulty of compromise, and the danger of being equally disliked by both Right and Left, is sympathetically presented in Stendhal's comments on Cardinal Consalvi; and there is no doubt that he had in mind, too, certain of the more enlightened ministers of Louis XVIII.

4. A natural sympathy with rebels, conspirators, impatient nationalists and republicans, but the certainty that the Republic is the surest road to military dictatorship.

5. The danger of *la haine impuissante*, which leads to the search

75. *Correspondance* (22 décembre 1817), vol. i, p. 1251.
76. *Ibid.*, p. 885.   77. See p. 28 and Bibliography.

for that power by which the hatred can be expressed in revenge and cruelty. The danger of fear, as the cause of tyranny and cruelty. 'Entendez toujours par avilissement moral, malheur et scélératesse. Le scélérat qui vous fait horreur comme assassin, vous ferait pitié comme père de famille'.[78]

6. Stendhal, by ambition and temperament, was inclined to accept the rigid social classifications of his time; the more egalitarian attitudes of our times would have appeared grotesquely eccentric in his. The Restoration period, like our own, was obsessed with class distinctions, but from a different point of view: the preoccupation then being to re-establish a social hierarchy on relatively new, financial, criteria. It is Balzac who best presents this process. Stendhal, because of his concern with the tribulations of the *âme généreuse*, and with *la chasse au bonheur*, is more interested in individuals than in classes and categories. An *âme généreuse*, after all, may be found in any class of society. Looking back on the childhood of Henry Brulard, Stendhal makes the distinction between his great friend, his grandfather's servant Lambert, and this young man's brother, and continues frankly:

Car il faut l'avouer, malgré mes opinions alors parfaitement et foncièrement républicaines, mes parents m'avaient parfaitement communiqué leurs goûts aristocratiques et réservés. Ce défaut m'est resté. . . . J'abhorre la canaille (pour avoir des communications avec), en même temps que sous le nom de peuple je désire passionnément son bonheur, et que je crois qu'on ne peut le procurer qu'en lui faisant des questions sur un objet important. C'est-à-dire en l'appelant à se nommer des députés.[79] [And he adds] Mes amis, ou plutôt prétendus amis, partent de là pour mettre en doute mon sincère libéralisme. . . .

In the later, 1826, version of *Rome, Naples et Florence*, he summed up his attitude towards the society of the Restoration, in an entertaining report of a conversation about it in an Italian salon; the most interesting case for him is that of the intelligent young nobleman: 'Voilà une triste position pour un homme de coeur: être toute sa vie marquis et libéral, et cependant jamais complètement ni libéral ni marquis.'[80] And again in *Henry Brulard*: 'J'avais et j'ai encore les goûts les plus aristocrates, je ferais tout pour le bonheur

78. *Rome, Naples et Florence*, vol. ii, p. 221.
79. *Vie de Henry Brulard*, ch. 14, p. 166.
80. *Rome, Naples et Florence*, vol. i, p. 301.

du peuple mais j'aimerais mieux, je crois, passer quinze jours de chaque mois en prison que de vivre avec les habitants des boutiques.'[81] As can be seen, in this honest statement Stendhal carried his dislike of cant and affectation to unusual lengths. A lifelong supporter of liberal principles, he disliked the society of the working classes, and preferred to admire the energy and dynamism that he always saw in them, from a distance. But common as this attitude may be, it is not always so openly admitted. He has, in fact—and this emerges very clearly at the time of *Rome, Naples et Florence*—the imagination that enables him to enter into other lives, and therefore to see the problems confronting sincere supporters of any political party. The desire to be just and generous in judgement is always predominant with him; and it is not surprising that he should have been greatly preoccupied, during his Italian years, with thinking out his attitude to Napoleon. The effect of the Revolutionary and Napoleonic wars on Italy, the effect of the Empire, is of course a major theme of *Rome, Naples et Florence en 1817*. Particularly in the last twenty pages or so he reflects on his conversation with three Italian officers, at Lake Como, and sums up his ideas on the Napoleonic era in Italy: 'Je m'enferme dans une chambre du second étage of the villa Melzi—là, je refuse mes yeux à la plus belle vue qui existe au monde après la baie de Naples; et arrêté devant le buste de Melzi, tout transporté de tendresse pour l'Italie, d'amour de la patrie et d'amour pour les beaux-arts, j'écris à la hâte le résumé de nos discussions.'[82] These pages form a fitting climax to so rich and varied a work, and contain many of the themes of his later works, briefly stated. Stendhal had been a servant of the Emperor, had reached the height of his administrative career in his service. But his contempt for the court life and society of the Empire was frequently expressed in letters and journal; he had no tendency to glamorize war or courage in battle: 'Je quittai Moscou le 16 octobre 1812. Les généraux étaient des modèles d'égoïsme sordide, prêts à sacrifier leur vie pour de l'avancement, et bien autre chose que leur vie. Ces âmes sales et sordides. . . .'[83] Like the majority of

---

81. *Vie de Henry Brulard*, ch. 27, p. 258.
82. *Rome, Naples et Florence*, vol. ii, p. 259.
83. *Mémoires intimes et Marginalia*, vol. ii, p. 312.

European liberals, he had admired the Revolutionary general, Bonaparte, and deplored the establishment of the Empire, even though he himself had profited from it. Trying as always to balance emotion and reason, a strong sense of drama and equally strong common sense, he had, shortly after the writing of *Rome, Naples et Florence*, come to the conclusion: 'J'abhorre Napoléon comme tyran, mais j'abhorre tout juste les pièces à la main. Napoléon condamné, j'adore poétiquement et raisonnablement une chose si extraordinaire: le plus grand homme qui ait paru depuis César.'[84] And to one of the versions of his 'epitaph' he added the name of Napoleon to those of Cimarosa, Shakespeare, Mozart, and Correggio—'Il respecta un seul homme: NAPOLÉON.'[85] He made two attempts to write a life of Napoleon; both were abandoned unfinished. The first, the *Vie de Napoléon*, written in Milan in 1817 and 1818, was taken largely from articles in the *Edinburgh Review*, but he made no pretence about this; 'Les auteurs de cette vie,' he says, 'sont deux ou trois cents. Le rédacteur n'a fait que recueillir les phrases qui lui ont semblé justes.'[86] The later attempt, the *Mémoires sur Napoléon*, owes much to the *Mémorial de Sainte Hélène*;[87] it was written in Paris in 1836-7. Neither work was published in his lifetime. Undoubtedly, although in his novels he allows his characters to pay tribute to the Emperor Napoleon, because of the historical fact of the persistence and growth of the Napoleon legend during the Restoration and July Monarchy, his own most deeply felt tribute is reserved for the young general Bonaparte, in the opening pages of *La Chartreuse*. What is particularly interesting is to see how he is gradually working towards the form of the opening sentence. In *Rome, Naples et Florence*, 'Le 14 mai 1796 fera une époque remarquable dans l'esprit humain. Le général en chef Buonaparte entra dans Milan; l'Italie se réveilla, et, pour l'histoire de l'esprit humain, l'Italie sera toujours la moitié de l'Europe.'[88] Between this and the final version of 1839 there comes a more intense effort to recollect emotion: 'Je me rappelle fort bien l'enthousiasme dont sa jeune

84. *Mélanges de littérature*, (19 juin 1818) vol. i, p. 189
85. *Oeuvres intimes* (Pléiade) *Essai d'autobiographie* 5, 1837, p. 1534.
86. *Napoléon* (Divan edition) vol. i, p. 3.
87. Comte de Las Cases. Published 1822–3.
88 *Rome, Naples et Florence*, vol. ii, p. 261.

gloire remplissait toutes les âmes généreuses.'[89] And there is also
a process of absorbing and transforming into something finer and
less grandiloquent the rhetoric of the Imperial proclamations. Like
the distant sound of the horn so beloved by the Romantic imagination, the sound of 'A la voix du vainqueur d'Austerlitz . . .' can
be heard faintly in 'Le 15 mai 1796, le général Bonaparte fit son
entrée dans Milan à la tête de cette jeune armée qui venait de
passer le pont de Lodi, et d'apprendre au monde qu'après tant
de siècles César et Alexandre avaient un successeur. Les miracles de
bravoure et de génie dont l'Italie fut témoin en quelques mois
réveillèrent un peuple endormi . . .'[90] but what is entirely typical,
and is already so in 1817, is the ironical and deflating conclusion;
'huit jours encore avant l'arrivée des Français, les Milanais ne
voyaient en eux qu'un ramassis de brigands, habitués à fuir
toujours devant les troupes de Sa Majesté Impériale et Royale:
c'était du moins ce que leur répétait trois fois la semaine un petit
journal grand comme la main, imprimé sur du papier sale.' But
after a brief comment on the decadence of the social life of Lom-
bardy under the Habsburgs, he works up again to the key of the
opening phrases: 'Il y avait loin de ces moeurs efféminées aux
émotions profondes que donna l'arrivée imprévu de l'armée
française. Bientôt surgirent des moeurs nouvelles et passionnées.'
'Emotion', 'profonde', 'imprévu', 'nouvelle', 'passionnée; all key
words. Dominique's lorgnette is steadily trained upon 'le monde
sublime'. The 'temps héroiques de Napoléon' have receded into
the 'lointains si nobles', far from the prosaic realities of the foreground. Of course, *La Chartreuse* lies far ahead; but its origins are
constantly apparent in *Histoire de la peinture* and *Rome, Naples et
Florence*, in the letters, journal, and various other writings of the
Italian years.

The year 1817, besides being memorable for the publication of
both the *Histoire de la peinture en Italie* and *Rome, Naples et
Florence en 1817*, was the year in which Stendhal first visited
England, and in which he first read Destutt de Tracy's *Commentaire
sur 'De l'Esprit des lois' de Montesquieu*. It appeared during this year
in a Belgian edition, to which Stendhal refers in a marginal note:

89. *Napoléon*, vol. ii, p. 329.
90. *La Chartreuse de Parme*, ch. 1, vol. i, p. 9.

'à Liège, chez Desoer, en 1817',[91] and in a letter to Mareste: 'Le *Com[mentaire] sur Montesquieu* contient exactement mon *credo* politique. De plus je veux le g[ouvernement] actuel jusqu'en 1860. Lorsque l'auteur me donna le livre, il me dit de n'en pas parler; c'est pourquoi je vous le dit de Jefferson.'[92] He frequently refers to the work as 'Jefferson', the latter having first been responsible for publishing it, in America. For the rest of Stendhal's life it remained one of his most valued books; he considered it an essential political document. 'Les Julien Sorel', he wrote in 1831, 'ont lu le livre de M. de Tracy sur Montesquieu.'[93] These, the ambitious young, with the example of those who had risen from obscurity to fame and fortune under the Empire always in their minds, will be the next revolutionaries—the 'deux cent mille Julien Sorel qui peuplent la France'. The reflection of the work can be seen too in *La Chartreuse*; in describing the political life of Parma, Stendhal reverses each of the terms of Tracy's description of a government founded upon reason. His Italy is just such a nation of which Tracy warns, 'composée d'éléments trop divers'[94] of which the state of Parma, too small a unit, is one. This dry, lucid, humane work must indeed have helped Stendhal, during his years in Italy, to redefine his own liberalism. His starting point might well have been Tracy's blunt statement of the inviolability of individual freedom and the sanctity of individual life: 'tout être animé, une fois né et capable de jouissance et de souffrance, n'est la propriété de personne, ni de son père, ni de l'état; il est la sienne propre. Par son existence même, il a droit à sa conservation.'[95] Individual liberty and liberty of the press are indispensable for a happy and well ordered society; these two principles were stressed again and again by Stendhal in later years.

He had met the Comte Destutt de Tracy in 1817 during a visit to Paris, and records this fact in *Souvenirs d'égotisme*, referring to 'l'homme que j'ai le plus admiré à cause de ses écrits, le seul qui ait fait révolution chez moi. . . .'[96] His account of the Tracy salon

91. *Mélanges intimes et Marginalia*, vol. ii, p. 10.
92. *Correspondance* (24 oct. 1818), vol. i, p. 943.
93. Ibid. (17 mars 1831), vol. ii, p. 254.
94. *Commentaire* (Paris 1828), pp. 208–13.
95. Ibid., p. 350.
96. *Souvenirs d'égotisme*, ch. 4, Pléiade, p. 1444.

in this chapter is detached and even caustic; but in this work no one, not even Tracy himself or Lafayette, entirely escapes Stendhal's irony. However, the enduring nature of his admiration for the *Commentaire* is hardly in doubt; politically, it must have had an influence equal to that of Tracy's *Idéologie* and *Logique* upon his view of human character.

It came at the right time for him. So, too, did Constant's *De l'Esprit de conquête et de l'usurpation dans leurs rapports avec la civilisation européenne*, which he read in May 1814 (it had appeared at the end of January), and to which he refers in a letter to his sister as 'un chef-d'oeuvre'.[97] So it is, and it could not have failed to clarify his thoughts about the regime that was ending. He seems to have maintained a careful balance between his artist's appreciation of the dramatic quality and extraordinary genius of Napoleon, and consternation at the deplorable results of his policies. Stendhal's published correspondence includes a curious letter, written on 26 June 1818 to an unknown correspondent:

Vous parlez à un Français, Monsieur, et à un of[ficier] qui meurt d'envie de ne pas être emporté au-delà des convenances, mais qui meurt d'envie de donner quelque marque de dévouement non point au Souverain qui eut des torts graves envers la liberté, mais au grand homme qui lui a donné des jours heureux. Avec le même dévouement et la même allégresse que je serais mort pour lui sur les bords de la Bérézina, je soutiendrai le feu de qui l'a appelé un étranger et un Corse. . . .[98]

It is interesting to contrast this with the one written to the Duc de Feltre, the Minister of War, in the previous year, in which Stendhal refers to 'Buonaparte', and protests 'je n'ai jamais varié dans ma fidélité et mon dévouement au souverain légitime'.[99] In *Henry Brulard* he looks forward to a period when France shall no longer be subjected to political revolutions every fifteen years: 'Le gouvernement fort et violent de Napoléon (dont j'aimai tant la personne) n'a duré que quinze ans, 1800–15. Le gouvernement à faire vomir de ces Bourbons imbéciles (voir les chansons de

97. *Correspondance* (23 mai 1814), vol. i, p. 775.
98. Ibid., p. 926.
99. Ibid. (26 avril 1817), p. 864. For the significance of the 'u' in 'Buonaparte' see *Rome, Naples et Florence*, vol. ii, p. 117.

Béranger) a duré quinze ans aussi, de 1815 à 1830. . . .'[100] It may
be concluded that he was fully aware of the fascination and danger
of the Napoleonic saga; the complexities of his own attitude
towards it were, as always, perfectly apparent to him, and affected
his future political judgements.

The social and political interest of *Rome, Naples et Florence en
1817* is very great, its biographical interest equally so; but in
discussing a writer so apparently self-revealing and so actually
secretive and elusive, it is possible that the real significance of the
book lies elsewhere. It is possible for example, to find it in the
creation of a mood of quiet, contemplative delight, touched with
the melancholy of recollected mortality, which is established at
the beginning and made to recur at very long intervals, so that
the reader tends to look for expressions of it as for the recurrence
of a beautiful theme in music. Thus the epigraph of the first edition
of *Rome, Naples et Florence* establishes such a mood. The epigraph
had already appeared as a footnote to Chapter 130 of *Histoire de
la peinture*, and was taken in 1816 from Hazlitt's review, in the
June 1815 number of the *Edinburgh Review*, of Sismondi's *De la
Littérature du midi de l'Europe*. Stendhal never attributed it correctly,
seeming to imagine that it came from Hazlitt's *Memoirs of Holcroft*
(this probably explains the even vaguer attribution in the *Histoire*
—Biography of the A[uthor]). Hazlitt's passage is worth quoting
in full (though Stendhal's extract begins only at 'The smile . . .'):

M. Sismondi wishes that the connection between Petrarch and Laura
had been more intimate, and his passion accompanied by more interesting circumstances. The whole is in better keeping as it is. The love of a
man like Petrarch would have been less in character, if it had been less
ideal. For the purposes of inspiration, a single interview is quite sufficient.
The smile which sank into his heart the first time he ever beheld her,
played round her lips ever after; the look with which her eyes first met
his, never passed away. The image of his mistress still haunted his mind,
and was recalled by every object in nature. Even death could not
dissolve the fine illusion: for that which exists in imagination is alone
imperishable. As our feelings become more ideal, the impression of the
moment indeed becomes less violent, but the effect is more general and

100. *Henry Brulard*, ch. 40, p. 379.

permanent. The blow is felt only by reflection; it is the rebound that is fatal.[101]

The quotation ends here; but the next sentence too is significant, since it anticipates one of the main themes of *De l'Amour*: 'We are not here standing up for this kind of Platonic attachment; but only endeavouring to explain the way in which the passions very commonly operate in minds accustomed to draw their strongest interests from constant contemplation.' Stendhal's choosing of epigraphs for whole works and chapters may simply have reflected a fashion of the period. Certainly he seems to have chosen them in a haphazard sort of way, misquoting, attributing wrongly, even sometimes requesting Crozet to find him something suitable. Yet this hit-or-miss method resulted in some extraordinarily interesting effects, and it is very probable that his selection of epigraphs, giving him the opportunity for the literary allusions which were so important a part of the total impression he wished to produce, was by no means as casual as it may appear. Here, at the outset of *Rome, Naples et Florence en 1817*, he associates two of his loves, the country of Italy and the literature of England; he affirms his belief in the 'monde sublime' and in the immortalizing power of memory and of the imagination. Behind the restless, wandering life of the author and the social and political changes and upheavals he is recording, lies something changeless, beautiful, and immortal. M. de Stendhal, jauntily pronouncing on all aspects of Italian life, blithely skipping from opera-box to salon, is an indispensable shield protecting the interests of the *âme généreuse*. Stendhal takes up again in the very last paragraph the same note of gentle defiance and faith in the intangible, that distinguish the epigraph:

J'y ai réfléchi, je recommencerais mon voyage, si c'était à refaire: non pas que j'aie rien gagné du côté de l'esprit; c'est l'âme qui a gagné. La vieillesse morale est reculée pour moi de dix ans. J'ai senti la possibilité d'un nouveau bonheur. Tous les ressorts de mon âme ont été nourris et fortifiés; je me sens rajeuni. Les gens secs ne peuvent plus rien sur moi; je connais la terre où l'on respire cet *air* céleste dont ils nient l'existence; je suis de fer pour eux.[102]

101. Hazlitt, review of Sismondi's *De la Littérature du midi de l'Europe* (Paris 1813), in the *Edinburgh Review*, June 1815. (Complete Works of William Hazlitt. Centenary edition, vol. 16, p. 45.)

102. *Rome, Naples, et Florence*, vol. ii, p. 293.

Between these passages, and spaced out through the book, come the 'reprises' of this mood; for example, at Naples, at a ballet of Vigano: 'L'âme, emportée par le plaisir de la nouveauté, a des transports pendant cinq quarts d'heure de suite; et, quoique ces plaisirs soient impossibles à exprimer par la parole, de peur du ridicule, on s'en souvient après de longues années. On ne peut pas peindre cet effet en peu de mots, il faut parler longtemps, et émouvoir l'imagination des spectateurs.'[103] And after hearing the Mombelli sisters in *Evelina*, he finds the mediocrity of the libretto and music transformed by the art of the singers:

Ce sont les mouvements les plus beaux et les plus tendres d'une âme généreuse qui va à la mort, peints avec une fidélité, et je dirais même une clarté dont je n'avais pas idée: cela seul vaut le voyage en Italie. Je ne sais comment peindre la sensation de bonheur vive et profonde dont j'ai été pénétré. . . . Ces voix me transportent au-delà de tout ce qu'il y a de commun dans la vie.[104]

Then after several pages on the Italian language, and on aspects of Italian life, he writes from Bologna, of the view from the hill of San Michele in Bosco: 'Tous les vains intérêts des villes semblent expirer à nos pieds; on dirait que l'âme s'élève comme les corps; quelque chose de serein et de pur se répand dans les coeurs.'[105] At this point Stendhal quotes the sonnet by Manfredi 'Vidi l'Italia col crin sparso, incolto . . .' imagining it declaimed by one of his companions at San Michele, and relating it to the crossing of the Saint Bernard by the reserve Army of Italy. In *La Chartreuse* Fabrice expresses his enthusiasm for Napoleon as liberator of Italy in the words of Monti.) Then, at Pesaro, on 24 May, comes a passage on the emotion created by the beauty of his surroundings, and the difficulty of conveying it in words. By contrast, the paragraph on Venice by moonlight (26 June) seems designed simply to prove that Stendhal can 'chateaubrillanter' on occasion. Even to the sentence 'Que j'abhorre Buonaparte de l'avoir sacrifiée à l'Autriche!'[106] As a contrastingly astringent touch, he ends the paragraph with a few statistics, on the construction price and sale of one of the palaces. The simple comment on his feelings in the îles Borromées: 'Nous y sommes depuis deux jours;

103. Ibid. vol. i, p. 393 and notes.   104. Ibid., vol. ii, pp. 148, 149.
105. Ibid., p. 167.   106. Ibid, vol. ii, p. 234.

je n'en puis rien dire, sinon qu'on m'y eût appris que je venais
d'obtenir le plus beau grade, que je ne me serais pas seulement
donné la peine d'ouvrir la lettre'[107] seems more personal and
authentic.

At this time of stock-taking and rethinking, the solitariness of
Stendhal is striking. He seems the prototype of the Romantic
wanderer, rootless, without family affections or home. Milan must
have been the nearest approach to a home that he knew after
leaving Grenoble at nineteen. Whatever desperate attempts he
made to understand his situation, to sort out the chaotic impressions remaining from the Revolutionary years, had to be made
alone. It is difficult to imagine him in a settled retreat, with
devoted companions, as for example Wordsworth was when,
overwhelmed and almost thrown off balance by a mass of
experiences, mostly disillusioning and involving the sacrifice of
cherished opinions of men in general and himself in particular, he
came back to be restored and cared for by his sister and friends,
and to discover his own poetic genius. Stendhal's situation in Italy
can perhaps best be imagined in contrast to one almost ludicrously
different—that of the society assembled on a summer day in 1797
in Coleridge's small cottage at Nether Stowey: Samuel and Sara
Coleridge and Hartley; William and Dorothy Wordsworth; and
Charles Lamb. The impatient and humorous intelligence of
Stendhal cuts sharply in, as it does into most gatherings of the
Romantic era that one may imagine. No doubt his experiences
up to 1817 could have provided the material for a *Dominique* to
match *Werther*, *René*, or *Adolphe*. But the direct exploitation of
personal experience for the creation of art was foreign to his genius
at this period. His inclination was to turn away and dwell upon
something outside himself—the music of Haydn, the paintings of
the Italian renaissance, the politics of Italy. And whatever the
physical miseries, spiritual torments, intellectual uncertainties of
the writer, however unpromising his immediate circumstances,
the voice that speaks, often in borrowed words, in *Histoire de la
peinture en Italie* and *Rome, Naples et Florence en 1817*, is the voice
of one who is confident of the reality of joy.

107. Ibid., p. 281.

He was now thirty-four and still at an early stage of the slow progress of his genius towards its inevitable flowering. For an artist of potential greatness there must be at this point some experience which connects things up, gives energy and direction to his effort. Fortunately, this experience came in the next year. He had already found, and quoted, the words which expressed it, in Hazlitt's description of the meeting of Petrarch and Laura. It had yet to be 'felt in the blood, and felt along the heart'.

3 De l'Amour

Julie D'Etanges to Saint-Preux: 'Je vois, mon ami, par la trempe de nos âmes et par le tour commun de nos goûts, que l'amour sera la grande affaire de notre vie.'[1] *La Nouvelle Héloïse* was perhaps the most important of all the many literary sources of *De l'Amour;* for this book, which he read in his youth against his father's wishes (a fact which of course made it all the more memorable) is the one of which he wrote: 'Je haïssais les hommes tels qu'ils sont à force de chérir des êtres chimériques tels que Saint-Preux, milord Edouard, etc.'[2] He echoes Julie in *Henry Brulard*: 'En effet, l'amour a toujours été pour moi la plus grande des affaires, ou plutôt la seule.'[3] The quest for an *amour-passion* similar to that of Julie and Saint-Preux (for like them he distinguished between 'le véritable amour' and 'l'amour sensuel') began for Stendhal, as for so many Romantics, in early youth, and his journal gives evidence that long before his meeting with Métilde Dembowski, some of the ideas most familiar to readers of *De l'Amour* were taking form in his mind, particularly in relation to his love for Victorine Mounier. On 22 September 1804 he notes that if he had more money 'Je pourrai *have a fair woman of the society, this is necessary for loving absolutely* Vict[orine], même *in the case nel quale trovarei in lei quel alma, grande e veramente amante, che forse ho sognata.'*[4] This division of the sensual and spiritual experiences of love was of course further investigated by Stendhal himself in *Armance*, and the most notable comments since then are probably those of Gide in his preface to *Armance*, and of G. Blin, in *Stendhal et les problèmes de la personnalité*. Among Stendhal's entries in his journal, one is of particular importance for the genesis of *De l'Amour*:

25 nivose XIII. [15 janvier 1805]
Dans ma première grande lettre à V. lui dire tout ce que je sens sur le grand amour, celui entre les grandes âmes, tel que la nature nous le

1. *La Nouvelle Héloïse*, Lettre xxxv, (Garnier, p. 83).
2. *Correspondance* (29 oct.–16 nov. 1804), vol.i, p. 162.
3. *Vie de Henry Brulard*, ch. 25, p. 246.   4. *Journal*, p. 544.

représente naturellement sublime dans Héloïse et Abélard; ça lui prouvera que je l'ai senti.

L'amour violent, subsistant sans être alimenté (tel que celui que j'ai eu pour elle du 14 prairial XI [3 juin 1803] au 23 nivose XIII [13 janvier 1805]), ne peut subsister qu'avec une imagination ardente et vaste. Je me figure tous les plaisirs que pourrait me donner tel caractère, je me figure cela pendant trois ans, je vois la figure qui me promet ce caractère. Avant de la voir, déjà toutes mes espérances de bonheur étaient concentrées dans ce caractère idéal que je me figurais depuis trois ans; lorsque je la vois, je l'aime donc comme le bonheur, je lui applique cette passion que je sens depuis trois ans et qui est devenue *habitude* chez moi.

Si j'ai changé de climat, que j'ai habité l'*Italie* dans ma jeunesse, que j'y ai goûté des sentiments délicieux qui ont contribué à former cette passion, que j'y ai imaginé dans mes rêveries (rêvé) ce bonheur que cette physionomie me promet, dès que je l'ai vue, je lui transporte le charme du regret que je sens pour cette suave Italie. Même au sein du bonheur, je porte le charme de la mélancolie. Je ne puis penser à l'Italie sans songer à elle, elle embrasse toute ma vie.

On voit que toutes les causes qui empêchent l'imagination et qui, avec de l'imagination, lui empêchent cette manière de s'exercer, empêchent cette passion préparatoire de l'amour, qui en est le commencement.[5]

This rather long quotation has little need of commentary; it is perfectly eloquent on its own, and certainly forms, with the surrounding entries in the journal, an important preparatory text to *De l'Amour*. Not that chronology is particularly important in the life of an artist. Stendhal's amused anticipation, with the admission in *Henry Brulard* that he was in love with his mother, of Freud's theory of infantile sexuality, ends typically:

En l'aimant à six ans peut-être, 1789, j'avais absolument le même caractère qu'en 1828 en aimant à la fureur Alberthe de Rubempré. Ma manière d'aller à la chasse du bonheur n'avait au fond nullement changé, il n'y a que cette seule exception: j'étais, pour ce qui constitue le physique de l'amour, comme César serait s'il revenait au monde pour l'usage du canon et des petites armes. Je l'eusse bien vite appris et cela n'eût rien changé au fond de ma tactique.[6]

---

5. *Journal*, p. 594.
6. *Vie de Henry Brulard*, ch. 3, p. 60.

For anyone with a taste for following Mr. Yorick in his amorous peregrinations through France and Italy, there is plenty of scope. But there is something more interesting to observe, for the 'étude du coeur humain'. In Stendhal's letters, and in the autobiographical works not intended for immediate publication, there is evidence of the desire to 'passer pour homme d'esprit', and to seek reassurance in social and sexual success; and this vanity, of which he was fully aware, can lead to a fastidious shrinking away from himself, to a focusing of attention upon the 'sublime' which is responsible for his best work, and which he knows can be fully enjoyed only by playing out to the last the role that nature has cast him in. Malvolio to Métilde Dembowski's Olivia? In *Lucien Leuwen*, Stendhal is certainly by turns Lucien, M. Leuwen *père*, Coffe, Du Poirier; but he is also M. de Busant de Sicile: 'A son arrivée à Nancy, se méprenant sur l'accueil dont il était l'objet, et oubliant sa taille épaisse, son regard commun et ses quarante ans, il s'était porté amoureux de Mme de Chasteller. Il avait constamment ennuyé son père et elle de ses visites, et jamais elle n'avait pu parvenir à rendre ces visites moins fréquentes.'[7] Métilde Dembowski had at least been able to reduce to one a fortnight the number of Stendhal's visits to her; a fact to which he frequently refers in marginal notes and, indirectly, in his published works.

His meeting with her in 1818 seemed at last to confirm his intuition that the noble form of love so enchantingly celebrated by the poets and novelists he had admired, actually existed in reality. To write of her, he found again the expression of rapt delight that he had managed to create in his first works. It is not likely that he himself failed to realize that Métilde was partly the creation of his imagination; but the importance of *cristallisation* is of course that the 'rameau d'arbre effeuillé par l'hiver' once arrayed in its glittering crystals never can be entirely commonplace again. In any case, the witness of contemporaries suggests that she was beautiful, intelligent, a devoted Liberal willing to take risks for her political beliefs; she did not return Stendhal's love for her; she died young.[8]

7. *Lucien Leuwen*, ch. 14, vol. i, p. 243 ('Le Chasseur Vert') and vol. ii, p. 192.
8. On Métilde Dembowski, her circumstances, political activities, the spelling of her name, etc., see P. P. Trompeo, *Nell 'Italia Romantica sulle orme di Stendhal*. Rome, 1924 ('Altri Ricordi di Métilde'); and B. Pincherle, *In Compagnia di Stendhal*. ('Métilde nel Processo dei Carbonari') Milan, 1967.

When he says that his was 'un amour qui ne vit que d'imagination',[9] he means of course that there was so little affection on Métilde's part for his own to feed on, that he was obliged to imagine an ideal relationship and the conversations to which it would have given rise; and so he did in all his novels. What he wrote before the novels, under the inspiration of Métilde Dembowski, is already among his best and most deeply felt work—*De l'Amour*, the 1826 *Rome, Naples et Florence*, the *Vie de Rossini*. It is as though he had been waiting to return to the key of the epigraph to *Rome, Naples et Florence en 1817*—Hazlitt's paragraph about the meeting of Petrarch and Laura—which prefigured his own experience, and whose gentle tones he now recalled. On 4 November 1819 he wrote the few pages now known as the 'Roman de Métilde', an uncompleted sketch for a novel. 'On ne pouvait oublier cette tête sublime lorsqu'on l'avait vue une fois, mais il faut dire aussi que tous les êtres vulgaires et prosaïques ne l'avaient jamais vue. Elle n'était que singulière à leurs yeux. . . .'[10] But his most complete description of her appearance comes not in *De l'Amour*, but in the 1826 *Rome, Naples et Florence*; in a portrait-painter's studio he sees several pictures of 'la beauté lombarde', among them one of 'Mme M. . . .':

Mais comment exprimer le ravissement mêlé de respect que m'inspirent l'expression angélique et la finesse si calme de ces traits qui rappellent la noblesse tendre de Léonard de Vinci? Cette tête qui aurait tant de bonté, de justice et d'élévation, si elle pensait à vous, semble rêver à un bonheur absent. La couleur des cheveux, la coupe du front, l'encadrement des yeux, en font le type de la beauté lombarde. . . .[11]

And in *Promenades dans Rome*, he recalls her personality, associating it with his happiest recollections of Italy:

Rome, 7 juin 1828.—Ce soir, après une représentation d'*Elisa e Claudio*, qui nous avait fait un plaisir infini, car Tamburini chantait et nos âmes étaient disposées à la candeur et à la tendresse, la jeune marchesina Mathilde Dembos . . . a été d'une éloquence admirable; elle a parlé du dévouement sincère, plein d'alacrité, sans ostentation mais sans bornes, que certaines âmes ont pour leur Dieu ou pour leur amant. C'est ce

9. *Mélanges intimes et Marginalia*, vol. i, p. 326.
10. *Mélanges de littérature*, vol. i, p. 19.
11. *Rome, Naples et Florence*, vol. i, p. 118.

que j'ai entendu, dans ce voyage-ci, de plus voisin du beau parfait. Nous sommes sortis de chez elle, comme enivrés par notre enthousiasme subit pour une simplicité réelle et complète.[12]

Many of Stendhal's most illuminating comments on his love for Métilde Dembowski are to be found in the margins of books he was reading; he records his experiences, and the chronology of the writing of *De l'Amour*. He also makes the following observation: 'Il fallait faire effort sur *myself* et violer pour ainsi dire la pudeur pour *speak*, même en des termes aussi peu développés, de mon amour *for* Métilde.'[13] Why then publish the book? Because it was an essential stage in his development as an artist, another and still more difficult exercise in getting the life-giving emotion to run in the veins of the book rather than lie exposed on the surface. *De l'Amour* is concerned not only with relationships in love, but with the lover's view of other aspects of life; to this extent it is a book about politics, art, and literature as well as about love. Stendhal takes care to place himself, in a long early footnote, under the protection of the Idéologues. 'Si l'idéologie est une description détaillée des idées et de toutes les parties qui peuvent les composer, le présent livre est une description détaillée et minutieuse de tous les sentiments qui composent la passion nommé l'*amour*. . . .'[14] He conceals behind a mock diffidence his pride in the word *cristallisation*, encouraging those readers who dislike it, to close the book. 'Une âme comme celle de Mme Roland me pardonnera, je l'espère, non seulement le mot de *cristallisation* employé pour exprimer cet acte de folie qui nous fait apercevoir toutes les beautés, tous les genres de perfection dans la femme que nous commençons à aimer, mais encore plusieurs ellipses trop hardies. . . .'[15] Having written a sentence which seems to betray some deep personal emotion, he immediately adds a footnote: 'C'est pour abréger et pouvoir peindre l'intérieur des âmes que l'auteur rapporte, en employant la formule du *je*, plusieurs sensations qui lui sont étrangères, il n'avait rien de personnel qui méritât d'être cité.'[16] And he uses the prefaces, too, as a hide. The first one, for the

---

12. *Promenades dans Rome* (7 juin 1828), vol. ii, pp. 194–5.
13. *Mémoires intimes et Marginalia*, vol. ii, p. 45.
14. *De L'Amour*, ch. 3, vol. i, p. 27.
15. Ibid., p. 28.   16. Ibid.

edition published during his lifetime, was entirely borrowed (this being acknowledged) from Simond's preface to his *Voyage en Suisse*; it is short, directed against the spirit of nationalism in literary judgement, and says nothing about *De l'Amour*. The next draft for a preface was written probably in 1825 when Stendhal was revising the whole work; in this preface he denies that any personal experience lies behind his use of the first person; 'jamais il n'a éprouvé aucun sentiment personnel qui méritât d'être raconté; et si l'on veut lui supposer l'orgueil de croire le contraire, un orgueil plus grand l'eût empêché d'imprimer son coeur et de le vendre au public pour six francs. . . .'[17] He discourses at some length on the kind of readers he does and does not want; stresses the mathematical, precise nature of his work. But he makes it clear all the same that he is writing for 'les coeurs tendres', and not for those whose lives are dedicated to the 'positif' and the 'utile'. The keynote of this preface and of the other two, much shorter, composed respectively in 1835 and 1842, is a certain tone of persiflage, a certain impudent independence of attitude. Take it or leave it; and if the prospective reader decides after all to leave it, the author shrugs his shoulders. This pretence of indifference is of course a possible way of attracting the interest of the reader. But Stendhal's independence and scorn of the slavish following of literary fashion were certainly as real as his desire to be read. The third preface is longer and more obviously relevant to the subject of the book than the others; it gives a half-true account of the origins of the book, omitting of course any reference to Métilde Dembowski, and it introduces the idea that *De l'Amour* is also a book about politics, governments, and social history, through its references to the influence of the Revolution and the succeeding regimes on the French character. The reason for referring to all these drafts of prefaces is to stress that for him a preface is a first line of defence. In any preface that he ever wrote to one of his works, he invariably emphasized the most prosaic aspect of his subject. No one would guess from the prefaces to *Armance* or *Lucien Leuwen*, for example, that the main theme in each case is the working of an *amour-passion* upon all the attitudes and

17. Ibid., vol. ii, p. 265.

activities of a life. *L'amour-passion* is the first of the four forms
of love which he lists and briefly illustrates in the first chapter,
the other three being *l'amour-goût*, which appears as a kind of
eighteenth-century salon game; *l'amour physique* ('on commence
par là à seize ans') and *l'amour de vanité*, which gives him the
opportunity for some sharp observations: 'Le cas le plus heureux
de cette plate relation est celui où le plaisir physique est augmenté
par l'habitude. Les souvenirs la font alors ressembler un peu à
l'amour. . . .'[18] 'Quelquefois, dans l'amour de vanité, l'habitude
ou le désespoir de trouver mieux produit une espèce d'amitié. . . .'[19]
The random remarks which conclude the chapter contain a statement of one of the main themes of the book: 'Le plaisir physique,
étant dans la nature est connu de tout le monde, mais n'a qu'un
rang subordonné aux yeux des âmes tendres et passionnées. Ainsi,
si elles ont des ridicules dans le salon, si souvent les gens du monde,
par leurs intrigues, les rendent malheureuses, en revanche elles
connaissent des plaisirs à jamais inaccessibles aux coeurs qui ne
palpitent que pour la vanité ou pour l'argent.'[20] In fact, *De l'Amour*
is chiefly concerned with a quality of experience which, in this
as in all other departments of life, according to Stendhal, is
accessible only to the *âme généreuse*.

The establishing of these categories of love, and the distinguishing of the seven stages of the development of love, form the basis
of the theorizing in the first volume. The whole book has a plan
of sorts; the first volume is concerned mainly with analysis, the
second with illustration, anecdote, and the maxims known as
'Fragments divers'. But the impression made by the whole, however careful and erudite the editing, is of something haphazard,
formless; this is inevitable because of the extraordinary wealth of
his own and other people's experience upon which, by this time,
he can draw. The peculiar charm of the work is likely to go on
defying analysis; but its variety is important. 'Sécheresse' and
'tendresse'[21] certainly; but it is the fusing of the two at the crucial

---

18. *De l'Amour*, ch. i, vol. i, p. 15.
19. Ibid.
20. Ibid., p. 16.
21. The reference here is to one of the most illuminating of all the writings
about Stendhal: J.-P. Richard's essay: 'Connaissance et tendresse chez Stendhal' in
Littérature et sensation (Editions du Seuil, 1954).

points that is perhaps the sign of Stendhal's peculiar genius. In the first two or three chapters, the technique is that of the Shakespearean serio-comedy of enumeration—the slightly pedantic classification, the compression of a large subject into a small pattern of words—illustrated by Jaques in the seven ages of man speech, by Polonius in the speech on the repertory of the players, by Rosalind on the movement of time, by Touchstone on the degree of the lie, and so on. It is in the second chapter that the famous explanation of the term *cristallisation* occurs. Since this passage shows Stendhal in complete command of his style, it is worth quoting in full:

Aux mines de sel de Salzbourg, on jette, dans les profondeurs abandonnées de la mine, un rameau d'arbre effeuillé par l'hiver; deux ou trois mois après on le retire couvert de cristallisations brillantes: les plus petites branches, celles qui ne sont pas plus grosses que la patte d'une mésange, sont garnies d'une infinité de diamants, mobiles et éblouissants; on ne peut plus reconnaître le rameau primitif.

Ce que j'appelle cristallisation, c'est l'opération de l'esprit, qui tire de tout ce qui se présente la découverte que l'objet aimé a de nouvelles perfections.[22]

This paragraph seems to illustrate well a complete command of the structural and tonal beauty of the French language used without any emphasis or striving for effect.

At the end of the first chapter he introduces the imaginary author of the work, which Stendhal professes to be translating—Lisio Visconti, a young man of great distinction, who has recently died in his native town of Volterra. It is Lisio Visconti who introduces Salviati and Delfante, thus providing Stendhal with an even more indirect means of writing out his own experiences. Léonore/Métilde does not appear until the end of Chapter 8. This chapter, a discussion of the different ways of loving of the two sexes, is already a summary of the relationship of Lucien Leuwen and Mme de Chasteller. 'Une femme est capable d'aimer et, dans un an entier, de ne dire que dix ou douze mots à l'homme qu'elle préfère. Elle tient note au fond de son coeur du nombre de fois qu'elle l'a vu; elle est allée deux fois avec lui au spectacle, deux autres fois elle s'est trouvée à dîner avec lui, il l'a saluée trois fois

22. *De l'Amour*, ch. 2, vol. i, p. 20.

à la promenade . . .' and the chapter ends simply 'nous disait Léonore.'[23] At this point it begins to be apparent that the book owes a good deal to the conversation of 'Léonore'. At any rate it contains a number of conclusions that it is doubtful whether Stendhal or any other man could have come to on his own. He suggests that he realises this: 'un homme ne peut presque rien dire de sensé sur ce qui se passe au fond du coeur d'une femme tendre, quant à une coquette c'est différent; nous avons aussi des sens et de la vanité.'[24]

By this time it has also become evident how varied is the style, grave and light-hearted, mocking and serious, often conversational; and how the effect of spontaneity is helped by the apparently capricious difference in chapter lengths. But this effect is calculated: 'Il est bon, comme Montesquieu et Chateaubriand, de faire les chapitres de longueurs très inégales, pour la variété.'[25] And very effective it is. After the name of Léonore, Chapter 9 consists of four famous Musset-like lines: 'Je fais tous les efforts possibles pour être *sec*. Je veux imposer silence à mon coeur qui croit avoir beaucoup à dire. Je tremble toujours de n'avoir écrit qu'un soupir, quand je crois avoir noté une vérité.'[26] All the following longer chapters are supposed to reflect the experience of Lisio Visconti, and culminate in the Chapter 24 which Stendhal introduces, then retires behind the double screen of Visconti and Salviati in order to be able to speak of his own love for Métilde Dembowski. This chapter, entitled 'Voyage dans un pays inconnu' is, says Stendhal, about orange trees and the countries where they grow; he spins out a page of introductory observations on the North and the South, on credulity, good faith, and the attempt of each writer to record what seems true to him, before remarking that what follows was written by Visconti in one of the places where orange trees grow, in Sorrento, birthplace of Tasso. What follows is the record of Visconti's experience of the difficulties confronting the *âme généreuse* in love; pride, sensibility, and imagination create insuperable difficulties of communication. Visconti is aware that he talks too much for fear of silence, and the interesting thing here

23. Ibid., ch. 8, p. 45. 24. Ibid., p. 43.
25. *Mélanges de littérature*, vol. iii, p. 116.
26. *De l'Amour*, vol. i, p. 47.

is that this awareness illuminates for him a completely different area of experience: 'Je comprends la lâcheté, et comment les conscrits se tirent de la peur en se jetant à corps perdu au milieu du feu.'[27] The *âme vulgaire* on the contrary is always confident of success. Visconti agrees that 'Tout ceci paraît une extravagance' but then quotes a still more extreme case, that of Salviati, condemned by his love to visit her only twice a month (as Métilde had condemned Stendhal). The description of the actual misery of these longed-for visits is one of the most poignant pages in a book full of them.

There are many unexpected, piquant comments on situations in literature; for example, the idea that the Princesse de Clèves would have regretted the past if she had lived to be old; and that in the whole of *Les Liaisons dangereuses*, the présidente de Tourvel is far happier than Valmont. The art of introducing a sudden complete change of mood is well illustrated. In the middle of Chapter 29, Stendhal suddenly exclaims: 'Je viens de relire cent pages de cet essai; j'ai donné une idée bien pauvre du véritable amour, de l'amour qui occupe toute l'âme, la remplit d'images tantôt les plus heureuses, tantôt désespérantes, mais toujours sublimes, et la rend complètement insensible à tout le reste de ce qui existe . . .'[28] and here he introduces the comte Delfante, the third of his aliases, discovered alone, and lost in sad meditation on the love that he believes unrequited, 'dans un bosquet de lauriers du jardin Zampieri'.

One of the main chapters is Chapter 31, in which Stendhal's experience forms the substance of Visconti's description, with quotations from a journal, of Salviati's passion for Léonore; 'il voyait dans une réception sévère de Léonore le triomphe des âmes prosaïques et intrigantes sur les âmes franches et généreuses.'[29] It is here that Salviati says the words already quoted: 'Comme la reformation de Luther . . .' which are really the heart of the matter; the whole view of the world has changed for the *âme généreuse*, his conception of the events of history, his understanding of art. 'C'est ainsi que les grandes ombres des tableaux du Corrège, loin d'être comme chez les autres peintres, des passages peu agréables, mais nécessaires à faire valoir les clairs, et à donner du

27. Ibid., ch. 24, p. 100.   28. Ibid., ch. 29, p. 139.   29. Ibid., p. 140.

relief aux figures, ont par elles-mêmes des grâces charmantes et qui jettent dans une douce rêverie.'[30] So Salviati accepts the sorrows of love rather than return to a state of unenlightened tranquillity. Visconti and Salviati are hardly distinguishable from each other; the important thing is the love for Léonore and the remarkable penetration and lucidity with which it is described. The following chapter, on intimacy, contains the important pages on that constant preoccupation of Stendhal, 'le naturel', and a discussion on the fact that 'plus on a de sensibilité, plus il est difficile d'être *naturel*'.[31] It becomes increasingly obvious that of all Stendhal's heroines, the nearest to Léonore is Mme de Chasteller—point after point of the relationship of *l'amour-passion* as described in *De l'Amour* is to be found more clearly illustrated in the first volume of *Lucien Leuwen*. In the succeeding chapters Stendhal examines the various hazards of love—jealousy, wounded pride, quarrels—but returns in the end, to Léonore: 'Mais auprès de Léonore, je trouvais un monde ou tout était céleste, tendre, généreux.'[32]

In all Stendhal's works of non-fiction, there are moments when he abandons personal emotion and experience, and seeks refuge in borrowed theories and generalizations. This happens in *De l'Amour* when at the beginning of the second volume he begins discoursing on the various temperaments, as he had done in the *Histoire de la peinture*, the sanguine, the phlegmatic, etc., and then on 'quelques traits généraux du caractère de l'amour chez les diverses nations'. This part of the second volume, in spite of certain memorable observations and lively anecdotes, has the restricted interest of most generalizations, especially when they are the *idées reçues* of the distant past. There is nothing more boring than dated pronouncements on national temperament and education. These chapters are 'padding'—he keeps up the fiction of Lisio Visconti's journal, honestly quotes his sources (some of them, at least; certain borrowings from the *Edinburgh Review* appear to have slipped in unacknowledged) and adds enlivening comments of his own. But there is a certain aridity in this section, compared with the first one. All the same, it must be admitted that these chapters contain many essential points of Stendhal's thought, and above all that they illustrate the way he inevitably passes, from

30. Ibid., p. 153.   31. Ibid., ch. 32, p. 162.   32. Ibid., ch. 39, p. 212.

any subject, to sociological and political considerations. As he disarmingly says at the beginning of Chapter 41, 'Je cherche à me dépouiller de mes affections et à n'être qu'un froid philosophe.'[33] However, these chapters evidently owe much to the discussions at which Stendhal was present in Métilde Dembowski's salon, and the relatively long chapter entitled 'Une Journée à Florence'[34] is really concerned with his recollections of Milanese society; so that they have a certain basis of lived reality as well as borrowed generalization. The chapter 'De ce qu'on appelle vertu' is particularly interesting in that here he takes up again the definition widely used at the time of the Revolution: 'Moi, j'honore du nom de vertu l'habitude de faire des actions pénibles et utiles aux autres.'[35] In this connection, he again makes sarcastic comments on the Christian idea of self-mortification, on the conduct of St. Simeon Stylites, (as he already had in the *Histoire de la peinture*), on the Carthusian habit of eating nothing but fish and speaking only on Thursdays, and on Mme de Tourvel's resisting the advances of Valmont mainly for fear of going to hell. 'La vertu philosophique qui explique si bien le retour de Régulus à Carthage, et qui a amené des traits semblables dans notre révolution . . . prouve au contraire générosité dans l'âme.'[36] This distinction is one that he made again and again throughout his works, and as he uses the word, 'vertu' rarely has the sense of self-righteous adherence to a code of behaviour—the sense in which Balzac uses it when he speaks of the 'difficile problème littéraire qui consiste à rendre intéressant un personnage vertueux';[37] a problem that he may fairly be considered rarely to have solved, and with which Stendhal was totally unconcerned.

The climax of the book is generally considered to come with the chapter on 'Werther et Don Juan'.[38] It is an eloquent and penetrating analysis of the two forms of love, the *amour-vanité* of Don Juan and the *amour-passion* of Werther, on the part of one who recognizes the pleasures of both, but gives an infinitely greater importance to the *amour-passion* whose joys cannot be explained

33. Ibid., ch. 41, p. 221.   34. Ibid., ch. 49, vol. ii, pp. 27–36.
35. Ibid., ch. 57, p. 107.   36. Ibid., p. 108.
37. Balzac, 'Avant-propos', *Comédie humaine*, ed. Conard, vol. i.
38. *De l'Amour*, ch. 59, vol. ii, pp. 123–37.

to those who have never experienced them. There is a touch of the 'carte du tendre' in Stendhal's presentation of *l'amour-passion*. It would never be surprising to discover a copy of *Clélie* with the first volume or two containing marginal notes in Stendhal's hand. Clélie's definition of *la tendresse*, during the long discussion between all the lovers on love, must certainly have met with his approval: 'C'est une certaine sensibilité de coeur, qui ne se trouve presques jamais souverainement, qu'en des personnes qui ont l'âme noble, les inclinations vertueuses, et l'esprit bien tourné. . . .'[39] While the letters from Aronce and Horace to Clélie illustrate excellently the difference between *amour-passion* and *amour-goût*.

But although Stendhal makes it clear that the experience of *l'amour-passion* is priceless to those who know it, he has no inclination to despise those who are not destined for it. He respects the demands of the individual *chasse au bonheur*: 'et tous ont raison, s'ils se connaissent bien, et s'ils courent après le genre de bonheur qui est le mieux adapté à leurs organes et à leurs habitudes. . . . Mais enfin chaque homme, s'il veut se donner la peine de s'étudier soi-même, a son beau idéal, et il me semble qu'il y a toujours un peu de ridicule à vouloir convertir son voisin.'[40] But in this chapter, one of the most important developments is the one in which Stendhal, reflecting on the character of Don Juan, makes the link between his conduct in love and his conduct in society, so that one finds that he has moved the analysis on to the plane of politics: 'L'idée de l'égalité lui inspire la rage que l'eau donne à l'hydrophobe; c'est pour cela que l'orgueil de la naissance va si bien au caractère de don Juan. Avec l'idée de l'égalité des droits disparaît celle de la justice. . . .'[41] For Stendhal, there is no subject which in half a page cannot be made to lead directly back to the Declaration of Rights.

The section which follows this chapter, 'Fragments divers', is most aptly titled. Lisio Visconti's 'morceaux de papier de toute grandeur écrits au crayon'[42] provide him with a charming mixture of aphorisms, anecdotes, literary and political comments, among which it is difficult to choose the most interesting and significant.

39. Mlle de Scudéry, *Clélie, histoire romaine* (10 vols.), 1654-60. Paris, Courbé, vol. i, p. 211.

40. *De l'Amour*, ch. 59, vol. ii. p. 137.   41. Ibid., p. 129.

42. Ibid., 'Fragments divers', introductory paragraph, vol. ii, p. 141.

They could be considered as forming a notebook for the novels, since they contain numerous passages that prefigure the stories of Julien Sorel, Lucien Leuwen and Mme de Chasteller, the Abbesse de Castro, Fabrice del Dongo, etc., and also many statements of belief on which the novels are based. What emerges most clearly is perhaps the ideal and even mystical nature of the *amour-passion*. Fragment 121—'Rêverie métaphysique'—is one of the most interesting. It records a conversation between the author and the 'contessina Fulvia', in which they agree that love is in no way necessarily connected with happiness as it is generally understood. The end of the conversation is another statement of the experience of the *âme généreuse*, and Fulvia concludes with a paradox: 'Oui, pour vous et pour moi, l'amour, même malheureux, pourvu que notre admiration pour l'objet aimé soit infinie, est le premier des bonheurs.'[43] And in Fragment 163, Stendhal tells without comment the story of Geoffroy Rudel and the princesse de Tripoli.

Yet he is a great attacker of Romantic clichés, for example on the nature of first love (Fragment 126), and of all forms of posturing and affectation. He describes what *he* considers as 'le triomphe du naturel ' on the part of a girl whose reserved manner makes the man she loves believe that she does not love him, but who would rather lose him to a rival than assume a more demonstrative style. 'Elle n'aurait qu'à changer un peu ses manières: mais elle regarde comme une bassesse qui aurait des conséquences durant toute sa vie de s'écarter un instant du *naturel*'.[44] Here he is on the plane of *Armance*, that novel to which it is useless to apply the criteria of common sense.

One could continue indefinitely meditating on the 'Fragments' and their great importance for the understanding of the *âme généreuse* and the later novels; but there is among the various sections discovered and published after Stendhal's death (these include the chapter 'Des Fiasco', considered so shocking in Stendhal's time and omitted from the first edition) a short story called 'Ernestine',[45] about the composition of which little is known. This story must have been one of Stendhal's earliest attempts at

43. Ibid., vol. ii, p. 200.   44. Ibid., Fragment 34, vol. ii, p. 152.
45. Ibid., 'Ernestine ou la Naissance de l'Amour', vol. ii, pp. 303–43.

fiction, and it bears exactly the relation to the later novels of an over-ture to an opera. This story is intended to illustrate the seven stages of falling in love which are described in Chapters 2 and 4. In fact the first sentence of the story is almost the same as the first of Chapter 4, which suggests that the story may belong to the same period.

The novels as a whole contain a good deal of action. 'Le roman,' as Stendhal later said 'doit raconter, c'est là le genre de plaisir qu'on lui demande.'[46] And of some of his plots and anecdotes it might well be said, as Evelyn Waugh said of the plot of Major Ludovic's novel in *Unconditional Surrender*, that it 'was Shake-spearean in its elaborate improbability'. Now the sign of the appearance of the *amour-passion* is that the action of the story practically ceases, or what action there is is confined to a restricted space—a prison, a garden, a library, or drawing-room—while the interest passes to the minds of the main characters. In 'Ernestine', the scene is an isolated country estate, the action consists of the hero leaving a bouquet in the hollow of a tree by the lake, the heroine taking the bouquet or not taking it. Reading this short work before the novels, one would surely recognize the humour, the irony, the undercurrent of profound seriousness, even of melancholy, the ability to laugh at what one secretly treasures, all of which are characteristics of the mature Stendhal novel. As it is, the reader's pleasure in the little story is increased by glimpses of characters familiar from the great novels: Clélia—'Le vieux comte de S. remarque qu'elle passe sa vie à soigner une volière qu'elle a établie dans les combles du château'; Hélène de Campiréali and Jules Branciforte—'S'il croit qu'on ne fait aucune attention à ses bouquets, il en conclura qu'on méprise son hommage'; all the heroes—'Le sentiment du devoir s'y oppose', the duty here being Ernestine's duty to herself, the promise she has made herself not to accept this homage. After the meeting in the church between Ernestine and her unknown lover (who is the same age as Stendhal then, and also 'n'avait pas même de croix') she finds that he has disappeared without speaking to her and immediately concludes that she has displeased him. 'C'est clair, se disait-elle; Mlle de C. me dit une fois que je n'étais pas jolie et que j'avais dans le regard

---

46. *Mélanges intimes et Marginalia*, vol. ii, p. 260.

quelque chose d'impérieux et de repoussant [here the shadow of
Armance falls across the page] il ne me manquait plus que de la
gaucherie; il me méprise sans doute.' But she finds another
bouquet, and a letter, protesting eternal devotion and saying fare-
well for ever. In her delight at being loved, it becomes obvious
to her that 'il est impossible d'aimer un homme qui n'a pas
quarante ans.' If he should also be poor, what joy! She dresses to
look as old as possible, to the great amusement of her family. But
the revelation of the unknown's name destroys her happiness. He
is known to be the lover of an elegant Parisian widow living
nearby. And Ernestine's reaction is one that will become familiar
to readers of the novels: 'Ce qu'il y avait de plus affreux dans son
état, c'est qu'elle était obligée de se mépriser elle-même.' From
this moment the pride which is always the greatest obstacle to the
amour-passion governs her actions. Stendhal then goes back over
the ground he has covered, to examine the point of view of Philippe
Astezan, who appears as a kind of sketch for all the heroes. 'Il fut
touché de la beauté de ses traits et surtout d'une sorte de simplicité
noble qui faisait le caractère de sa physionomie.' He experiences
self-distrust, the gradual realization of love, its sudden cessation
and renewal, the triumph of emotion over reason. But misunderstanding, suspicion, and pride combine with Stendhal's
perversity to separate the lovers. He decides to marry Ernestine
to 'un vieux lieutenant général fort riche et chevalier de plusieurs
ordres.' These characters are as yet but shadows; however, in that
they are at once victims of his mockery and the way of expressing
some of his deepest emotions, they point the way forward.
'Ernestine' shows too his mastery of the current Romantic style,
which always, when he uses it, has a faintly ridiculous charm. 'O
ciel! il y a un petit papier presque imperceptible, il est attaché au
noeud du bouquet.' It is always necessary to remember when reading Stendhal, or any other writer of the early nineteenth century,
that this is the period when the emphasis and exaggeration so often
attacked by Stendhal were to be found in conversation and correspondence as well as in literature. What he describes as 'mettre 4
dièzes à tous les sentiments' when expressing one's feelings, and
'noyer tout dans un plat d'épinard infini'[47] when describing land-

47. *Mélanges intimes et Marginalia*, vol. ii, p. 392.

scape, was a feature of the times. Though possibly less marked at
the time of the Restoration than during the Revolutionary wars
when Nelson's father, writing to his son in 1797, after the Battle
of Cape St. Vincent, expressed himself thus: 'Joy sparkles in every
eye, and desponding Britain draws back her sable veil and smiles.'

Without Métilde Dembowski, Stendhal could not have written
De l'Amour, though he had had the idea of writing it long before.
As he had quoted in an entry in his journal for March 1811. ' "Thou
canst not speak of what thou dost not feel . . ." Je lis *Roméo*, il
me semble que je relis quelque chose que j'aurais écrit le mois
passé, tant ces sentiments découlent naturellement de ma manière
de voir. . . .'[48] But as he looked back from the standpoint of 1819
on some of the notes he had made in 1806 on his passion for
Victorine Mounier and on love, he commented, 'j'étais amoureux
de l'amour', and referred to his notes as 'tout ce fatras'.[49] He had
already, in 1803, made a formidable list of works he intended to
write; among those in verse is *L'Art d'aimer*, and he comments
'en d'autres termes l'art de séduire. Sujet délicieux. Il faut pour
l'entreprendre, bien connaître les femmes. Une teinte de douce
sensibilité. Histoire de l'art d'aimer. Histoire de l'amour au temps
de la chevalerie.'[50] Seduction and 'douce sensibilité'—Don Juan
and Werther again. The theories of *De l'Amour* have their origin
in earlier experience and often in other writers' pronouncements;
but the note of authentic feeling which brings the work to life is
due to Métilde Dembowski. All his critics, even the least senti-
mental, seem willing to regard his love for her as one of the main
forces of his life. From the day in March 1818 when he met her
until the one in June 1821 when he was forced by an accumulation
of unhappy circumstances to leave Milan, she occupied his life,
and during this time he produced no work but notes for *De l'Amour*.
The preceding years in Italy, foreshadowing the withdrawal of each
of his heroes to a place of meditation for the recuperation of
mental force, had been followed by three years of intense emotional
life and even of intense despair, the completing factor in what was
by this time a remarkable total of human experience. It is from
De l'Amour onwards that memory and imagination work together,

48. *Journal* (27 mars 1811), p. 1047.
49. Ibid., p. 797.   50. Ibid., p. 470.

memory of the Milan years which are the homing-place of all his
enthusiasms in art, music, literature, and politics as well as the
period of his experience of *amour-passion*. Henceforward his
precise and shrewd observation of men and events, his pursuit of
happiness in material well-being and absorption in other loves,
was always to be interrupted, as in the case of each of his heroes,
by laying aside the concerns of daily life and wandering off into
the 'magie des lointains'. 'Elle devint pour moi comme un fantôme
tendre, profondément triste, et qui, par son apparition, me
disposait souverainement aux idées tendres, bonnes, justes, indul-
gentes.'[51] A favourite quotation for all writers on Stendhal and
Métilde Dembowski; but one whose importance is not perhaps
always fully recognized. This is not merely gentle nostalgia, a
Romantic elegy; it is a statement that a certain moral height can
be reached only by way of the *amour-passion*. Justice, tolerance,
magnanimity are displayed by Métilde's lover not towards her
but towards other human beings, fellow-inhabitants of the world
after her death. The death of Métilde in 1825 would not have been
presented by Stendhal (had he written of it at all except to
record in the margin of a copy of *De l'Amour* 'Death of the
author') dramatically, as a blow from which he never recovered,
one thing that his study of the human heart had taught him being
that it is much tougher than the Romantic cares to pretend. But
his experience of love proved aesthetically the climax of his career,
giving him the power to create inimitably in his novels not only
heroes but relationships. Not only is there no self-knowledge
without *amour-passion*, he seems to say, there is no self to know—
only a *peut-être*. If this is so, then the Stendhalian hero is largely
the creation of the Stendhalian heroine. It is Mme de Chasteller
and Mme de Rênal who have from the start the profound inward
life and the 'nonchalance profonde' for the pettinesses of social life
that Lucien and Julien later learn to acquire. And, as all the heroes
learn, 'Le véritable amour rend la pensée de la mort fréquente,
aisée, sans terreurs, un simple objet de comparaison, le prix qu'on
donnerait pour bien de choses'[52]—a statement of what is a simple
truth for many people, and not necessarily inspired by melo-

51. *Souvenirs d'égotisme*, ch. I, p. 1438.
52. *De l'Amour*, Fragment 46, vol. ii, p. 156.

dramatic thoughts of suicide on the part of the author at the time of his break with the comtesse Clémentine Curial. There is in Stendhal's works, as J.-P. Richard has memorably pointed out,[53] a great deal about overcoming the fear of death; not despair, but a certain intensity of living, seems to be the best way.

The experiences of Lisio Visconti, Salviati, and Delfante form the most original and valuable part of *De l'Amour*; but the social and political considerations, the theorizing without which Stendhal never felt secure—the firm scientific stake to which his rather wayward plant of feeling was tied—which occupies mainly the second volume, is not surprisingly concerned with the subjects which had preoccupied him in *Histoire de la peinture* and *Rome, Naples et Florence en 1817*: the effect of climate, national character, forms of government, social fashions, on the behaviour of individuals. But already in the first volume, his tendency never to study any human emotion or activity in isolation is apparent. In Chapter 11, he passes from the process of *cristallisation* to the question which arises from it; what is beauty? His answer is typical in that it is a complete repudiation of the generalizations on which he so often depends: 'Les plaisirs de chaque individu sont différents, et souvent opposés: cela explique fort bien comment ce qui est beauté pour un individu est laideur pour un autre. . . .' 'Del Rosso entend par amour, apparamment l'amour physique, et Lisio l'amour-passion. Rien de plus évident qu'ils ne doivent pas être d'accord sur le mot beauté. La beauté que vous découvrez étant donc une nouvelle aptitude à vous donner du plaisir, et les plaisirs variant comme les individus.'[54] Having arrived at this extreme point of individualism, he immediately takes refuge in new generalizations about human beings in society. It is evident that one of his greatest interests is the study of the pressures which turn *l'homme* into *le citoyen*, and those which from time to time compel him to assert that he is unique. This interest governs the structure of *De l'Amour*, and of all Stendhal's writing. To this extent it is perhaps not true to say that his characters are exceptional beings; they *appear* exceptional because of the power of the artist's microscope. It is the personal experience of Lisio Visconti which leads to the

53. J.-P. Richard, op. cit., (see p. 43 and Bibliography).
54. *De l'Amour*, ch. 11, vol. i, pp. 53, 54.

extraordinarily rich and compressed writing of Chapters 14 to 25, which occupy no more than twenty-five pages, and during which, in a footnote, the writer concludes that 'La beauté n'est que la *promesse* du bonheur.'[55] For these chapters alone *De l'Amour*, with its record of acute sensibility and far-ranging intelligence, would have an assured place of its own among the readers for whom Stendhal said he was writing. Visconti, writing of Salviati, remarks that the 'caractère généreux' is 'renouvelé et retrempé par l'amour', and concludes that 'après deux ans de cette passion généreuse et sans bornes, son caractère avait contracté plusieurs nobles habitudes. . . .'[56] Salviati's greater understanding, because of his love for Léonore, of the devotion of the Romans to their Republic, gives point to a later marginal note: 'Il y a une véritable *cristallisation* en politique pour le parti que l'on adopte. Cette cristallisation se fait à coups de journal; ainsi, dans le combat de l'esprit de parti contre l'amour, ce sont deux cristallisations qui se battent.'[57] But at this period *De l'Amour* marks the moment at which the ability to experience an *amour-passion* in love, and to hold with unswerving fidelity liberal views in politics, became inseparably associated as the distinguishing marks of the *âme généreuse*. Métilde Dembowski, a Liberal and associated with the Carbonari in this turbulent and dangerous period of Italian history, confirmed him in this association of all the virtues of the *âme généreuse* with the liberal ideals of the European nations.

And in saying of his love for Métilde 'C'est un amour qui ne vit que d'imagination' he emphasized the very great importance that is given, in *De l'Amour* as in all his works, to imagination as the source of a total spiritual liberty, relying upon the unattainable delight, the hope rather than the fulfilment. *De l'Amour* contains much that is well within the compass of the *âme commune* that inhabits us all and is a source of pleasure to most of us; but its importance lies in the evidence it gives of a poetic sensibility not quite at full stature, of the artist's instinct acting in the same way as the one which 'impels the chrysalis of the horned fly to leave room in its involucrum for antennae yet to come.'[58]

55. Ibid., p. 74. (See also *Rome, Naples et Florence*, vol. i, p. 46.)
56. Ibid., ch. 31, p. 155.   57. *Mélanges intimes et Marginalia*, vol. ii, p. 47.
58. Coleridge, *Biographia Litteraria*, ch. 12.

4 The Years in Paris

De l'Amour, once the manuscript, lost for many months in the post, had been recovered and prepared, was published in 1822, its subsequent failure being one more disappointment and humiliation to add to those already suffered by Stendhal at this time. After the more poetic chapters of *De l'Amour*, it is interesting to read *Souvenirs d'égotisme*; though it was not written until 1832, to while away long evenings in Civita-Vecchia, it is an attempt to make a truthful record of the life of the man who had returned in such despair from Milan to Paris, in 1821. Looking back over ten years, Stendhal turns upon himself an even more pitiless eye than upon the society he frequented. The object of the exercise is of course self-study in the interests of understanding the human heart.[1] But Stendhal, with all the writing of the Restoration years behind him, including *Le Rouge et le Noir*, is still aware only of what is provisional and precarious. '... mes jugements varient comme mon humeur. Mes jugements ne sont que des aperçus.'[2] Not that there is any suggestion, or ever was, of hesitation or diffidence; Stendhal writes as one who is sure of his readers. In the opening pages he asks himself a number of questions, among them 'Aurai-je le courage de raconter les choses humiliantes sans les sauver par des préfaces infinies?'[3] He has this courage, not only in the direct record of physical defects and humiliations (though the admission of these is tempered with a certain vanity: '... je ne l'aimais pas assez pour oublier que je ne suis pas beau. Elle l'avait oublié.'),[4] but also in showing himself to be capable of waspish comments on friends and acquaintances, moments of triviality, and a selfish lack of involvement—he accepts human beings only on his own terms, resisting any demands made upon him, any responsibilities.

---

1. 'Si ce livre est ennuyeux, au bout de deux ans il enveloppera le beurre chez l'épicier; s'il n'ennuie pas, on verra que l'égotisme, *mais sincère*, est une façon de peindre ce coeur humain dans la connaissance duquel nous avons fait des pas de géant depuis 1721, époque des *Lettres persanes....*' *Souvenirs d'égotisme*, ch. 6, p. 1482.
2. Ibid. ch. 1, p. 1427. 3. Ibid., ch. 1, p. 1428.
4. Ibid., ch. 5, p. 1461.

Mercifully he never married; he seems in any case to see no connection between marriage and love. It is when one is most inclined to think, as one reads this social tittle-tattle, that Métilde Dembowski was perfectly right to reject him, that one realizes that he has achieved his object, and is directing the thoughts of his 'hypocrite lecteur' towards the inevitable results of 'l'égotisme, *mais sincère*'. 'J'étais au désespoir, ou pour mieux dire profondément dégoûté de la vie, de Paris, de moi surtout. Je me trouvais tous les défauts, j'aurais voulu être un autre.'[5] But we are concerned here with what one might call a self-righting craft—he can always be relied upon to get back on an even keel eventually. The fact that one can see this almost not happening is what gives value to his record of experience. Spaced out through the work are the signs by which he communicates with the readers he wants, his indications of a persistent and deep grief, which must necessarily weaken in time because he has applied himself to the task of going on living. Any feelings of exasperation that the reader may have are always forestalled by references to 'ce bavardage' or fears that the book is 'ennuyeux' or 'fade'.

In the last chapter but one, he is correcting the proofs of *De l'Amour* in the woods at Montmorency. 'Les folles idées de retourner à Milan que j'avais si souvent repoussées, me revenaient avec une force étonnante. Je ne sais comment je fis pour résister.'[6] But there is the determination to break out of this despair; already, deprived of the *amour-passion*, his inclination is to make the most of 'les espèces subalternes d'amour'. In spite of the indiscretions in which the book abounds—even with changed names, the true identities of his victims would probably have been apparent—he intended that it should be published ten years after his death, and left instructions accordingly.[7] As an original literary exercise it is one of the most interesting he wrote. Although he intended that it should be the record of the whole nine years that he spent in Paris during the Restoration, it is obvious that he could never have maintained that exceptionally lucid honesty for so long. The great thing is that he never tries to pretend that the self so unflatteringly presented here is only a vision of a despairing moment; the whole

5. Ibid., ch. 6, p. 1470.   6. Ibid., ch. 10, pp. 1509-10.
7. Ibid., 'Appendice', pp. 1516, 1517.

point is that this is what he was like, and the problem is to keep the peace between Prospero, Ariel, Caliban, Stephano, and Trinculo when they are all confined, so to speak, in one cloven pine. Anyway, Stendhal abandoned *Souvenirs d'égotisme*; he leaves the reader on the way up the six flights of stairs leading to Delécluze's rooms, having decided that it was too hot to go on writing.[8] But before breaking off in the middle of a paragraph, he describes certain features of the rooms: 'Il y avait un superbe portrait du cardinal de Richelieu que je regardais souvent. A côté était la grosse figure lourde, pesante, niaise de Racine. C'était avant d'être aussi gras que ce grand poète avait éprouvé les sentiments dont le souvenir est indispensable pour faire *Andromaque* et *Phèdre*.'[9]

But to return to the Restoration period. He became known then as a journalist and pamphleteer; his articles and reviews during these years, all concerned with the political and social world which he now saw, perhaps, more clearly for having been absent from it for so long, form a background to the novels. The longer works, too, the *Vie de Rossini* (1823), the second *Rome, Naples et Florence* (1826), are works of the writer's maturity, drawing upon all the many forms of his experience which he had so great an imaginative power of associating one with another. But if one has been tracing the very gradual accumulation of all the elements that were to find expression eventually in the work of a novelist of genius, then his first novel, *Armance*, may prove disconcerting. Certainly the facts about the composition of the work, excellently set out in the recently revised Champion edition, expose Stendhal to several charges: of attempting to exploit a fashionable theme, since the subject and plot were inspired by notorious works by Mme de Duras and Henri de Latouche; of pusillanimity, since the subject of the sexual impotence of the hero is not mentioned in the text, but is relegated by Stendhal to an extremely explicit letter to Mérimée and to the marginal notes of a copy of his own; of inability to construct a plot, since he cannot manage to get to the end of this short work without recourse to such well-worn Romantic devices as a forged letter and a note written by the hero in his own blood; and of dishonesty, since the so-called second

8. Ibid., ch. 11, p. 1515 n.   9. Ibid., ch. 11, p. 1514.

edition consisted of unsold copies of the first with the addition of
new covers and title pages.

Stendhal's own foreword, as usual, seems designed to distract
attention from all that is most important in the book. But since
then so much has been written about it, and about the physiological and psychiatric problems of the hero, and of the heroine
too, and of all the circumstances of its composition, that it is
tempting simply to refer the reader to the summary of critical
opinions contained at the end of the revised Champion edition,[10]
return to the original text, and try another approach. This time by
way of *Cymbeline*. In *Armance*, all depends upon a certain intensity
of feeling. A critic, of course, has a perfect right to object to this
and to subject the work to other more measurable criteria; but
then Stendhal has the right to say, as he said of Dr. Johnson's
criticism of *Cymbeline*, 'Johnson nous paraît avoir eu trop de
science, et pas assez de sentiment. . . .'[11]

Cymbeline was, as is well known to Stendhalians, one of
Stendhal's favourite plays. What is interesting is that his direct
references to it, and his evocations of it, run through the whole
of his work from the time he first read it in the Letourneur
translation, in Grenoble, at the age of thirteen. It seems that he
uses references to it as he uses other literary allusions, as a kind of
emotional code for himself. In that classic of Stendhalian criticism
La Création chez Stendhal, in the chapter on *Souvenirs d'égotisme*,
Jean Prévost comments on the corrections to the manuscript, and
the misspellings, which, he says, indicate a writer '*qui se dicte à
lui-même*, qui reçoit sa phrase par l'oreille et la transcrit avec une
faute de copiste . . . sa pensée est orale, toute parole intérieure.
. . .'[12] There is an interesting example of this, not included
by Prévost, in Chapter 10. 'De même comme on sera bien plus
détrompé des *Kings*, des nobles et des prêtres vers 1870 qu'aujourd-
'hui, il me vient la tentation d'outrer certains traits contre cette
vermine de l'espèce humaine. Mais j'y résiste, ce serait être *infidèle
à la vérité*, "Infidèle à sa couche", Cymbeline.'[13] The quotation
seems to have nothing whatever to do with the rest of the passage.

10. *Armance*, Postface, pp. 337–57.
11. *Histoire de la peinture en Italie*, ch. 101 (footnote). See pp. 41–2.
12. Prévost, op. cit., p. 289.   13. *Souvenirs d'égotisme*, p. 1510.

It is the word *infidèle* which acts like the opening notes of a musical phrase, to start a parallel mental process. But as Stendhal very well knew, this reminder of another work could create, perhaps momentarily, perhaps for a longer period, an emotional climate totally opposed to the one he thought he was creating. Here, he pushes it out of the way and gets immediately back to the matter in hand. In *Armance*, he offers it no resistance. In *Le Coeur de Stendhal*, Martineau mentions his reading *Cymbeline* on 2 January 1821 just before visiting Métilde Dembowski.[14] Among the books he was obliged to leave behind in Milan was the complete Letourneur edition of Shakespeare. He had also, for many years, as the *Cymbeline* note in the *Histoire de la peinture* shows, been using the Malone edition.[15] Although it is usually considered that certain of the *Armance* epigraphs had been chosen by Mérimée at Stendhal's request,[16] while he read the manuscript, it seems likely that Stendhal himself chose the *Cymbeline* ones, and probably the others from Shakespeare and other English writers.

The use of epigraphs was a prevailing fashion of the times, and Stendhal treats this fashion with typical nonchalance. His quotations are often inaccurate, occasionally invented by him and light-heartedly attributed to Byron or any other name that happened to come to mind. But when later he made notes in a copy of *Armance*, he appeared to take the matter more seriously: 'L'épigraphe doit augmenter la sensation, l'émotion du lecteur, si émotion il peut y avoir, et non plus présenter un jugement plus ou moins philosophique sur la situation'.[17] In any case, suppose for a moment that one imagines *Armance* as a work by an unknown author, and let it stand on its own, forgetting the circumstances of its writing or the names of the author's friends. It is undeniable that the *Cymbeline* epigraphs, then, inaccurate as they both were in the first edition, do create for any lover of the play a kind of further dimension, at the particular place in the novel at which they occur.

Armance is a poor relation of the Maliverts, companion and adopted niece of the marquise de Bonnivet; she loves her cousin

14. Op. cit., vol. i, p. 421.
15. The quotation from Johnson which he uses in his footnote appears in Malone, vol. 8, p. 473.
16. *Armance*, Avant-propos, p. xxxvi.
17. *Mélanges intimes et Marginalia*, vol. ii, p. 78 (May 1830).

Octave de Malivert and is loved by him. What Stendhal is
concerned with in the presentation of this relationship is the
obstacle to love caused by pride and the desire for independence;
he takes an extreme form of the case for illustration, providing
Octave with an unexplained catastrophe in his life, upon which
he constantly broods, and giving Armance her poverty and inferior
social position. Until Chapter 5, the two characters are presented
mainly in relation to the law of indemnity which is about to restore
the fortune of the Maliverts; this leads to misunderstanding,
Octave believing on hearsay that Armance is jealous of his fortune,
and Armance believing that he has changed and become arrogant
because of it. It is in Chapter 5 that Stendhal explains the circumstances and character of Armance. She is the first of Stendhal's
heroines to show the profound nonchalance for 'les petits événements de la vie' coupled with the passionate feelings of an intense
inward life that they all share. 'On voyait qu'Armance ne se
permettait pas une foule de choses que l'usage autorise et que l'on
trouve journellement dans la conduite des femmes les plus dis-
tinguées. Pour tout dire en un mot, je ne doute pas que sans son
extrême douceur et sa jeunesse, les ennemics de mademoiselle de
Zohiloff ne l'eussent accusée de pruderie.'[18] In fact, this accusation
has frequently been made by critics of the novel.

Octave's efforts to win the esteem of his cousin, because he
misses her intelligent companionship (and not, as Stendhal ironically implies, because of any realization on his part that he loves
her), are rewarded after three months of merely formal social
contacts, but three months in which their thoughts of each other
have progressed. Armance's brief reply to Octave's frank attempt
to break down the barrier: 'Vous avez toute mon estime',[19] and
her brusque departure, to conceal her tears, appear cold to Octave,
but to her as a shameful revelation of her feelings. It is not the
circumstances of the story, but the inward life of the characters,
that prompt their thoughts. 'O Dieu! après une telle honte comment oser reparaître devant lui?'[20] is absurd unless seen as an
extreme expression of the intense pride that invariably in the *âme
généreuse* is an obstacle to love. And for Armance, to love someone who apparently does not return her love is a desperate fall

18. *Armance*, p. 56.   19. Ibid., ch. 6, p. 79.   20. Ibid., ch. 7, p. 82.

from grace: 'un homme d'autant d'esprit aura vu toute l'étendue de ma faiblesse, et cette faiblesse est du nombre de celles qui doivent le plus choquer sa sévère raison.'[21] In this Chapter (7) Stendhal presents with humour and sympathy the exaggerated despair of the two lovers; it is Armance's character even more than Octave's that inspires in him that simultaneous expression of mockery and understanding which became so typical of his attitude towards his characters. He is here entirely taken up with the intensity of emotions and scruples, with difficulties of communication, that he has himself experienced or divined in others; the difficulty and perhaps the fault is to try to invent circumstances to match the emotions. But for a man who could accept the plot of *Cymbeline* without criticism, even Posthumus' vision and the descent of Jupiter on his eagle at the end, a few illogicalities in the actions of his heroes are to be expected. In any case, *Armance* is about love, not about rational conduct.

To continue: Armance, so overwhelmed at having revealed, as she supposes, her feelings to Octave, determines that the only solution is to enter a convent; she half-confides in her friend Méry de Tersan, but 'Armance serait morte de honte plutôt que de prononcer le nom d'Octave',[22] and this inability to trust even her closest friend is an additional grief. At the end of the chapter Octave, in the salon of Mme de Bonnivet, seeks distraction from his anxiety about his relationship with Armance by making greater efforts than usual to please the society there, which is full of affectation and malice. Then Stendhal comments: 'Ce qui est admirable, c'est que notre philosophe n'eut pas la moindre idée qu'il aimait Armance d'amour.'[23] Which suggests the irony of the earlier exclamation that Stendhal records for Octave: 'Tout ce que j'ai pu faire, c'est de me connaître.'[24]

It is at this point that Stendhal opens the next chapter, Chapter 8, the first of the next book, with the epigraph

> What shall I do the while? Where bide? How live?
> Or in my life what comfort, when I am
> Dead to him?
>
> *Cymbeline*, Act III[25]

21. Ibid., p. 83. 22. Ibid., p. 87. 23. Ibid., p. 90.
24. Ibid., ch. 1, p. 15. 25. Ibid., ch. 8, p. 91.

He has made an adaptation to suit his text by replacing Shakespeare's words 'my husband' by 'him'. He then outlines the situation of Armance, aware of her love for Octave, but also convinced that she would be universally despised if she revealed it. She therefore avoids him, and for Octave 'En sortant de l'hôtel de Bonnivet, le vestibule, la façade, le marbre noir au-dessus de la porte, le mur antique du jardin, toutes ces choses assez communes, lui semblèrent avoir une physionomie particulière qu'elles devaient à la colère d'Armance.'[26] But three days later she is there; with Mme de Bonnivet they go for a drive in the fine weather, visit the tomb of Abelard in the Père Lachaise, and here, in response to a formal enquiry after her health, she invents, as an explanation of her apparently troubled manner at their last interview, a project of marriage, about which she has some uneasiness. This short chapter leads without interruption into Chapter 9, the first paragraph of which explains Armance's decision to invent the report of a projected marriage, and continues with a delicate analysis of their relationship, according to the findings of *De l'Amour;* Octave sees the world in a new and happier light, while for Armance, 'Tous les sentiments que l'amour le plus exalté, le plus tendre, le plus pur, peut faire naître dans un coeur de femme, Armance les éprouvait pour lui. L'espoir de la mort, qui formait toute la perspective de cet amour, donnait même à son langage quelque chose de céleste et de résigné, tout à fait d'accord avec le caractère d'Octave.'[27] The chapter ends with Armance's confronting Octave with a charge of wild and dissolute conduct in houses of ill fame; her tone is decidedly priggish. But Octave simply replies 'tout ce qu'on vous a raconté est vrai . . . mais ne le sera plus à l'avenir.'[28] Armance is at first shocked and afflicted, but later finds in his frank acknowledgement, additional reason for loving him. This odd episode has a precise origin. 'Un soir, Métilde me parlait de Mme Bignami, son amie. Elle me conta d'elle une histoire d'amour fort connu, puis ajouta: "Jugez de son sort; chaque soir son amant, en sortant de chez elle, allait chez une fille." Or, quand j'eus quitté Milan, je compris que cette phrase morale n'appartenait nullement à l'histoire de Mme Bignami, mais était un avertissement moral à mon usage.' This comes in the third chapter of *Souvenirs*

26. Ibid., p. 92.   27. Ibid., p. 102.   28. Ibid., p. 106.

d'égotisme.[29] He has taken this memory and embellished it for *Armance*.

The epigraph to Chapter 9 is 'Que la paix habite dans ton sein, pauvre logis, qui te gardes toi-même.' It is a translation of Belarius' words in *Cymbeline*, III, vi, '. . . Now peace be here,// Poor house, that keep'st thyself!', as he and the two brothers Guiderius and Arviragus return to their cave home after hunting. There are three difficulties here. The first is that Stendhal began by attributing the quotation to Burns. The second is that when he eventually corrected this mistake, he made the note 'Cymbeline (Imogène entrant dans la caverne)', still not attributing the words to the right character. And the third, that the epigraph appears to have nothing whatever to do with the hôtel de Bonnivet or the hôtel de Malivert, or in fact with any place in *Armance*, or any circumstance mentioned in the novel. In fact, the epigraph here seems only to illustrate a carelessness not infrequent when Stendhal was quoting from other writers? The first attribution to Burns one has to accept as a piece of absent-mindedness. What is undeniable, however, is the impact of this quotation, with its context recalled, when it is associated with the one in the previous chapter. What Stendhal had remembered was the climax in the affairs of Imogen, and the whole emotional tone of the relevant scenes—the extremes of joy and despair, as she is first informed by a letter from Posthumus that he is at Milford Haven, and sets out with Pisanio to seek him; then on the way is given by the faithful Pisanio the letter in which Posthumus bids him kill her for her supposed infidelity with Iachimo. From this point, the accent is upon the total moral isolation of Imogen. She has no resource but her own resolution and courage. So it is with Armance. The *Cymbeline* epigraphs at this point shed upon the figure of Armance a pathetic and even a tragic light. The understanding between these two lovers is too fragile and fleeting. Their tranquillity exists only because they are deceiving themselves and each other. *Armance* is a tragedy because of the hero's failure to understand not only himself, but also Armance. Octave's belief in the forged letter that Armance is supposed to have written to her friend Méry, declaring that she no longer loves him, shows

29. Op cit., p. 1443.

that he has no understanding of her character. One recalls Posthumus' immediate belief of the false report of Imogen's infidelity. Octave dies because he believes that Armance's apparent love for him is simply a pretence maintained by a sense of duty. He sends back to her the false letter, which she sees for the first time after his death, together with a letter which he had written to her before his marriage but never sent. It is therefore not until the end of the book that Armance feels the shock experienced by Imogen at the point of the two epigraphs; the sense of the annihilation of the whole personality caused by the knowledge of total misunderstanding on the part of the person most deeply loved, that is wonderfully conveyed by Shakespeare, and symbolized by the disguise of Imogen as the page Fidele. It is just before Belarius' words 'Now peace be here . . .' that the desolate Imogen, disguised as Fidele, and wielding an inexpert sword, enters the cave, the 'poor house'. It is not only the death of Octave, but the undescribed despair of Armance at her receipt of his letter, that make tragic the end of the book. The contrast between this ending, and the ending of *Cymbeline*, where divine intervention restores confidence and harmony, is poignant.

Armance is not, as a character, the human being that Mme de Rênal and Mathilde de la Mole, Mme de Chasteller, or Gina Sanseverina, was each to be. But like them, extremely sensitive to the demands of the social conventions of their times, she is ready if the occasion demands it to disregard convention at whatever cost to her pride or reputation. Having heard that Octave is gravely wounded in a duel, 'Armance avait envoyé chercher une voiture, et ne songeait qu'à trouver un prétexte qui lui permît d'aller à Clamart. Tout lui parut devoir céder à l'obligation de secourir Octave dans ses derniers moments s'il vivait encore. Que me fait le monde et ses vains jugements? se disait-elle, je ne le ménageais que pour lui; et d'ailleurs, si l'opinion est raisonnable, elle doit m'approuver.'[30]

The intensity of feeling which is the keynote of *Armance* is worked to a climax in Chapter 16, where Octave, realizing at last the nature of his feeling for Armance, is given a moment of intense happiness before the return of reason 'le précipita du comble

30. *Armance*, ch. 22, p. 207.

de la félicité dans un malheur affreux et sans espoir.'[31] It is not surprising to find at the head of this chapter the quotation from *Antony and Cleopatra* beginning 'Let Rome in Tiber melt . . .' The brief moment of joy and understanding of the two lovers is expressed in lines which sum up one of the most important aspects of the experience of the *âme généreuse*: 'Ce fut un de ces instants rapides que le hasard accorde quelquefois comme compensation de tant de maux, aux âmes faites pour sentir avec énergie. La vie se presse dans les coeurs, l'amour fait oublier tout ce qui n'est pas divin comme lui, et l'on vit plus en quelques instants que pendant de longues périodes.'[32]

At the beginning of the second volume of *Lucien Leuwen* there is a passage describing a form of love which closely resembles that of Armance for Octave; it is necessary to realize the nature of this love, if the tragedy of the end is to be understood. It is this: 'Pourquoi parler le langage de la raison? Quand j'aurais trouvé en elle des défauts choquants, que dis-je? des vices déshonorants, j'aurais été cruellement combattu, mais je n'aurais pu cesser de l'aimer.'[33] Whatever Stendhal may have intended when he began *Armance*, what he finally achieved was a delicate and complex study of the minds of two *âmes généreuses* in love; drawing upon his own experience, recalling the works that by now were so closely woven into his way of thought as to be inseparable from it, but also, though obviously moved by the sorrows of his hero and heroine, keeping enough detachment to be able to mock.

This is why it is possible to consider *Armance*, like all the others, to be a political novel. There are times when one may be tempted to think that, in a novel where the interest is so predominantly in a love relationship, the importance of the political and social side must be about as slight as it is in *Cymbeline*. But this would be impossible. The background of *Armance* is not a world of legend, but the world of all the post-Revolutionary problems that Stendhal had been thinking and writing about for years. He is not of course concerned with historical accuracy, but with using facts so as to create an *impression* of life in the Faubourg Saint Germain towards the end of the Restoration. The hero and heroine, because of their

31. Ibid., p. 158.   32. Ibid., p. 156.
33. *Lucien Leuwen*, ch. 38, vol. iii, p. 146.

incapacity for action and the sterility of their lives, have often been seen as symbolical of the class to which they belong. Stendhal sees the dilemma of the nobility as that of fidelity without object and without faith. Octave and Armance are the young members of a class for whose way of life there is no place in a changed world. Octave is a *Polytechnicien*, thoughtful, intelligent, intellectually capable of working in society, emotionally unable to leave the caste to which nine centuries of tradition attach him. 'Ces gens ont la sottise d'avoir peur, il se croient dans une ville assiégée et s'interdisent de parler des nouvelles du siège. La pauvre espèce! et que je suis contrarié d'en être!'[34] But he belongs irrevocably to this class. Chapter 14, which consists mainly of a discussion between Octave and Armance on the society of the times, is a remarkable condensation of years of reading, observation, and thought. But it is not only the social and political traditions of the nobility that imprison Octave and Armance— they are also the prisoners of a death-seeking romanticism. 'Alas! I have nor hope nor health//Nor peace within nor calm around...' Shelley's *Stanzas* (*written in dejection near Naples*) seem to express exactly the state of mind of Octave de Malivert during his last voyage to Greece. Stendhal's very few and brief references to Shelley may conceal a profound impression made upon him by 'ce grand poète, cet homme si extraordinaire, si bon et si calomnié...'[35] whom he said he met in Bologna in 1816, and who is mentioned in one of the drafts of a will published in *Mélanges intimes et Marginalia*: 'Je... demande à être enterré près de mon ami Shelley (Pyramide de Cestius).'[36] The date he gives for the meeting is as usual wrong; it could not have been until 1818.

Octave, always presented as one of those mysteriously doomed beings so frequently to be found in Romantic literature, expends, like Hamlet, all his energy on soliloquy and discussion. Only the devotion of Armance could have given him the confidence to act. 'Il a besoin de mes consolations, se disait-elle, pour se pardonner à lui-même.'[37] She thinks this after a false 'confession' by Octave of youthful misdeeds which he has invented; but her diagnosis is the right one, whatever the guilt or deficiency may be. Without

34. *Armance*, p. 138. 35. *Rome, Naples et Florence*, vol. i, p. 183.
36. Vol. 1, p. 23. 37. *Armance*, ch. 24, p. 234.

his fatal mistrust of her, she could perhaps have induced him to make the necessary movement towards change and discovery that his century demanded and that his talents made possible. Armance is the one who wants to escape from the prison of the Faubourg Saint Germain; she might have helped him to do so. As it is, Octave's treadmill of thought inhibits action. There is really no need for any action at all—sooner or later his complete inability for faith and hope will cause him to distrust and misjudge Armance, and to seek death. Having chosen to set his story in 1827, Stendhal can hardly rely upon the descent from heaven of Jupiter on his eagle, as in *Cymbeline*, to create order out of human chaos. And in any case the creation of such order here is not logically possible; Octave is a far more complex and eccentric character than Posthumus.

The background characters and their frivolous or vindictive activities are necessary because, like all Stendhal's novels, and in spite of the fact that he liked to pretend that politics have no place in the novel, *Armance* is a brilliant glimpse—no more than a glimpse admittedly—of the world of the Restoration. The extraordinary economy and compression with which he writes is nowhere better illustrated. He wrote once of *De l'Amour* 'l'auteur saute quelquefois du commencement d'une proposition ou d'une théorie à la conclusion, en omettant la plupart des idées intermédiaires, et en laissant son malheureux lecteur haletant et qui tâche vainement de le suivre.'[38] This is absolutely true of all his works, and one comes to accept it. In *Armance*, his mockery of Romantic attitudes is entirely implicit in the nuances of the style. He makes a more direct statement in one of the letters in the form of articles on the contemporary scene that he wrote in 1825. He was attacking Lamartine: 'M. de Lamartine rend, avec une grâce divine, les sentiments qu'il a éprouvés. Ces sentiments vagues et mélancoliques, partagés par beaucoup de jeunes gens riches de l'époque actuelle, sont tout simplement l'effet de l'oisiveté. Napoléon faisait remuer cette jeunesse; de son temps, on connaissait peu l'ennui mélancolique.'[39] Stendhal, in spite of this robust middle-aged attitude, knew 'l'ennui mélancolique' perfectly well; but for him it was something to be dispelled by work.

38. *Courrier anglais*, vol. i, p. 358.   39. Ibid., p. 162.

Armance itself, after all, was completed as a distraction from yet another access of amorous despair, his mistress, Clémentine Curial, having finally left him in September 1826. But to find the explanation of the writing of the work in personal misfortune, or the desire to exploit a contemporary literary fashion, is to take too narrow a view of it; *Armance* has a necessary and logical place in the development of Stendhal's work. It is the culmination of years of human experience and reflection, as its remarkable insights show, he achieves in it some of his most subtle, concise and exquisite effects of style; and it is not difficult to see, though he prefers not to make it too obvious, that Armance herself is the most important and interesting character in it. It is typical of his manner that the tragedy and anguish of Armance are suggested, nothing more, on the last page: 'Il écrivit à Armance, et mit dans sa lettre celle qu'il avait eu le courage de lui écrire dans un café de Paris, et la lettre à son amie Méry de Tersan qu'il avait surprise dans la caisse de l'oranger.'[40] The reader needs only to look back to the first page of Chapter 30 to see the contents of this forged letter, which Armance now reads for the first time, after Octave's death. It is possible to dismiss the various improbabilities or inconsistencies of the plot as Stendhal did those of *Cymbeline*: 'fautes que le premier homme médiocre corrigerait en une heure d'attention'[41] and to regard them as having little importance beside the profoundly moving record of two minds, their inescapable solitude, their imprisonment in physical humanity and in the limitations of their times.

But if they could have escaped from the Ultra stronghold, where would Stendhal have had them go, and how could Octave have employed his intelligence? He would have been happy to be an industrial chemist; he had considered a way of entering 'les sociétés où c'est la richesse qui donne le pas et non la naissance.'[42] And an extraordinarily roundabout way it is—via England and the Liberal nobility, whose interest in the intellectual and scientific life of France would give him an excuse, on his return, for seeking an introduction to the leaders in these fields in France. No wonder

40. *Armance*, p. 302.
41. *Histoire de la peinture en Italie*, ch. 101 (footnote). See pp. 41–2.
42. *Armance*, ch. 14, pp. 144–5.

'Armance se taisait.' Stendhal's satirical intention is evident; on the whole Octave represents the youth of his class, and it is only at certain moments that Stendhal remembers that as a Romantic hero he must also be sombre, accursed, singled out by a mysterious affliction.

The difficulty is that Stendhal was contemptuous not only of the exclusive and backward-looking society of the Ultras, but also of the dynamic industrial society that was replacing it, because he saw the glorification of money and the criterion of practical utility as inimical to all that he valued most in human life. It is not the progress of industry and technology that he despises, but its self-adulation, and this is the basis of his attack on the Saint-Simonists and their new journal *Le Producteur* in his pamphlet *D'un nouveau complot contre les industriels*, published in December 1825, less than two years before *Armance*. 'Pendant que Bolivar affranchissait l'Amérique, pendant que le capitaine Parry s'approchait du pôle, mon voisin a gagné dix millions à fabriquer du calicot; tant mieux pour lui et ses enfants. Mais depuis peu il fait faire un journal qui me dit, tous les samedis, qu'il faut que je l'admire comme un bienfaiteur de l'humanité. Je hausse les épaules.'[43] And the indifference to moral considerations of the great money-lenders revolts him: 'dès que le huit pour cent se présente, le banquier oublie bien vite la liberté. Quant à nous, notre coeur ne pourra pas oublier de sitôt que vingt maisons, prises parmi tout ce qu'il y a de plus industriel et de plus libéral, ont prêté l'argent au moyen duquel on a acheté et pendu Riego.'[44] In fact, what Stendhal is perturbed about, by the end of the Restoration period, is the debasing of the term 'liberal'. No one, in this complex, fascinating, and dramatic period, the period of so many beginnings—large scale banking, large industrial enterprises, party politics—was more aware of the conflicting meanings given to the word 'liberalism', and of how it could become a political label for those whose struggle for power was based on hatred of the privileged by birth and fear of those with no privileges at all. In every subsequent work, Stendhal launched his broadsides at the 'Liberals' of the Restoration and the July Monarchy as well as at the 'Ultras'. Octave and Armance are too

43. *Mélanges de littérature*, vol. ii, p. 222.   44. Ibid., pp. 223–4.

perplexed and timid. But the clearer-sighted adversaries are called Julien Sorel and Altamira, Lucien Leuwen (at the end of the novel), Gauthier, Coffe, Ferrante Palla, Mosca. And even M. Leuwen *père*, who attacks from within the camp by being (though one of the richest bankers of the period) indifferent to money, cynical in politics, and bankrupt in the end. Political and financial expediency dressed up as humanitarian zeal, this is what Stendhal objects to; a self-deception which he is always quick to unveil. To present the values and way of life of the currently powerful group as praiseworthy, even beneficent, is always the tendency of governments; the self-righteous evangelism of the Jacobins was very persistent, and survived their fall from power. But here Stendhal goes back to the thought and style of the Revolutionary years: 'pour arriver à une haute estime, il faut, en général, qu'il y ait *sacrifice* de l'intérêt à quelque noble but.'[45] If his readers here start quibbling about the meaning of his words, he himself has always given them encouragement to do so. According to his Helvétian principle, self-sacrifice is simply a form of self-interest. And what is the sense of the vague expression 'quelque noble but'? Some lofty state of beatitude unconnected with money and manufacturing? The man who could reason that in certain cases 'la laideur est beauté', and could prove that Racine had been a Romantic, would in certain moods have turned that sentence inside out and destroyed his own argument for amusement.

But since his return from Italy he had been absorbed by the political, literary, artistic life of Paris, and as a journalist had kept closely in touch with as many aspects as possible of the Parisian scene. He had observed, read, listened, discussed, frequented the most notable salons, established a reputation as a wit. He was equipped to write with understanding about the Restoration period, but wisely elected to stand back from the picture from time to time, and get it in perspective. In July 1827 he left Paris for Italy, and remained there until January 1828. It was during this visit that he went to Milan, at the end of December, and was turned away by the Austrian police as an undesirable alien. Métilde Dembowski had died three years before. He never lived again in Milan.

45. Ibid., p. 227.

In 1817 he had written in a copy of the *Histoire de la peinture en Italie*, 'A Paris, je vis sur une surface agréable, mais dès que je veux approfondir, je trouve le tuf le plus pauvre et le plus sec. A Milan, je vis sur une surface légèrement ennuyeuse par le manque de vie, mais dès que je veux approfondir, soit illusion, soit réalité, je trouve les sensations les plus brillantes, les plus passionnées, les plus exemptes de toute langueur.'[46] This experience was undoubtedly renewed in 1827, though Milan was closed to him; the result is that *Promenades dans Rome*, written after his return to France, is like a re-statement of the faith of the *âme généreuse*.

46. Quoted by A. Paupe: *La Vie littéraire de Stendhal*, p. 27.

5 Promenades dans Rome

Promenades dans Rome, like all Stendhal's works of non-fiction, is to a certain extent a work of imagination. It is the record of a journey, and of daily excursions in and around Rome, made by a party of seven congenial companions; there are four men, Frédéric, aged forty-six: 'beaucoup de sagesse, de bonté, d'indulgence, de douce gaîté'; Paul, not yet thirty: 'infiniment d'esprit ... impossible d'être plus amusant et meilleur.' 'Il y a deux autres voyageurs d'un tour d'esprit assez sérieux' (one of these is Stendhal, at the times when he is not also Frédéric or Paul); and three ladies 'dont l'une comprend la musique de Mozart.'[1] This constitutes for Stendhal the ideal party of travellers, and, with their three servants, they plan to spend several months in Rome. What follows is a mixture of fact (mostly borrowed from other writers), fiction, and reflections on all subjects of interest to the author. Stendhal says that the work is an authentic journal, written at the end of each day's excursion. In fact it was written in Paris, at a time of poverty and almost suicidal depression, between June 1828 and September 1829. It was undertaken with no enthusiasm, but because he hoped to make money by writing the kind of guidebook popular at the time. His cousin and friend Romain Colomb, who had recently visited Italy and intended to write an account of his own journey, gave him help and encouragement by working with him from June 1828 until March 1829.

The work aroused, in his own times and later, many well-founded objections. As research has progressed, so these have increased. He had spent not more than a few weeks altogether in Rome, and had not been there since 1824. His intention, undoubtedly, was to pretend a more intimate knowledge of Rome than he actually possessed, and to do it by letting other people's work fill the gaps in his own knowledge. In fact, *Promenades dans Rome* is pieced together from passages that he had had to leave out of the second *Rome, Naples et Florence*, and the spoils of an

1. *Promenades dans Rome*, vol. i, p. 18.

unprincipled plundering of works of history and travel, many of them by writers then still living. When padding was necessary, he used pieces of *Histoire de la peinture* or *Rome, Naples et Florence*. 'Il n'y a pas d'amour-propre,' he later wrote to Mareste, 'à vanter ce livre, dont les trois quarts sont un extrait judicieux des meilleurs ouvrages.'[2] All that it is necessary to know about *Promenades dans Rome*, with what it has to reveal about Stendhal's methods and source-books, is contained in Armand Caraccio's admirable volumes in the revised Champion edition. Other excellent critical studies have appeared. But the fascination of this strange master-piece is never likely to diminish with time.

If we accept that the facts and dates are often wrong, that the borrowed passages were adapted and put together with the intention of deceiving, that some of the details and old anecdotes like the ones about Pope Joan are boring, the truth is that none of this matters very much beside the fact that this is one of those remarkable and unforgettable works that creates itself through the imagination of the reader, becoming something more than itself. It is a matter of establishing, minutely and elaborately, a spiritual climate, that of the novels to come, in which the world of the *âmes généreuses* can be enjoyed fully only in contrast to the everyday world in which they live. The Rome of this work is no more or less real than, say, that of Piranesi; what matters is the slow forming of the artist's vision of his times. With *Promenades dans Rome*, Stendhal makes another pause for reflection, reaffirms his faiths, discards what is no longer necessary. He has reached a point beyond which he has no intention of advancing. Duvergier de Hauranne's review in the *Globe* stresses this, but obviously from the point of view of a reader of 1829, with no knowledge of the later works.

Tandis qu'il y a dix ans nous croyions encore à la tragédie classique, à la barbarie de Shakespeare, à l'immobilité absolue du beau, déjà M. de Stendhal riait de La Harpe, admirait Macbeth, proclamait le beau infini dans son essence et mobile dans sa forme . . . il est vrai que depuis nous avons marché, tandis que M. de Stendhal est resté au même point. Peut-être est-il aujourd'hui en arrière, mais n'oublions pas qu'il

2. *Correspondance* (15 janvier 1829), vol. ii, p. 155.

y a dix ans il était en avant. . . . Il a bâti sur Helvétius toutes ses théories et pour recommencer il n'est plus assez jeune.[3]

Precisely; by refusing to advance for the sake of advancing and in defiance of his deepest convictions, he was spared disappearing without trace among the fashionable nonentities of the day. Stendhal was interested in beginnings—the early Revolution, early Romanticism—rather than in their development into established institutions. 'Etre passionné pour une chose, et puis l'oublier tout à fait. . . .'[4] So, having been regarded as one of the leaders of the Romantic movement in France, he had lost interest in it as it became accepted.

In *Promenades dans Rome*, it is through selection and emphasis that he reveals his own judgement of the Restoration period, and his own position as 'homme' and as 'citoyen'. Rome is for him the city of antiquity, the great Republic which had been the inspiration of the Revolutionaries, rather than the centre of the Catholic faith; it is his intransigent anti-clericalism that is fascinated by the history of the Popes, the Papal government, the exercise of temporal power. In the course of what might well be considered a definitive study of Stendhal's views on the Papacy and his expression of them in *Promenades dans Rome*, H.-F. Imbert comments: 'Il y a des chances que pour Stendhal la religion, sous toutes ses formes, n'ait été qu'une gigantesque machine d'exploitation politique.'[5] In fact, Stendhal's whole interpretation of history confirms this, and in a marginal comment on *Rome, Naples et Florence* he sums it up: 'C'est l'astuce italienne qui a créé aux trois quarts cette religion, que nous croyons celle de J[ésus]-C[hrist], mais qui, au contraire, a changé de direction tous les 200 ans et qui a eu une si profonde influence sur les idées et les habitudes de l'Europe. . . .'[6] And he contrasts this antiquated, self-perpetuating and reactionary structure with the inevitable progress of 'ce sentiment profond de la justice que l'on désigne en ce moment par le nom d'*idées libérales*.'[7]

But the ideas on the Papacy expressed in this book differ little

3. *Promenades dans Rome*, vol. i, Avant-propos bibliographique, (cxiv–cxvii).
4. *Journal*, p. 1278.　　　　　5. Imbert, op. cit., p. 333.
6. *Mélanges intimes et Marginalia*, vol. ii, pp. 33–4.
7. *Promenades dans Rome*, vol. iii, p. 93.

from those to be found in the earlier works. And although the importance of Stendhal's political views in the *Promenades* is considerable, and though he always writes of the past in such a way as to force reflections on the problems of France and Italy in the late Restoration period, there are other considerations equally important for the perspective of his work as a whole. For example, it is in the *Promenades* that the different interpretations that he gives to the word 'energy', emerge particularly clearly. It may be an extrovert energy, the way of ruthless self-expression, in individuals, or of progress in the fight for liberty, in nations; or it may be a passionate feeling not necessarily translated into action at all, but turned inward. It is through this distinction that he manages not only to pass from consideration of politics to consideration of art, but also to convey to the attentive reader certain fears, presentiments and predilections of his own.

In the entry for 20 November 1828, he distinguishes in the French character a lack of feeling for the arts, even in certain famous writers, which he says will give him a reputation for 'méchanceté'.

Cette méchanceté, qui repousse par un sentiment pénible les âmes bonnes et tendres, telles que Madame Roland, Mademoiselle de Lespinasse, etc., pour lesquelles seules on écrit, recevra une nouvelle preuve de l'explication bien simple que voici. L'esprit français ne peut exister sans l'habitude de l'attention aux impressions des autres. Le sentiment des beaux arts ne peut se former sans l'habitude d'une rêverie un peu mélancolique. L'arrivée d'un étranger qui vient la troubler est toujours un événement désagréable pour un caractère mélancolique et rêveur. Sans qu'ils soient égoïstes, ni même égotistes, les grands événements pour ces gens-là sont les impressions profondes qui viennent bouleverser leur âme. Ils regardent attentivement ces impressions, parce que des moindres circonstances de ces impressions, ils tirent peu à peu une nuance de bonheur ou de malheur. Un être absorbé dans cet examen ne songe pas à revêtir sa pensée d'un tour piquant, il ne pense nullement aux autres.

Or, le sentiment des beaux-arts ne peut naître que dans les âmes dont nous venons d'esquisser la rêverie.[8]

Shortly after this, while writing of the history of Rome from 891 to 1073, he dwells upon the story of Crescentius, whom he has

8. Ibid., pp. 109–10

already mentioned and who indeed appears as a kind of hero of
Promenades dans Rome. In the passage dated 1 June 1828, Crescentius
is described as seeking the liberty of his country, as a man not
really of his period: 'Notre révolution s'est chargé de fournir un
nom à cette espèce d'hommes généreux et malhabiles à conduire
les affaires: c'était un *girondin*. Pour agir sur les hommes, il faut
leur ressembler davantage; il faut être plus coquin'.⁹ Apart from
the fact that, like Michelangelo and Leonardo, Crescentius now
becomes a Stendhalian hero, this definition reinforces the impression to be gained from many other references in his works, that
Stendhal's deepest affinity was with the Girondins, to whom, after
all, his favourite Mme Roland belonged; to the contrasted categories Tom Jones/Blifil; Werther/Don Juan; Don Quixote/Sancho
Panza, must be added Girondin/Jacobin. But in a later reference
to Crescentius he continues that if one examines his story one
finds that 'les âmes tendres et généreuses restent en butte à toutes
les mauvaises chances. Elles ne devraient songer qu'aux beaux-
arts.'¹⁰ And this is precisely what he says of Julien Sorel, in his
next work: 'Les âmes qui s'émeuvent ainsi sont bonnes tout au
plus à produire un artiste.'¹¹ This is to say that Julien is mistaken
about the kind of energy with which he is endowed.

And here we come to the heart of *Promenades dans Rome.* This
is the fear, already expressed in *Histoire de la peinture en Italie* and
elsewhere, that 'Le siècle des budgets et de la liberté ne peut plus
être celui des beaux-arts'¹² or, as he put it in *Rome, Naples et Florence,*
'Les choses qu'il faut aux arts pour prospérer sont souvent contraires à celles qu'il faut aux nations pour être heureuses....'
And in the 1826 edition he ends this paragraph typically: 'Qu'
importe? la liberté est le nécessaire, et les arts un *superflu*, duquel
on peut fort bien se passer.'¹³ He never ceases to welcome the
movement towards democratic institutions, impartial justice,
freedom of speech and of the press, and his examples of 'energy'
in the working classes of France and Italy suggest that he sees the
eventual assumption of power by the majority as inevitable.
What he calls 'l'idée *nivelante*' works against all that he most

9. Ibid., vol. ii, p. 174.　　　10. Ibid., vol. iii, p. 127.
11. *Le Rouge et le Noir*, ch. 28, vol. i, p. 332.
12. *Promenades dans Rome*, vol. ii, p. 301.　　　13. Op. cit. p. 15.

values in art and civilization. *Promenades dans Rome* is a passionate appreciation of all that is beautiful in painting, music, architecture, landscape, and in that which, to use a phrase frequent in Stendhal, 'prête des ailes à l'imagination'; all threatened by the very advancement of democracy that he hopes for.

He records, for 6 January 1829, a meeting with a rich American, who has a conversation with him entirely about financial matters. 'Toute cette conversation avait lieu en présence des plus beaux monuments de Rome. L'Américain a tout examiné avec ce genre d'attention qu'il eût donné à une lettre de change qu'on lui aurait offerte en paiement; du reste il n'a absolument senti la beauté de rien.'[14] He is a man of intelligence and even subtlety of mind; but he declaims in the manner of someone used to being listened to. It is after the record of this encounter that Stendhal comments: 'Suivant moi, la liberté détruit en moins de cent ans le *sentiment des arts.*'[15]

The struggle for this liberty, and the various forms it can take, is a major theme of all his work. Violence is inseparable from it, whether it comes from the 'canaille romaine, à la fois hideuse et admirable par l'énergie',[16] or the sans-culottes of the Revolution, or the brigands of sixteenth-century Italy who form the 'opposition' to autocratic power, or the young and poor of 1829, who, like Napoleon, and like the young Laffargue whose *crime passionnel* Stendhal describes at length, have a good education and ardent imaginations, but are also extremely poor. It is at the end of his account of the Laffargue case that he brings the subject of art once again to the fore; he concludes that to escape from the disastrous pressures of journalism, from the temptation of titles, crosses of the Legion of Honour, and commissions won by cultivating influential directors, it will be necessary for the artist to be noble and rich by birth. But—since energy of all kinds seems to have deserted the higher classes—'comment se soustraire à l'élégance, à la delicatesse, etc., et garder cette surabondance d'énergie qui fait les artistes et qui rend si ridicule?'[17]

There is of course the eternal threat of the barbarians. Without any preparation or comment, Stendhal includes under the date

14. *Promenades dans Rome*, vol. iii, p. 213.   15. Ibid., p. 214.
16. Ibid., vol. ii, p. 189.   17. Ibid., vol. iii, p. 149.

23 December 1828, the beginning of an article on the barbarians, who for the most part 'avaient la bravoure et la liberté', but set out to ravage and destroy. 'En 527, Vitiges, roi des Goths, assiège Rome, que Bélisaire défend pendant un an, et que le barbare ne peut prendre; il s'en venge en ordonnant à ses troupes d'anéantir dans la Campagne de Rome tout vestige de civilisation. . . .'[18] Here, it is as though he were unknowingly looking to the future as well as the past; as he does also when he refers to the horror-pictures of the martyrdom of saints in the church of San-Stefano-Rotondo: 'ces affreuses peintures du Pomarancio et du Tempesta, si célèbres parmi les hommes vulgaires que le hasard fait passer à Rome; cela est intelligible pour ces messieurs, comme la guillotine en action. Cette réalité atroce est le sublime des âmes communes.'[19] And his last comment is perhaps the most interesting—that this art is not great enough to make the subject tolerable.

But what gives life to *Promenades dans Rome* is not so much the general and political reflections on Italy and France, nor even the evocations of the splendours of art, as the nostalgia of the writer for a country of the mind inhabited by Métilde Dembowski and her friends, which he had long remembered as though from a place of exile. Not that he had failed to enjoy, on a different plane but with great verve, the other activities, loves, and diversions of his years in Paris. But in one of the most revealing sentences of the *Promenades* he speaks of the effect of the Villa Ludovisi: 'Un instant vous révèle ce dont votre coeur avait besoin depuis long-temps sans se l'être avoué à lui-même.'[20] In Stendhal's time, his critics wondered, practically, whether or not it was possible to visit the Villa Ludovisi when Stendhal said he had. In ours, the name 'Villa Ludovisi' may be understood simply as six notes at the beginning of a musical phrase evoking a memory. In fact, on a later page he recalls a jasmine-covered arbour in a garden near the sea at Pizzo-Falcone, at Naples. 'Le plaisir indicible que je rappelle par ce peu de mots est bien voisin de celui que donnent la musique de Cimarosa et la Madone du Corrège à la bibliothèque de Parme.'[21] In the second *Rome, Naples et Florence*, which adds to the first his experience of love for Métilde Dembowski and there-

18. Ibid., p. 194.   19. Ibid., vol. ii, p. 330.
20. Ibid., vol. ii, p. 114.   21. Ibid., vol. iii, p. 151.

fore enriches it greatly, he speaks of Milan at much greater length
than in the 1817 edition. He tries on several occasions to express
what life in the city had meant for him. 'Quand je suis avec les
Milanais, et que je parle milanais, j'oublie que les hommes sont
méchants, et toute la partie méchante de mon âme s'endort à
l'instant.'[22] What he misses so much is 'l'ensemble des moeurs . . .
le naturel dans les manières, c'est la bonhomie, c'est le grand art
d'être heureux qui est ici mis en pratique avec ce charme de plus,
que ces bonnes gens ne savent pas que ce soit un art, et le plus
difficile de tous.'[23] And he recalls the society in a box at the Scala,
where all the habitués have known each other for years and
understand each other. Distinctions of birth or wealth are unimportant. What he does in *Promenades dans Rome* is to take as his companions a group of friends from a box at La Scala.

Jean Prévost points out that though Stendhal thought he was
writing a guide-book to sell as well as possible, once he had begun
writing he wrote entirely for himself. Prévost speaks of the
'hommage funèbre à Métilde, inutile au livre, étranger à Rome,
mais poignant dans sa douceur obscur.'[24] Yes, but it is a most
essential part of the book; and one might say that Stendhal was
writing not only for himself but in memory of people he loved,
those who alone could help him to discover what he might be,
or what his aspirations were. He had wished for a language that
only they would understand ('Que ne puis-je écrire dans un langage
sacré compris d'elles seules!')[25] and might almost be considered to
have discovered it, by the way he arranges and comments upon
his largely borrowed material, so that what is most important to
him is kept in the background, touched upon very lightly. On
3 June 1828 he remarks on the form that the *chasse au bonheur* takes
in Rome: 'A Rome, on cherche à être heureux en satisfaisant ses
passions; chacun suit l'impulsion de son âme, et *cette âme ne prend
nullement la couleur du métier dont l'homme se sert pour gagner sa vie.*'[26]
This tells us more about Stendhal than about Rome; he could
perfectly well reconcile an administrative post with the world of

22. *Rome, Naples et Florence*, vol. i, p. 153.
23. Ibid., pp. 155–6.   24. Prévost, op. cit., p. 215.
25. *Promenades dans Rome*, vol. ii, p. 218.
26. Ibid., p. 265 (my italics).

art and literature to which he was devoted, and the cares of office would simply give greater value to this world. *Promenades dans Rome* reveals a need for experiences opposed to the ones he had in Paris; the need to replace preoccupation with money by indifference to it; physical infatuations by an ideal and unattainable love; fashionable journalism by a return to unfashionable convictions; the foreground of getting and spending by the 'lointains sublimes.'

A. Caraccio, while fully admitting the inaccuracies, plagiarisms, and longueurs of the *Promenades*, sums it up admirably: 'Avec l'amertume et la douceur des souvenirs, il déverse dans ce livre, en de menues phrases discrètes, le grand désir inassouvi des "vastes portiques" et d'une vie sans entraves.'[27] The echo of Baudelaire is very apt here. Stendhal could be one of the exiles so innumerable in the poet's thought that the end of 'Le Cygne' dies away into silence: 'à bien d'autres encor!' Prospero in permanent exile from Milan, perpetually conjuring up visions.

Promenades dans Rome has been a favourite guide to many travellers in its time. Perhaps now it is of most value to a solitary reader in a cold northern spring. Then its warmth, its long detailed descriptions, its unaffected and brief evocation of the emotions of an *âme passionnée* can have their most beguiling effect. After the necessary preliminary of the Cercle du Bibliophile edition, it could best be read with no introduction or notes, in a large, elegant volume illustrated with seventeenth- and eighteenth-century engravings, a memorial to past splendour and the dangerous nostalgia for a heroic age.

27. Ibid., vol. i, p. lxxxi.

6 The Tourist

Shortly after the publication of *Promenades dans Rome*, on an autumn evening in 1829, Stendhal's 'great years' as a writer may be considered to have begun. '1829, nuit du 25 au 26 octobre, Marseille je crois, idée de *Julien*, depuis appelé, en mai 1830, *Le Rouge et le Noir*.'[1] 'Idée' in this context means not the first conception of the work, but the inspiration of how to treat a subject already waiting for development. There are signs of Julien Sorel in *De l'Amour*, as there are signs of Fabrice del Dongo in *Rome, Naples et Florence en 1817*. But the sombre and beautiful tones of *Promenades dans Rome* form a prelude to the story of the grave, humourless, ambitious young man setting out to conquer the world of Restoration France; and 'Vanina Vanini', a story of the Carbonari, published in December 1829 in the *Revue de Paris*, is in the same key. The character of Julien Sorel owes perhaps more to that of the young Napoleon than to any other of the many sources, autobiographical, literary, or judiciary, that have been suggested.

The next ten years were the long-delayed and sustained climax of Stendhal's career as a writer, as novels, stories, autobiographical works, innumerable notes, plans, and articles accumulated, during the long solitary evenings at Civita-Vecchia where he had become Consul in April 1831, or during extended periods of leave in France. Altogether about thirty works were begun in the years between December 1829 and Stendhal's death in March 1842. Of these, two major novels—*Le Rouge et le Noir* and *La Chartreuse de Parme;* a travel journal, *Mémoires d'un touriste*; seven stories of various lengths, including 'L'Abbesse de Castro', were completed and published during his lifetime. The rest, ranging from long but incomplete works like *Henry Brulard, Souvenirs d'égotisme*, and *Lucien Leuwen*, to manuscripts of a page or two, were either directed by Stendhal to be published after his death, or were discovered and published much later.

1. *Mélanges intimes et Marginalia*, vol. ii, p. 91.

In 1829 only the obstinate wish to be a playwright seemed to hold him back from commitment to the novel. Even so, after *Le Rouge et le Noir* it must have been clear to him that the novel was the only literary form which would offer him the freedom his talent demanded. In any case, he shortly decided that the novel was replacing the drama as the most important literary genre in the nineteenth century.[2] His long study of the human heart had by now provided him with inexhaustible resources for creating and inventing variations on precisely four characters—the young hero, the two women, one gentle and reflective, the other lively and brilliant—and the older man of experience and wit. *Le Rouge et le Noir*, *Lucien Leuwen*, and *La Chartreuse* were constructed round these characters. *Armance* had revealed to him the danger of putting too great a strain on the intuition of his readers, and of writing for too small a public. He also knew that a ready-made plot, like the two court cases that he adapted for *Le Rouge et le Noir*, gave him the best opportunity to concentrate on the characters. He had already determined years before what he thought the function of the plot to be—'pour peindre un caractère d'une manière qui plaise pendant plusieurs siècles, il faut qu'il y ait beaucoup d'incidents qui prouvent le caractère, et beaucoup de naturel dans la manière d'exposer ces incidents.' He had written this in 1811, in the criticism of *Cymbeline* that formed the footnote to Chapter 101 of *Histoire de la peinture*.[3] He repeated it in the margins of a copy of Montesquieu in January 1815; 'Résumé of all my dramatic doctrine. Pour peindre un caractère d'une manière qui me plaise, il faut qu'il y ait beaucoup d'incidents qui le prouvent et beaucoup de naturel dans la manière d'exposer ces incidents.'[4] Hence the melodramatic incidents and the succession of escapades that are a feature of all his stories, the extreme situations which will force the character to reveal itself. Characters do not 'change'. They are gradually revealed by events. In life these essential events may not occur; but in literature the writer can see that they do. The Shakespearean conception of plot is then early established; from

---

2. Ibid., pp. 122, 130, 134; and *Mélanges de littérature*, vol. iii, ('La Comédie est impossible en 1836').

3. Vol. ii, pp. 81–4.

4. *Mélanges intimes et Marginalia*, vol. i, pp. 299–300.

the drama, too, Stendhal had only to take what was to be his
greatest resource as a novelist—the soliloquy, which became his
'interior monologue'. Among all the examples of the wonderful
use that he makes of this device it is difficult to select one. Perhaps
his demonstration, in the scenes of Julien Sorel in prison, of the
fact that human thought is not naturally logical and orderly, and
can only become so by a painful process, constantly repeated,
of self-discipline; and that any chance may destroy the conclusion
so laboriously arrived at. Or Gina Sanseverina, alone after hearing
of the capture and imprisonment of Fabrice, in Chapter 16 of
La Chartreuse, where Stendhal takes the opportunity of emphasiz-
ing the extreme complexities of the situation as well as the
character of Gina; the style of the monologue recalls Mosca's
judgement of her formed years before: 'où trouver ailleurs cette
âme toujours sincère, qui jamais n'agit avec prudence, qui se livre
tout entière à l'impression du moment, qui ne demande qu'à être
entraînée par quelque objet nouveau?'[5] But because Stendhal was
not convinced of his power to create life and drama out of the
record of thought, without the need for constant action, he
tended, when he had no precise limit imposed by a ready-made
plot, to go on too long. *Lucien Leuwen* could perfectly well end
where he left it, and there was no need to plan a third volume. Even
in its unrevised and in parts sketchy condition, it is still a major
work, to be ranked with *Le Rouge et le Noir* and *La Chartreuse*.

The young heroes may represent the destructive energy of a
passionate commitment to an imagined heroic past or a totally
absorbing ideal world; but there is also the possibility of survival
because of another form of energy, a vitality and curiosity stronger
than the intransigent idealism of youth. In *Souvenirs d'égotisme*
Stendhal, remarking that as far as his relations with women were
concerned, he had the good fortune to be as gullible at forty-nine
as he had been at twenty-five, goes on to say 'C'est ce qui fait que
je ne me brûlerai jamais la cervelle par dégoût de tout, par ennui
de la vie. Dans la carrière littéraire je vois encore une foule de
choses à faire. J'ai des travaux possibles, de quoi occuper dix
vies. . . .'[6] So interest and curiosity triumph over despair, and

5. *La Chartreuse de Parme*, ch. 6, vol. i, p. 186.
6. *Souvenirs d'égotisme*, ch. 10, p. 1513.

reason must be made to co-exist with emotion. There is, too, the duty to maintain a kind of fidelity to what has seemed beautiful— the sense that there must continue to exist in the world a conscious- ness to reflect and perpetuate for as long as possible, this beauty and its life-transforming power.

Qui se souvient de Lambert aujourd'hui, autre que le coeur de son ami?

J'irai plus loin, qui se souvient d'Alexandrine, morte en janvier 1815, il y a vingt ans?

Qui se souvient de Métilde, morte en 1825?[7]

And who will remember Gina, Fabrice, and Clélia, if it is not Count Mosca? But Mosca is a creation of the artistry of Stendhal; the traveller of *Mémoires d'un touriste* appears not as an artist, but as the middle-aged servant of a 'juste-milieu' regime, bitterly aware that the bourgeois way of life, the life of the 'bourgeoisie orléaniste', has powerful advantages, at a time of life when, as the Tourist frequently implies, it is important that the roads should be well paved and hot water readily available for making tea.

The choice of the narrator for each of Stendhal's travel books has a certain symbolical value; thus the Italy of two years after Waterloo is seen by a cosmopolitan of taste and some wealth, a cavalry officer, an aristocrat frequenting the most distinguished society of the cities he visits. The narrator of *Promenades dans Rome* is one of a small group of *âmes généreuses*, the chosen companions summoned from a past that differed in every way from the France of 1828; and for *Mémoires d'un touriste* the narrator, Philippe L., is rather a sad widower of thirty-four, travelling for his own iron and steel firm, and tells the story of his life in the Introduction. This man is closely accompanied by the consul for Civita-Vecchia, casting a sardonic eye upon life in the 1830s. Philippe L. has lived in the colonies, and hopes to return there: 'C'est un grand rampart contre la sottise vaniteuse qui est le péché de notre siècle, que d'être obligé de sortir en chapeau de paille et en jaquette de toile les trois quarts de l'année.'[8] As Philippe L.'s circumstances and character are divulged, one suspects that, for Stendhal, if anyone who makes a fortune by commerce

---

7. *Henry Brulard*, ch. 14, p. 166.
8. *Mémoires d'un touriste*, vol. i, p. 13.

or banking is to be worth writing about, it is essential that he should, like Philippe L., dislike the commercial world, or like M. Leuwen *père* be indifferent to money. Philippe L., then, has enough of Stendhal's attitudes and tastes for it to be possible to forget for long stretches of the book that he is supposed to be the narrator, and that he is at least twenty years younger than Stendhal. The familiar tone of voice is soon unmistakable. Already, the remark about the straw hats and linen jackets of the tropics suggests the pleasure of the sardonic observer in the victimization of the human being by his environment.

From the beginning, the tone is disenchanted. Nothing could be further from the enthusiastic opening of *Rome, Naples et Florence en 1817*. And indeed, on the second page Stendhal sketches a symbolical landscape:

Le pays que je parcours est horriblement laid; on ne voit à l'horizon que de grandes lignes grises et plates. Sur le premier plan, absence de toute fertilité, arbres rabougris et taillés jusqu'au vif pour avoir des fagots; paysans pauvrement vêtus de toile bleue; et il fait froid! Voilà pourtant ce que nous appelons la belle France! Je suis réduit à me dire: 'Elle est belle au moral, elle a étonné le monde par ses victoires; c'est le pays de l'univers où les hommes se rendent le moins malheureux par leur action mutuelle les uns sur les autres' . . .

Everything points to 'à la fois l'absence des grands malheurs et des sensations profondes.'[9] As France moves towards universal suffrage and the rule of the majority, Stendhal maintains the position that has for some time given him a certain sharp pleasure—to be emotionally on the Left and intellectually moving to the Right.

For some time after the opening description the journal is rather flat, arid, with borrowed descriptions of ancient monuments, and anecdotes with no apparent point, except, no doubt, to relieve the tedium of the table d'hôte. This is the France of M. Valenod, who, we can be sure, is now a 'bourgeois orléaniste' one hundred per cent, and probably a member of parliament. But Stendhal himself gradually takes over the journal and appears as we have come to know him—by turns serious, mocking, lively, sarcastic, poetic, his individual judgements, comments, and evocations enlivening the pages of boring facts for which he always had

9. Ibid., p. 19.

a strange relish, and which were more often than not supplied by
his friends. At one point he breaks into a description of Vienne
to return to the character of Philippe L. and the reasons why he
should not be writing a travel journal. Firstly, he has not enough
time, 'je ne suis pas un curieux, mais un marchand',[10] and secondly, because his opinions are unfashionable. Here he becomes
Stendhal again: 'Le ciel m'a si peu donné l'instinct du succès, que
je suis comme forcé de me rappeler plus souvent une manière de
voir, précisément parce que l'on me dit qu'elle n'est pas à la mode.
J'ai du plaisir à me prouver de nouveau cette vérité dangereuse,
à chaque fait duquel on peut la déduire.'[11] He is writing, he says, to
put on record for his own pleasure a France which is changing
quickly. And he goes on to meditate on current fashions of thought
in France. France, unlike England, 'peut s'ennuyer même de son
intérêt. Les âmes nobles seront les premières à se révolter contre
le genre hypocrite et ennuyeux. Après la révolte, on pourra donner
une second édition plus complète, si dans l'intervalle personne n'a
mieux fait.'[12] This remarkable political forecast of the 1848 revolution, the short-lived Republic, and the continued bourgeois rule
of the Second Empire, seems to indicate the shrewdness of the
Consul's assessment of the way his countrymen were thinking.
No wonder that the political scene in this most politically sophisticated and quick-witted of nations could always fascinate him and
inspire him with the curiosity to see what would happen next.
There is no doubt that at this period of his life, it was a great
pleasure to him to be on leave from his post in Italy, and to spend
that leave in France. In a letter to Sainte-Beuve written on 21
December 1834, he admits 'L'Italie n'est plus comme je l'ai
admirée en 1815. Elle est amoureuse d'une chose qu'elle n'a pas.
Les beaux-arts pour lesquels seuls elle est faite ne sont plus qu'un
pis-aller. Elle est profondément humiliée dans son amour-propre
excessif de ne pas avoir une robe lilas [a constitutional monarchy]
comme ses soeurs aînées, la France, l'Espagne, le Portugal. Mais
si elle l'avait, elle ne pourrait la porter. . . .'[13] But as he observed
more closely the France of the July Monarchy, his nostalgia for
the Italy he had known increased.

10. Ibid., pp. 262–3.   11. Ibid., p. 263.
12. Ibid., p. 264.   13. *Correspondance*, vol. ii, p. 763.

Stendhal was always less interested in places than in the people who inhabited them, and *Mémoires d'un touriste* is, as might be expected, less a guide-book than a moral judgement of a regime. Going down the Rhône, he reflects upon the prosperity of the July Monarchy, which he views with a certain pride. In his judgements, the effort to be scrupulously fair is apparent, and he gives full weight to those aspects of the regime that seem to him to deserve credit—peace, prosperity as it was then understood, public order—but it all tasted flat. *La Chartreuse de Parme*, written a few months after the publication of *Mémoires d'un touriste*, marks perhaps a reaction against this long effort to make the best of the *juste milieu* regime and all its works. In the *Mémoires*, Stendhal, describing the centre of the town of Lorient, uses the word *snug*, and defines it: 'bien arrangé, petit, tranquille et silencieux'.[14] There must have been a certain enchantment and relief in creating the imperious, immoral, and passionate characters of *La Chartreuse*, a book in which everything is the antithesis of 'snug'.

Throughout the *Mémoires*, his comments are provoked by his admiration for the material achievements of the regime and his dislike of the spirit of the times. 'Les peuples furent électrisés par Napoléon. Depuis sa chute et les friponneries électorales et autres qui suivirent son règne, les passions égoistes et vilaines ont repris tout leur empire: il m'en coûte de le dire, je voudrais me tromper, mais je ne vois plus rien de généreux. Chacun veut faire fortune, et une fortune énorme, et bien vite, et sans travailler. . . .'[15] But on the next page, half-mockingly, he tells how he replied to certain deprecating comments on the government by quoting statistics of imports and exports, and maintaining that it would be impossible to do better under any government. It would not be Stendhal, however, if he did not also comment to the reader that any 'sot qui sait une date' or who can provide himself with 'quelques chiffres nécessaires'[16] can silence more distinguished and interesting thinkers.

It was in his interest that the regime should flourish; he held his official appointment from the government, he had friends in influential positions, and was protected by the comte Molé when

14. *Mémoires d'un touriste*, vol. ii, p. 46.
15. Ibid., vol. i, p. 105.   16. Ibid., p. 107.

the latter was Minister of Foreign Affairs. His admiration for the achievements of the July Monarchy was genuine; in the *Mémoires* he pays tribute to the enterprise and the constructive activity that he sees everywhere, in the north and south, in Paris and in the provinces. He refers again to the sale of the 'national lands' (émigré and Church property) during the Revolution, and the laws of inheritance which had provided for the equal distribution of property among the heirs. In a population of thirty-three million, there were, he says, five million landowners. He had already referred, in *Rome, Naples et Florence en 1817*, to the changed ownership of land as one of the most significant results of the Revolution. In the *Mémoires* he comments, 'Par la loi démocratique qui partage les successions, le nombre des proprié-taires tend à s'augmenter à l'infini. En présence de ce fait, comment craindre le retour de 93 qui alarmerait tous les propriétaires?'[17] He was proved right, surely, when the franchise was at last extended, after the revolution of 1848, and the exercise of universal suffrage ensured the triumph of conservatism. But the fear of 1793 remained, he constantly sees it and warns against it.

Another preoccupation that has remained from earlier years is the liberty of the press. Nothing marks him more as a liberal than his absolute devotion to this principle, in spite of any disadvantages it might have for the things which interested him personally: 'Le journal, *excellent, nécessaire pour les intérêts politiques*, empoisonne par le charlatanisme la littérature et les beaux-arts.'[18] The power of the critic to promote fashionable mediocrity, Girodet, for example, he deplores, but 'politiquement parlant, notre liberté n'a pas d'autre garanti que le journal.'[19] Having observed the immediate attacks made upon freedom of the press by govern-ments of the extreme left and the extreme right during and since the Revolution, he remained constantly watchful. At the same time, he could take an ironical view, as in his comments on the Moderates who had taken over a paper on the verge of failing: 'ils ont fait entre eux une souscription de cent francs par tête et ont appelé de cent lieues de là un écrivain spirituel auquel ils donnent trois on quatre mille francs par an. Ils ont ainsi le plaisir

17. Ibid., vol. i, p. 279.   18. Ibid., p. 35.
19. Ibid., p. 36.

de lire tous les matins un article qui les confirme dans leur façon de penser.'[20]

In a work which tends to be rather rambling and even repetitive, a section which allows the writer to draw together the main points of his political and social arguments, dispersed throughout the record of his travels, occurs when he leaves France briefly for Geneva. Here he reflects at length on the problems of his times, one of the chief of which seems to him to be: 'Comment ces deux grandes forces, la religion et la passion des peuples pour des Chambres discutantes, vont-elles s'arranger ensemble? Laquelle des deux l'emportera dans le coeur des hommes? Là est toute la destinée du XXᵉ siècle.'[21] He comes back to this question several times in the course of the rest of the book. His main objection to the education given to seminarists is that they are taught to 'mépriser le gouvernement des deux Chambres, qui régit la France, et à détester *la liberté de la presse*, qui en est l'âme.'[22] But the fear of 1793 plays into the hands of reactionaries; he finds in the current admiration for Gothic architecture a political sign: the upper classes thought that admiration for Gothic architecture would draw the faithful into the Gothic churches where priests are to be found, and that the priests, in gratitude, 'feraient remonter le bon peuple de France vers le degré de stupidité et d'amour pour ses maîtres qu'il montra en 1744. . . .'[23] These fears, which he illustrates in all his works as a most notable feature of the times, but which he does not share, seem to him to be based on a complete lack of understanding of the current situation. Saying that he would prefer even a bad king to a republic—a view he had held for many years—he states that there are no longer the terrible abuses against which the Revolution was made. 'Où sont aujourd'hui les abus atroces?' The sentence recurs in slightly different forms several times in the course of the book. Are we to suppose that Stendhal has gone over entirely to the side of the prosperous and powerful? A paragraph of the entry in his journal at Béziers, which again, like Geneva, marks a pause during which he can emphasize certain ideas that he particularly wishes to impress upon his readers, suggests otherwise. 'Voyez quelle suite de beaux

20. Ibid., vol. ii, p. 471.   21. Ibid., p. 284.
22. Ibid., p. 475.   23. Ibid., vol. i, p. 272

drames depuis quelques années: Fieschi, la rue Transnonain, les deux grands événements de Lyon, si différents entre eux.'[24] This reference to the attempt against the life of the king, and to the brutally suppressed workers' risings of the 1830s, should not be taken at its face value as the heartless comment of a complacent bourgeois. A terrible irony infuses all these pages, in which Stendhal, like his Lucien Leuwen, plays his part as a loyal servant of the regime, knowing that its values have worked upon him; but he continues:

Quand les ouvriers écrivirent sur leur étendard:
Vivre en travaillant
Ou mourir en combattant,
il gagnaient quatre francs par jour et il y avait beaucoup d'ouvrage.

A présent qu'ils meurent de faim depuis six mois, de novembre 1836 à juillet 1837, et sans voir de terme à leur misère, le gouvernement n'a aucune crainte. Ceci est une grande louange pour la sagesse du King et la marche actuelle du gouvernement.[25]

One seems to hear the voice of Coffe, in *Lucien Leuwen*: 'Si j'avais trois cents francs de rente seulement, je ne servirais pas le ministère qui retient des milliers de pauvres diables dans les horribles cachots du Mont-Saint-Michel et de Clairvaux.'[26] And the Tourist revenges himself for his complicity with the regime by innumerable evocations of people, places, and times that in all his works have engaged his imagination and heart. At Lyon 'j'étais absorbé dans la contemplation des temps héroïques où Madame Roland a vécu. Nous étions alors aussi grands que les premiers Romains. . . .'[27] Later he recalls 'ces jeunes gens si éloquents, si généreux, si connus sous le nom de Girondins.'[28] and the name of Barnave recurs from time to time. So eventually to the sentences which, in the whole long book, seem the most important for any understanding of the man and his art. He is crossing the Vilaine on the way to Vannes.

Par cette fin de journée sombre et triste, le danger sérieux et laid semblait écrit sur tous les petits rochers garnis de petits arbres rabougris qui environnent cette rivière fangeuse. . . . Je n'ai rien vu d'aussi

24. Ibid., vol. ii, p. 489.   25. Ibid., p. 490.   26. Op. cit., ch. 49.
27. *Mémoires d'un touriste*, vol. i, p. 141.
28. Ibid., vol. iii, p. 83.

semblable que le paysage du bac de la Vilaine et l'Ecosse désolée, triste, puritaine, fanatique, telle que je me la figurais avant de l'avoir vue. *Et j'aime mieux l'image que je m'en faisais alors que la réalité; cette plate réalité*, toute dégoûtante d'amour exclusif pour l'argent et l'avancement, *n'a pu chez moi détruire l'image poétique.*[29]

The last words in particular are his defiance of the July Monarchy on which he depends and of which, in many ways, he must approve.

Voici l'accident qui m'arrive: mon attention est empoisonnée pour toute une journée si je l'arrête sur des âmes basses, et les âmes basses qui se trouvent réunies à beaucoup d'esprit ne font que rendre le poison plus subtil; de là mes imprudences par inattention.

Ecrire ce journal le soir, en rentrant dans ma petite chambre d'auberge, est pour moi un plaisir beaucoup plus actif que celui de lire. Cette occupation nettoie admirablement mon imagination de toutes les idées d'argent, de toutes les sales méfiances que nous décorons du nom de prudence. La prudence! si nécessaire à qui n'est pas né avec une petite fortune, et qui pèse si étrangement et à qui la néglige et à qui invoque son secours![30]

In these paragraphs the nostalgia for all that is not the July Monarchy is as strong as the nostalgia he had felt years before for all that was not the Paris of Charles X. But close association with the daily reality of these regimes continues to be a condition of the full delight in what transcends them. He is not a detached and dreaming spectator. The weather affects him greatly, and he excels at creating an impression of cold and desolation, as in the description of the journey from Vannes to Auray, on 6 July:

Ce matin, à cinq heures, en partant de Vannes pour Auray, il faisait un véritable temps druidique. D'ailleurs la fatigue d'hier me disposait admirablement à la sensation du triste. Un grand vent emportait de gros nuages courant fort bas dans un ciel profondément obscurci; une pluie froide venait par rafales, et arrêtait presque les chevaux. . . . De temps à autre, j'apercevais un rivage désolé; une mer grise brisait au loin sur de grands bancs de sable, image de la misère et du danger. . . .[31]

29. Ibid., vol. ii, pp. 3–4 (my italics).
30. Ibid., vol. i, p. 311.   31. Ibid., vol. ii, p. 10.

These pages on the journey to Carnac and Ste Anne d'Auray are among the best in the book, and contain several very characteristic examples of the Stendhalian manner: the artist intent upon concentrating into the fewest possible words a visual and emotional effect, while at the same time guarding a certain detachment: 'Cette antique procession de pierres profite de l'émotion que donne le voisinage d'une mer sombre';[32] the ironical observer: 'Toutes les religions, excepté la véritable, celle du lecteur, étant fondées sur la peur du grand nombre et l'adresse de quelques-uns. . . .'[33] What is particularly interesting is the totally un-Romantic nature of his reactions to his surroundings. He extracts no poetic reverie from them; in fact, having at the start attributed his 'sensation du triste' to fatigue, he invites the conclusion that 'reality' is variable. The one certain thing is that to be cold and wet calls forth no Ossianic lyricism from him. He is rather impatient and caustic; with amusing asperity he passes in review the various explanations of the huge granite stones in this countryside, dismisses most of the explanations with contempt, and concludes by quoting from Caesar's Gallic Wars. He stresses the superstition and poverty of the region, and the fanaticism of the opinions he has encountered: 'Ainsi est la Bretagne, du moins celle que j'ai vue: fanatiques, croyant tout, ou gens ayant mille francs de rente et fort en colère contre les auteurs de la guerre civile de 93.'[34] And a remarkably detached statement about himself ends the narrative for 6 July: 'J'ai un talent marqué pour m'attirer la bienveillance et même la confiance d'un inconnu. Mais, au bout de huit jours, cette amitié diminue rapidement et se change en froide estime.'[35]

After this, the mood changes, and the genuine piety of the pilgrims to the chapel of Ste Anne d'Auray moves him to sympathy. This in turn leads to one of his most contemptuous indictments of the society of his times: 'C'est ici que devraient venir chercher des modèles ces jeunes peintres de Paris qui ont le malheur de ne croire à rien, et qui reçoivent d'un ministre aussi ferme qu'eux dans sa foi l'ordre de faire des tableaux de miracles, qui seront jugés au Salon par une société qui ne croît que par politique.'[36] He goes on to note the ideas on the times that occupied him on the

32. Ibid., p. 13.   33. Ibid., p. 15.   34. Ibid., p. 23.
35. Ibid., p. 24.   36. Ibid., p. 25.

coach journey from Hennebon to Lorient. And he comes to the
thought which is at the heart of all his presentation of character:
to escape from what he regards as the worst feature of the present
time, the propensity to hatred, and particularly impotent hatred,
that *haine impuissante* so frequently mentioned in all his works,
it is necessary to reflect on the life of any individual one is inclined
to hate: 'Chercher quels sont ses moyens de subsistance; essayez
de deviner ses manières de faire l'amour. . . .' And extend this
charity even to the 'rénégat vendu au pouvoir, qui examine votre
passeport d'un air louche.'[37] In fact this is the imaginative sympathy
of the *âme généreuse*, here presented light-heartedly but nevertheless seriously; a direct statement of an attitude illustrated in all his
great novels. One can only applaud the wisdom of what he says
and like him the more for saying it. He was obviously an observer
for whom a passer-by in the street, or a stranger on a journey,
carries with him not only his appearance of the moment, but a
whole aura of fortune or misfortune, a whole background of
family, home, town, or village. In spite of his impatience, asperity,
and comically vehement strictures on men and their opinions,
love, humanity, and generosity are what have impressed him most
in his study of the human heart. His constant awareness of the
difficulty of maintaining humanity and generosity in the face of
human stupidity and in spite of the inanity of facile exhortations
to universal tolerance and brotherhood, is one of his strong points.
It is not easy for human beings to tolerate each other, he constantly
reminds us; what is perhaps unusual is the matter-of-fact way in
which he recognizes that he himself was at times intolerable. He
follows these admirable paragraphs of personal experience, typically, with some pages of generalization on the 'three races' of
France—supplied by Crozet or borrowed from some even more
pedestrian writer.

  The difficulty of exercising tolerance and understanding demands
the compensating relief of frequent solitude. It is only in solitude
that he can get back on to that plane of spiritual enchantment that
exists in all his great works, and which in this one is to be found
under the heading 'Grenoble, le 24 août'. On the south side of the
picture gallery, he persuades the guardian to leave him alone at

37. Ibid., pp. 26, 27.

an open window to look at the superb view. He describes it briefly, and comments 'C'est dans ces instants célestes que la vue ou le souvenir d'un homme qui peut vous parler fait mal à l'âme.'[38] And the man destroys the enchantment by returning to talk; Stendhal goes quickly away, and comments 'Dans ces moments de générosité et de supériorité que fait rencontrer quelquefois la vue imprévue d'une très belle chose, il faut se jurer à soi-même de ne prendre humeur pour rien.'[39] But the resolution is difficult to keep. He is also only too well acquainted with the depths of nervous irritability and depression, though he recalls these with a comical vehemence. Between Dol and Saint-Malô he had as travelling companions several rich bourgeois, the July Monarchy triumphant. This encounter with the Crevels and Popinots of the period induces a black mood that can still be felt several pages later. 'Jamais je ne vis l'espèce humaine sous un plus vilain jour, ces gens triomphaient de leurs bassesses à peu près comme un porc qui se vautre dans la fange. Pour devenir député, faudra-t-il faire la cour à des êtres tels que ceux-ci? Sont-ce là les rois de l'Amérique?'[40] And he concludes 'Voilà donc ce peuple pour le bonheur duquel je crois qu'il faut tout faire.' But these are the leaders of the regime of which he is a uniformed official, decorated moreover with the cross of the Legion of Honour which he had at last obtained in 1835 after long efforts made, he affirmed, because the Consul of France was at a disadvantage without a decoration. Another cause of his contempt for these 'bourgeois enrichis' is that 'ils se sont mis à louer bêtement la liberté de façon à en dégoûter, la faisant consister surtout dans le pouvoir d'empêcher leurs voisins de faire ce qui leur déplaît.'[41] For this particular liberal, the problem is how to tolerate all the others. He speaks later of 'le sombre Alfieri, le poète aristocrate par excellence, qui se croyait libéral parce qu'il abhorrait tout ce qui était plus haut placé que lui dans l'échelle sociale. . . .'[42] And of course, further to the Left there were the dangerous Republicans who, however reasonable they might be on coming to power, eventually 'se mettraient en colère, et voudraient *régénérer*.'[43] His use of this verb is interesting; moral regeneration of the community was of course

38. Ibid., p. 199.   39. Ibid., pp. 199–200.   40. Ibid., pp. 69, 70.
41. Ibid., p. 69.   42. Ibid., p. 465.   43. Ibid., p. 401.

the sense of the expression 'le salut public' at the time of the Jacobins.

Considerable sections of the *Mémoires*, including the part about Geneva, and the 'Voyage dans le Midi', remained in manuscript and were not published until after the death of Stendhal. They figure, however, in modern editions, and it is interesting to see that the same attitudes and even expressions recur—the descriptions of places are the least important aspect of the work, and it is the journey that the writer is taking round his own mind that is significant. The mood in which he judged the 'bourgeois orléanistes' between Dol and Saint-Malô, towards the end of the shorter first edition, recurs towards the end of the 'Voyage dans le Midi': at Toulon he is depressed, tired, and disenchanted with the times; he feels that he will be without defence against the sadness caused by ugliness. 'Quelquefois mépriser est un supplice pour moi; et ceux qui connaissent la France de 1838 me rendront cette justice qu'il me faut quelque adresse pour n'être pas tué par le *mépris*. . . . Mais, grand Dieu! quelle laideur! Le monde a-t-il toujours été aussi vénal, aussi bas, aussi effrontément hypocrite? Suis-je plus méchant qu'un autre?'[44] But as before, in Brittany, this moment of *spleen* is overcome eventually by the pleasure of being near the sea and the activity of a port. And at last we return to the mood that heralds the beginning of *La Chartreuse*. 'Tout le monde avait vingt-cinq ans à l'armée d'Italie qui passa le pont de Lodi. Le général en chef, qui avait vingt-sept ans, était plus âgé que les neuf dixièmes de ses soldats. Du génie et de la jeunesse: *sic ita ad astra*.'[45]

The multifarious interests of the Tourist make it difficult not to give a false impression of his picture by concentrating too much on any one of them. And one can pick out sentences or paragraphs that suggest joy and youthful enthusiasm for beauty in nature and art, and overlook those that suggest an elderly and rather querulous preoccupation with material comfort. Or ignore the fact that at times the undoubted sincerity of his distaste for the *âme basse* merges into the fashionable scorn of the Artist for the Bourgeois. There is always the possibility of mockery—of the institutions he is praising, of the reader, above all of himself. Give

44. Ibid., vol. iii, p. 243.   45. Ibid., p. 261.

Stendhal a reader who is relying on comforting certainties of any description, particularly about Stendhal himself as a writer, and he will make it his business to remove them. But one might go so far as to suspect that, considering Stendhal's ambition, ever since the administrative reorganization of France, to be appointed to a prefecture, there is a slight emphasis in the *Mémoires* on politics and administrative questions. The *Mémoires* represent what he thought it was safe to publish at that time on the July Monarchy. *Lucien Leuwen* had been kept in reserve for later times, but it contains one passage in particular that comes very close to the *Mémoires*. The speaker is complaining to Lucien of the difficulties he has to encounter as president of the local council:

Le conseiller Ducros, auquel je reprochais son vote en faveur d'un cousin de M. Lefèvre, le journaliste libéral et anarchiste de Honfleur, n'a-t-il pas eu le front de me répondre: 'Monsieur le président, j'ai été nommé substitut par le Directoire auquel j'ai prêté serment, juge de première instance par Bonaparte auquel j'ai prêté serment, président de ce tribunal par Louis XVIII en 1814, confirmé par Napoléon dans les Cent-Jours, appelé à un siège plus avantageux par Louis XVIII revenant de Gand, nommé conseiller par Charles X, et je prétends mourir conseiller. Or, si la république vient cette fois-ci, nous ne resterons pas inamovibles. Et qui se vengeront les premiers, si ce n'est messieurs les journalistes? Le plus sûr est d'absoudre. Voyez ce qui est arrivé aux pairs qui ont condamné le maréchal Ney. En un mot, j'ai cinquante-cinq ans, donnez-moi l'assurance que vous durerez dix ans, et je vote avec vous.' Quelle horreur, monsieur, quel égoïsme![46]

Stendhal's attitude to the July Monarchy can perhaps best be seen if one understands that he both despises and sympathizes with Ducros.

Mémoires d'un touriste is the culmination of Stendhal's efforts to write about the July Monarchy; the *âme généreuse* is here walking on the edge of quicksands. His lifelines are memory and imagination. But there is no wish to turn back, or withdraw to safer ground. He will always, as well as making the best of the self he has to live with, make the best of the times he lives in. But with increasing difficulty. An unfinished novel, written in 1832 and 1833 and called *Une Position sociale*, is one of the most signi-

46. *Lucien Leuwen*, ch. 52, vol. iv, p. 111.

ficant pages in Stendhal's July Monarchy sketch-book. The hero
Roizand is an idealized self-portrait;[47] the heroine is obviously
a first sketch for Madame de Chasteller; and there is an exquisite
conversation between them on the fear of death that is surely one
of the most characteristic and memorable passages that Stendhal
ever wrote. But the peculiar difficulties created for the *âme
généreuse* by the political climate of the times are here described
in relation to Roizand: 'Malheureusement, à cette époque de 1832,
maintenant si reculée, les idées politiques entraient pour beaucoup dans la conduite et dans la façon de juger de la partie, dirai-je,
généreuse ou romanesque de la nation. Des larmes de colère et
d'indignation venaient aux yeux de Roizand en lisant certains
faits dans les journaux. Ce n'était pas un philosophe. C'était peut-
être encore moins un ambitieux. Rien de plus imprudent que ces
larmes. . . .'[48] Roizand's contempt for certain turpitudes is guessed,
and resented; he finds himself increasingly isolated in society.
The Tourist too has obviously learnt to accept solitude as the just
and necessary result of his inability to disguise his feelings.

There are undertones of bitterness in the *Mémoires*, regrets for
the past and fears for the future can be sensed in many judgements
of the present. There are undoubtedly tedious passages; there is
repetition. But there is also the sense of concern for the destiny
of the country that runs through the whole work; the desire to
admire, and the immediate response to beauty in nature and art;
the interest in individuals; the lively intelligence of a man deeply
involved in the life of his times. *Mémoires d'un touriste* prepares the
way for *La Chartreuse*, in which the *image poétique* is so beguiling
that it almost eclipses the *plate réalité* that is a condition of its
existence.

47. *Romans abandonnés*, ed. Crouzet (p. 158, note 17).
48. Ibid., p. 126.

7 The Dilemma of Count Mosca

It is difficult to consider *La Chartreuse de Parme* as a 'political' novel, except that it contains a disillusioned presentation of early nineteenth-century liberalism, and, in the form of the Ultra and Liberal 'parties' at the court of the hereditary Prince of Parma, an embryonic political confrontation. Where *Lucien Leuwen* is precise in its condemnation of electoral corruption, spying, and nepotism in the civil service, *La Chartreuse* retreats into the past, into a state where the 'deux Chambres' are unknown. Stendhal here makes his observations dramatically, or rather operatically; he is concerned with large generalizations about Freedom and Justice, which is why *La Chartreuse*, of all his works, seems the least bound by any one period of time. Count Mosca could have formed the nucleus of a political novel, had he been required to live in nineteenth-century France instead of the limbo of the post-Napoleon reaction in Italy, in an infinitely prolonged *fin de siècle*, and that century the eighteenth. And what do we know of him? Only how he reacts to a personal crisis, the danger created for him, as man and as minister, by the rash conduct of Fabrice del Dongo. Mosca, this passionate, intelligent, and benevolent man—all characteristics, by the way, which are revealed more by his treatment of Fabrice than by what we are told of his ministerial conduct—is tantalizingly incomplete as a character. He appears in Gina Pietranera's box at the Scala in Milan, taking refuge from the rigours of court intrigue at Parma in the pleasures of intelligent society, and recapturing the liberalism of his youth. The operatic inspiration of *La Chartreuse* is never more evident than in the character of Mosca—his great arias, the jealousy scene for example, are the highlights of the book, as are the dramatically conceived scenes in which he appears with Gina and Fabrice, or Gina and the prince. As for example the trio in Chapter 13 in which he and Gina wring from the prince a letter revoking the condemnation of Fabrice, and Mosca makes his fatal mistake of deleting, by an instinctive courtierly reaction, the words 'cette procédure

injuste n'aura pas de suite'; and the scene with Rassi, in which
Stendhal himself points to the operatic affinity by describing Rassi
as like 'Figaro pris en flagrant délit par Almaviva';[1] or the scene
of the burning of incriminating documents, where the participants
are once again Mosca and Gina, this time with young Ranuce-
Ernest V and his mother. In this one novel Stendhal brilliantly
compensates for years of fruitless attempts to write plays. But it
is as though the deep seriousness of *Fidelio* were constantly
interrupted by Mozartian overtones of hilarity. Mosca loves court
politics, his life of constant intrigue and manoeuvring fascinates him,
is indispensable to his lively restless intelligence; and he is financi-
ally dependent upon his post as a minister, as Leuwen *père* is upon
his banking, or Stendhal upon his consulate. But he does not take
it entirely seriously. Like all Stendhal's heroes, if he chooses to
participate in the particular form of games that are being played
in the times in which he lives, he can win. It is difficult to make
any moral judgement of Mosca from what we see of him in this
novel, even though the events in which he is concerned occupy
fifteen years or so. We know nothing of his life before he met
Gina, except that he fought with the French armies in Spain and
seems to date the fall of Napoleon from 1813. We are never told
his profound feelings on liberalism and *ultracisme*—we can only
speculate and deduce. According to Stendhal's chronology, never
very accurate, he must have been born in the early 1770s, and he
is between forty and forty-five when he meets Gina Pietranera
in 1815. He must have been about forty, then, at the time of the
Peninsular War in which he fought. What had he done until
then? How was he educated? What were his views on the French
Revolution? One must assume that they were Stendhal's, and that
his acceptance of service in the government of Ranuce-Ernest IV
is the result of necessity, as he himself suggests—a war pension,
an unfinished palace in Parma as sole assets, at the fall of Napoleon
—and that, just as Stendhal would have consented to serve the
Bourbons, if he had had the chance, in order to maintain the way
of life that he had enjoyed under the Empire, so Mosca would
never voluntarily accept poverty and obscurity in defence of
principle. He is first an aristocrat, and second a liberal. And he is

1. *La Chartreuse de Parme*, ch. 17, vol. ii, p. 75.

more interested in human beings and their relationships than in
political theory. He knows that, as Stendhal emphasized in 1817,
Italy is not ready for republicanism, nor for 'les deux chambres';
he loathes the antiquated forms of government of vindictive and
vain autocrats; his effort is therefore directed to strengthening the
power of the monarch in such a way that if he can be guided, it
shall be towards enlightenment and humanity, and if not, his
subjects shall be protected as far as possible against the results of
wounded vanity, spitefulness, and fear. He has a chance of success
with the young Ranuce-Ernest; the old one is a much tougher
proposition, complicated, wily, touchy, tortuous, and cruel by
nature, but also astute. Throughout the book, Mosca's comments
on the reactionary regime of Parma are witty, almost callous;
they cannot be thought to translate his deepest feelings. These are
revealed only in connection with Gina and Fabrice. At the period
at which we see Parma, the political life of the duchy depends
entirely upon relationships in love, in which Mosca, Gina, Fabrice,
Clélia, and both the princes, father and son, are concerned. Mosca,
ruefully and self-deprecatingly aware that at the age of forty-five
he has at last encountered an *amour-passion*, makes his main concern
the welfare of Gina, and of Fabrice, for whom she has made
herself responsible. The chapters in which Stendhal knots together
the relationships of Mosca, Gina, and Fabrice—Chapters 7, 8, and 9
of Part 1—must surely be among the most accomplished ever
written by a novelist. As an introduction to them, the long
Chapter 6 recounts Gina's meeting with Mosca, his courtship
of her, his highly immoral suggestion that she should marry the
renegade liberal Duke of Sanseverina-Taxis, from whom the
stigma of former liberalism will be lifted if he consents to this
marriage of convenience. (Mosca, it appears, is himself married,
but separated from his wife because she persisted in taking as a
lover one of the Raversi circle, Mosca's political enemies.) At
this point the moral climate is exactly that of Mozart's *Don
Giovanni*. Gina, then, is established at the court of Parma as the
Duchess Sanseverina, and Stendhal takes the opportunity for a
satirical description of the main personages of the court. The
charm of Gina helps Mosca to establish his position at the court
more firmly, and he becomes prime minister. Gina's favour with

the prince is such that she obtains the release of a political prisoner in the notorious Tour Farnese (Stendhal typically makes the sardonic comment that the man released happened to be unworthy of such fortune). There follows a witty and cynical discussion on what to do with Fabrice, forced to remain away from Austrian territories as a dangerous liberal, since his escapade at Waterloo. Mosca is anxious that he shall not be idle: 'quelle vie que celle qui à dix-huit ans ne fait rien et a la perspective de ne rien faire!'[2] The familiar 'rouge versus noir' argument follows, with the final decision that Fabrice shall study theology and become, eventually and as of right, archbishop of Parma. Stendhal gives to the duchess the speech in which Fabrice is ironically advised on his future behaviour.

Mosca's career is in danger from his enemies; he re-establishes his position and appoints Fabio Conti, leader of the court 'liberals', as governor of the prison which is full of liberals, and founds an ultra-royalist newspaper with the intention of letting it eventually be taken over by the 'ultra-furibonds' who will be hated for it. Gina establishes her influence over the prince, and finds the 'jeu d'échecs' of court life in Parma increasingly amusing. In fact Chapter 6 is devoted to establishing the claustrophobic atmosphere of intrigue and immorality at the court of the small state of Parma. Aesthetically the achievement of the following chapters is to rise gradually out of this *aria cattiva* of the court, to a higher region. At the beginning of Chapter 7 the four years of Fabrice's studies at Naples are concentrated into one paragraph, and he returns to Parma a Monsignore. Stendhal makes clear one of the peculiarities of Fabrice's character—that he is capable at the same time of sincere devotion to the memory of Napoleon, and also of sincere reactionary and ultra principles. During his interview with the prince, in Chapter 7, he expresses firm reactionary views, and Stendhal comments: 'Fabrice croyait à peu près tout ce que nous lui avons entendu dire. . . .'[3]

Later, in Chapter 12, he feels resentment towards the Archbishop Landriani for a slighting reference to Napoleon, and exclaims: 'O roi d'Italie . . . cette fidélité que tant d'autres t'ont

2. Ibid., ch. 6, vol. i, p. 216.
3. Ibid., ch. 7, vol. i, pp. 249–50.

jurée de ton vivant, je te la garderai après ta mort. . . .'[4] In fact, as with most of Stendhal's young characters, his liberalism is a matter of emotion rather than reflection. His aristocratic birth and his Jesuit education have between them made him, according to Stendhal, practically incapable of logical thought. It is at this point that Stendhal intensifies the complications of the personal relationships. Ranuce-Ernest, who, we learn, was 'parfaitement habile dans l'art de torturer un coeur',[5] and who is piqued by the indifference of Gina, and jealous of Mosca, suggests through an anonymous letter to Mosca that Gina and Fabrice are lovers. The rage and despair of Mosca's long and solitary meditation on this suggestion bring the reader much closer to the true nature of the man. Mosca's soliloquy here reveals his total lack of vanity, the fact that his irony is directed as much at himself as at others. 'Comment rapporter tous les raisonnements, toutes les façons de voir ce qui lui arrivait, qui, durant trois mortelles heures, mirent à la torture cet homme passionné?'[6] Against his better judgement, he goes to Gina's house, where he finds her alone with Fabrice and imagines his fears to be justified. It is here, as he watches them both, and imagines their exclusive absorption in one another, that Stendhal introduces some of the most moving lines in the book —Mosca's judgement of Fabrice. This is not only the clearest picture of Fabrice to appear in the story, it is made by a jealous rival who, looking at the young man in a moment of intense despair, can neither hate nor be unjust.

Le comte regarda Fabrice; jamais cette belle figure lombarde ne lui avait paru si simple et si noble! Fabrice faisait plus d'attention que la duchesse aux embarras qu'il [Mosca] racontait.

Réellement, se dit-il, cette tête joint l'extrême bonté à l'expression d'une certaine joie naïve et tendre qui est irrésistible. Elle semble dire: il n'y a que l'amour et le bonheur qu'il donne qui soient choses sérieuses en ce monde. Et pourtant arrive-t-on à quelque detail où l'esprit soit nécessaire, son regard se réveille et vous étonne, et l'on reste confondu.

Tout est simple à ses yeux, parce que tout est vu de haut. Grand Dieu! comment combattre un tel ennemi? Et après tout, qu'est-ce que la vie sans l'amour de Gina?[7]

4. Ibid., ch. 12, p. 357.   5. Ibid., ch. 7., p. 257.
6. Ibid., p. 260.   7. Ibid., pp. 262–3.

There is no doubt that this is an *âme généreuse*, likely to endure more suffering than he can ever bring himself to inflict. His instinct to kill Fabrice then, and himself afterwards, is overcome by his reason, still strongly on guard. After a night spent in 'les affreux transports de la plus cruelle jalousie', he does indeed sink to bribing the duchess's favourite maid to keep him informed of the progress of the relationship. It is interesting to notice that the style used by Stendhal is perfectly in keeping with the period and the passionate nature of the characters; the rhetorical expression translates strong emotion and also, since this is what he describes as 'putting all the feelings into four sharps',[8] serves to mock slightly a character with whom he sympathizes.

Meanwhile, Fabrice has begun to suspect the nature of Gina's love for him (which she never, at this or any other time, even when the Count's suspicions have been revealed to her by her maid, admits to herself) and reflects: 'Je suis bien sûr qu'elle ne parlera jamais, elle aurait horreur d'un mot trop significatif comme d'un inceste.'[9] He reviews his position; it is evident that, since the Waterloo escapade, he has grown up a good deal. 'Ces soirées si gaies, si tendres, passées presque en tête à tête avec une femme si piquante, si elles conduisent à quelque chose de mieux, elle croira trouver en moi un amant; elle me demandera des transports, de la folie, et je n'aurai toujours à lui offrir que l'amitié la plus vive, mais sans amour; la nature m'a privé de cette sorte de folie sublime.'[10] For he is convinced that, in spite of his many love affairs at Romagnano and Naples, he has not known true love and is incapable of feeling it. Deciding that, as far as Gina is concerned, 'tout est préférable au rôle affreux de l'homme qui ne veut pas deviner',[11] he embarks upon a 'petit amour de bas étage' for the leading actress in a group of strolling players at Parma, attracts the fury and jealousy of the girl's protector, and shortly finds himself in real danger of assassination. The Count, who has made a journey, ostensibly diplomatic but really strategic, to Bologna, is kept informed of these developments in Parma. At this point, given the climate of violence which exists in Parma, where there is no equality before the law since impartial law does not prevail,

8. See above, p. 76.　　9. *La Chartreuse*, ch. 7, vol. i, p. 265.
10. Ibid., pp. 266–7.　　11. Ibid., p. 266.

there being no separation of powers, nothing would have been easier than for Mosca to connive at the assassination of Fabrice. 'Qui eût songé à lui faire un sujet de reproche de la mort de Fabrice, arrivée en son absence, et pour une si sotte cause?'[12] But Mosca returns to save Fabrice by sending him away on a visit to his mother at Belgirate, and having the strolling players moved on in his absence. At this point Stendhal uses the sentence which finally makes it clear how he wants Mosca to be seen. 'Mais il avait une de ces âmes rares qui se font un remords éternel d'une action généreuse qu'elles pouvaient faire et qu'elles n'ont pas faite: d'ailleurs il ne put supporter l'idée de voir la duchesse triste, et par sa faute.'[13] In Stendhal's view, as he expresses it in the Helvétian fragment (91) of *De l'Amour*, this reaction is instinctive and as essential to the *âme généreuse* as the sap to the plant in whose veins it rises. What is certain is that Mosca's generosity, whatever its source, gives Fabrice the chance to live long enough to discover Clélia. The generous action may be in the interest of the *âme généreuse*—it also enhances the humanity of the fellow human being to whom it is directed, since the truly generous action, as distinct from the self-glorifying gesture, must be based upon a delicate assessment of the nature and well-being of the other person. To make a virtue of total self-absorption is a tendency of the twentieth century; in this, Stendhal is not 'modern'.

Stendhal conceived the function of the novel or play to be the statement of experience in its most extreme forms—'les incidents qui prouvent le caractère'—and the melodramatic action of *La Chartreuse* is directed to this end. At the end of a preface to *Lucien Leuwen* he puts the reader on guard against hatred and fear, seeing them always as the most stunting and diminishing emotions in human life, to be constantly resisted. When he remarks of Mosca 'Le comte n'avait pas de vertu; l'on peut même ajouter que ce que les libéraux entendent par vertu (chercher le bonheur du plus grand nombre) lui semblait une duperie; il se croyait obligé de chercher avant tout le bonheur du comte Mosca della Rovere . . .'[14] he is not confining the character in the bonds of a narrow egoism or in any way reducing him in stature; the fact

12. Ibid., ch. 8, p. 272.   13. Ibid.
14. Ibid., ch. 16, vol. ii, p. 64.

is that the 'bonheur du comte Mosca' is inseparable from that of Gina and therefore of Fabrice. It is Mosca's love for Gina that governs the action of the book, not his political views. He is less interested, in any case, in political theories than in their effect upon the actions of the human beings who hold them and more interested in individuals than in the masses for whom political theories are conceived.

Mosca never ceases to be jealous of Fabrice, even though he spares no effort to save him from his enemies. The spectacle of Fabrice's despair at the marriage of Clélia to Crescenzi, however,

le guérit enfin tout à fait de la jalousie que jamais Fabrice n'avait cessé de lui inspirer. Cet homme habile employa les tournures les plus délicates et les plus ingénieuses pour chercher à redonner à Fabrice quelque intérêt pour les choses de ce monde. Le comte avait toujours eu pour lui beaucoup d'estime et assez d'amitié; cette amitié, n'étant plus contre-balancé par la jalousie, devint en ce moment presque dévoué. . . . Le comte se mettait l'esprit à la torture pour faire naître un sourire sur cette figure d'anachorète, mais il n'y put parvenir. . . .[15]

Mosca's jealousy seems to have had as its chief result a more penetrating understanding of Fabrice; jealousy is something which he observes in himself and feels with terrible sharpness, but against whose prompting his reason is constantly watchful. Mosca observes himself in moments of crisis not with complacency but with irony, and occasionally with severity. Nowhere is this better illustrated than in his long account to the duchess of his repression of the popular rising after the death of Ranuce-Ernest IV. What he acknowledges here is the insidious delight of power and the attraction of fighting: 'Mais le plaisant, à mon âge, c'est que j'ai eu un moment d'enthousiasme en parlant aux soldats de la garde et arrachant les épaulettes de ce pleutre de général P——. En cet instant j'aurais donné ma vie, sans balancer, pour le prince; j'avoue maintenant que c'eût été une façon bien bête de finir. . . .'[16] Without his intervention, Mosca declares, 'Parme eût été république pendant deux mois, avec le poète Ferrante Palla pour dictateur.'[17] With Ferrante Palla, the true liberal, the dedicated revolutionary, we enter the world of Shakespeare's clowns.

15. Ibid., ch. 26, pp. 317–18.   16. Ibid., ch. 23, p. 244.
17. Ibid., p. 245.

Gifted, intelligent, willing to sacrifice for his principles not only
his own well-being but that of his mistress and their five children,
he sees it as his mission to 'réveiller les coeurs et de les empêcher
de s'endormir dans ce faux bonheur tout matériel que donnent les
monarchies.'[18] He is mad, the duchess's servants tell her, after her
encounter with him in the forest at Sacca; he is harmless, they say,
but 'parce qu'il aime notre Napoléon, on l'a condamné à mort.'[19]
It is he who becomes the instrument of the duchess's revenge by
killing Ranuce-Ernest IV and opening the way for the popular
demonstration which the Count suppresses. Ferrante is a pure
theorist—fanatical, impractical, reckless, out of touch with the
realities of the situation that he seeks to change; his is a world of
mad conspirators and fools in forests. At this point it is clear that
Stendhal, besides evoking the Italy of the early Restoration, is also
writing from the standpoint of the July Monarchy, whose servant
he was and whose material benefits he was enjoying.

Mosca undoubtedly regards it as one of his duties to protect
Parma from Ferrante Palla as much as from his own political
opponents. Mosca is referred to as a man who is widely considered
to be the foremost diplomat of Italy. He serves an ambitious
master, an absolute monarch of the old style, who hates and fears
Jacobinism, but is a man of considerable intelligence and even
finesse, with whom it is interesting for Mosca to fence. It is typical
of Stendhal that he allows Ranuce-Ernest to express the Left-wing
opinion that 'esprit'—liveliness of mind, wit, intelligence—is
always the prerogative of the Left: 'un homme d'esprit a beau
marcher dans les meilleurs principes et même de bonne foi [i.e.
expressing Right-wing sentiments] toujours par quelque côté il
est cousin germain de Voltaire et de Rousseau' (i.e. an infamous
Jacobin).[20] If this is so of Fabrice, in the prince's opinion, how much
more must it be so of Mosca? The prince knows perfectly well
that it amuses Mosca to play the Ultra, as well as being profitable
to him, while Mosca knows that his career and fortune depend
upon the whim of the prince. The sense of living on the edge of
an abyss is never unwelcome to a Stendhal character—Mosca is
always threatening to resign, or contemplating imminent disgrace.

18. Ibid., ch. 21, p. 178.   19. Ibid., p. 179.
20. Ibid., ch. 7, vol. i, p. 247.

Is one to assume that the fate of the political prisoners in the Tour Farnese is a matter of indifference to him, that he has renounced all liberal sympathies and gone over to the Ultra side entirely? Obviously not, as Stendhal has presented him as an *âme généreuse*, though the picture given by Stendhal of liberalism in Parma would make it not at all surprising if Mosca had renounced it altogether: 'le chef du parti libéral (Dieu sait quels libéraux!).'[21] Raversi, Fabio Conti, Rassi, they go from extreme meanness of spirit to extreme fanaticism. Rassi, the obsequious villain, and the Tour Farnese, represent all that Parma knows of justice. There is therefore no freedom. As one reads of the sinister practices of the jailers of the Tour Farnese, it seems that the most terrible sentence is Stendhal's description of the prisoners rejoicing at the recovery of Fabio Conti from the overdose of laudanum administered on the orders of the duchess:

il était abhorré de tout ce qui était dans la citadelle; mais le malheur inspirant les mêmes résolutions à tous les hommes, les pauvres prisonniers, ceux-la mêmes qui étaient enchaînés dans des cachots hauts de trois pieds, larges de trois pieds et de huit pieds de longueur et où ils ne pouvaient se tenir debout ou assis, tous les prisonniers, même ceux-la, dis-je, eurent l'idée de faire chanter à leurs frais un Te Deum lorsqu' ils surent que leur gouverneur était hors de danger. Deux ou trois de ces malheureux firent des sonnets en l'honneur de Fabio Conti. Oh! effet du malheur sur ces hommes! que celui qui les blâme soit conduit par sa destinée à passer un an dans un cachot haut de trois pieds, avec huit onces de pain par jour et *jeûnant* les vendredis.[22]

At the beginning of the Revolution it might have seemed that at last a society would determine to live in humanity and tolerance, and therefore justice and freedom; but this hope was short-lived. Yet the terms of the Declaration of Rights remained in the minds of successive generations of liberals, a revered but impossible ideal of human behaviour in society. Certainly they are remembered by Ferrante Palla, the self-styled 'tribun du peuple'. For both Palla and Mosca, the essential task is to empty the prisons of Parma, and break the power of Fabio Conti and of Rassi. The happiest state will be one in which the human impulse to cruelty symbolized by Barbone and his fellow-jailers, is at least not put to the service

21. Ibid., ch. 6, p. 205.   22. Ibid., ch. 21, vol. ii, p. 197.

of the lawful government of the country. The humiliating fact is that the lives and well-being of the people of Parma—humiliating, at least, for those who had heard of the 'peuple souverain' and the general will,—are dependent upon the character of the reigning monarch. Ranuce-Ernest IV, this absolutist, humourless autocrat, has the extraordinary ambition to become 'le chef libéral et adoré de toute l'Italie'.[23] What Stendhal clearly shows in this work is that the word 'liberal' has already gathered as many meanings as there are people to exploit and debase it. For Ferrante Palla, liberal means republican, and he is behind the people's revolt at the moment of the death of the prince. His methods are the surest way of filling the prisons with political prisoners; had his revolt succeeded, as Mosca well understands, the success would have been short-lived and the retribution terrible. The monarchy of Parma is backed by the victorious sovereigns of Europe. Later in his conversation with Gina about the events following the death of the prince, Mosca enlarges upon his idea of what would have happened if he had stood aside:

Les troupes fraternisaient avec le peuple, il y avait trois jours de massacre et d'incendie (car il faut cent ans à ce pays pour que la république n'y soit pas une absurdité), puis quinze jours de pillage, jusqu'à ce que deux ou trois régiments fournis par l'étranger fussent venus mettre le holà. Ferrante Palla était au milieu du peuple, plein de courage et furibond comme à l'ordinaire; il avait sans doute une douzaine d'amis qui agissaient de concert avec lui, ce dont Rassi fera une superbe conspiration.[24]

In the late twentieth century this pattern of events is still depressingly familiar, Mosca's assessment of the situation is perfectly correct, and he cannot do very much for Parma except attempt to make the new monarchy a more benevolent one. Even Ferrante Palla is forced to say 'Comment faire une république sans républicains?'[25] The people of Parma accept the hereditary principality, the court, and the social hierarchy that goes with it. Mosca has to do what he can for Parma as it is *now*, not in some imagined future. With the young prince there is some hope. In the remarkable Chapters 23, 24, and 25, both Mosca and Gina work upon

23. Ibid., ch. 17, p. 78.   24. Ibid., ch. 23, p. 248.
25. Ibid., ch. 24, p. 257.

him, firstly to save Fabrice, but also to educate the prince himself, by proving to him, to his consternation, that his jailers are poisoners, that the Minister of Justice is a dangerous rascal, and that, above all, there is no justice in his realm. It is Gina who tells him: 'Vous avez des jurisconsultes savants et qui marchent dans la rue d'un air grave; du reste, ils jugeront toujours comme il plaira au parti dominant dans votre cour.'[26] The duchess saves Fabio Conti from total disgrace because she wishes at all costs to bring about the marriage of Clélia Conti and the marquis Crescenzi, thus vindictively separating Fabrice and Clélia. When she has left Parma, she is followed by Mosca, who will forgive her anything; six weeks after Mosca's departure, 'Rassi était premier ministre, Fabio Conti, ministre de la guerre, et les prisons, que le comte avait presque vidées, se remplissaient de nouveau.'[27]

Fabrice, alone of the three to remain in Parma, living a life of withdrawn austerity because of his grief at the loss of Clélia, sees the wretched state of Parma and longs for the return of Mosca 'le comte, pour qui sa vénération augmentait tous les jours, à mesure que les affaires lui apprenaient à connaître la méchanceté des hommes.'[28] If, in the end, Mosca decides to return to Parma, it is on the invitation of the prince, who is disgusted by the party in power. The important thing here is that the Raversi crowd, who called themselves 'liberal' when in opposition, are 'ultra' when in power: 'le nouveau parti ultra, dirigé par ces deux bonnes têtes, Rassi et la marquise Raversi. . . .'[29] Stendhal, writing from the point of view of the July Monarchy, is probably concerned, in this book as much as in *Lucien Leuwen*, to stress that the party in power, everywhere and at all times, is always the 'parti ultra' insofar as its first consideration is to retain power for itself, reward its supporters, and silence its opponents.

With Mosca, the first consideration again becomes to empty the prisons. At the end his position is greatly strengthened; Gina, Fabrice, and Clélia are dead, and he was vulnerable only through them. Even after the death of Gina, which so closely follows that of Fabrice, it is possible to imagine Mosca once again taking

26. Ibid., ch. 25, p. 298.   27. Ibid., ch. 27, p. 337.
28. Ibid., p. 342.   29. Ibid., ch. 23, p. 251.

pleasure in the intrigues of political life in Parma. At the end he is actually, or nearly, sixty. Politics will provide the amusement of his old age, since the retirement with Gina to Naples or Milan is no longer possible; and the dream of the liberation and unification of his country will seem like the dream of exuberant youth.

Stendhal's judgement of Napoleon also has to be considered when one is interpreting the character of Mosca. In *Rome, Naples et Florence en 1817* there is a paragraph in which he makes it plain what Napoleon, in his view, had the power to do but failed to do:

Au reste, aucune des idées qui auraient occupé Washington n'arrêta l'attention du César moderne; ses vues étaient toutes personnelles et égoïstes. Donner d'abord au peuple français autant de liberté qu'il en pouvait supporter, et graduellement augmenter l'importance du citoyen à mesure que les factions auraient perdu de leur chaleur et que l'opinion publique aurait paru plus éclairée, n'était pas l'objet de sa politique; il ne considérait pas combien de pouvoir on pouvait confier au peuple sans imprudence, mais cherchait à deviner de combien peu de pouvoir il se contenterait. . . .[30]

Perhaps it lay in Mosca's power to foster the desire for political responsibility by increasing the importance of the individual citizen, in an enlightened community. If so, what Mosca obviously requires is a life-span of at least double the normal length, since at the end of the book, and on the threshold of old age, he has only just embarked upon the first stage of what Stendhal well understood to be a long, slow and painful process.

There is no doubt that Stendhal has reflected back on to the problems of his Parma those of Louis-Philippe's France, and above all the impasse of liberalism. The liberalism which values personal liberty above everything is usually that of property-owners: 'les droits naturels . . . sont la liberté, la propriété, la sûreté, et la résistance à l'oppression'. 'La propriété étant un droit inviolable et sacré . . .'[31] But Julien Sorel, Ferrante Palla, Coffe, and their like have no property to preserve; it is they who want, or think they want, a strong state which will defend their interests. Complicating Stendhal's appreciation of the intense difficulties of

30. *Rome, Naples et Florence*, vol. ii, p. 265.
31. *Déclaration des Droits . . .* 1789. See also B. Constant, *De l'Esprit de conquête* etc.

defining liberalism in post-Napoleonic Europe, there is his own reluctance to maintain one position for any length of time. To be able to escape is constantly necessary—from France to Italy, from Italy to France, from the real to the ideal. This is what makes him change the emphasis at a key point in his story, and move away from the preoccupations of court life to the world of Clélia.

The placing of the first long description of Clélia reveals the artistry of Stendhal as well as anything in a book which is full of examples of it. Chapter 14 is concerned with the prince's betrayal of Mosca and the duchess, and with the low intrigues among Mosca's enemies which lead to the capture of Fabrice. The next chapter opens with the description of Fabrice's journey under arrest to the Citadel, where he arrives at the moment when Clélia and her father are leaving for an evening party at the house of the Minister of the Interior, Count Zurla. Stendhal makes the transition to Clélia from the courtiers and jailers by way of the paragraph describing the meeting of Fabrice with her. 'Durant ce court dialogue, Fabrice était superbe au milieu de ces gendarmes, c'était bien la mine la plus fière et la plus noble . . .' the contrast with his captors is of course complete. It forms 'la partie extérieure de sa physionomie', this expression of contempt; more important is that he is 'ravi de la céleste beauté de Clélia.'[32] After this, the chapter is almost wholly concerned with Clélia, her appearance, her father's wish to exploit her beauty by some advantageous marriage, her behaviour at the soirée, during which the duchess is told of the arrest of Fabrice. Although, like most of the members of the court, Clélia believes the duchess to be the mistress of Fabrice, and might therefore already feel jealous of her, her reaction is to pity her: 'Les yeux de Clélia se remplirent de larmes en voyant passer la duchesse au milieu de ces salons peuplés alors de ce qu'il y avait de plus brillant dans la société. Que va devenir cette pauvre femme, se dit-elle, quand elle se trouvera seule dans sa voiture?'[33] The care with which Stendhal presents this imaginative sympathy that is always to be found in his favourite characters, is an indication of the importance he attaches to it; and to those readers who have had the good fortune to observe it and value it

32. *La Chartreuse de Parme*, ch. 15, vol. ii, p. 36.
33. Ibid., p. 45.

too, it always forms one of the most precious signs of the *âme génereuse* in life as in his novels. 'Quelle terrible passion que l'amour! . . . et cependant tous ces menteurs du monde en parlent comme d'une source de bonheur!'[34] concludes Clélia after a meditation entirely devoted to the difficulties of other people concerned in the intrigues of Parma. Stendhal here seizes the opportunity not only to make clearer the nature of Clélia, but also to sum up in one paragraph the complexities of the action of his novel. But it is particularly in the paragraph 'Les courtisans, qui n'ont rien à regarder dans leur âme, sont attentifs à tout'[35] and the one following that Stendhal establishes most strongly the effect of contrast between the *monde sublime* of which Clélia is an inhabitant until love forces her into the world of intrigue and action; and the world of the *âmes communes*, uniquely occupied with material concerns, position, wealth, titles, and the calculations necessary to obtain these. In the Citadel of which her father is governor, Clélia 'dans son appartement si élevé', high up in the Tour Farnese, has the solitude necessary for a profound inward life. But it is the second of these worlds, that of the *âmes communes*, that much of Mosca's life is passed, from choice and inclination. His strength is that he admires, as his earlier thoughts about Fabrice show, the inhabitants of the other world even though he mocks their ineptitude in the one he so expertly inhabits. Expertly— though to be sure this great statesman is capable of making grave mistakes, for example the suppression of certain words in a document, leaving the prince free to have Fabrice arrested and imprisoned. The anger of Gina, and her severe judgement of him: 'Cette âme vulgaire n'est point à la hauteur des nôtres'[36] stresses one fact: that the *amour-passion* that the count has for her is not returned. But even at this unhappy moment, his reflections on the course of action that will be necessary, restore a certain measure of calm: 'L'oeil du comte avait repris toute sa finesse satirique.'[37] It is shortly after this that he realizes, when calculating his financial resources, that he has neglected to make his fortune while in office—another *étourderie* that he promises himself to remedy if he can manage to stay in office. Actually, to become rich is a distrac-

34. Ibid., p. 46.   35. Ibid., p. 41.
36. Ibid., ch. 16, p. 58.   37. Ibid., p. 72.

tion he allows himself at the end, when he is alone. But the condition of Mosca's success in the ministerial affairs of Parma is that he shall continue to take refuge, in imagination, in the world represented in the novel by Gina, Fabrice, and Clélia—that of youth, passion, energy, and beauty, inaccessible to politics, a world of beginning and becoming, not of terrible established realities: 'mes jours les plus heureux sont toujours ceux que de temps à autre je puis venir passer à Milan; là vit encore, ce me semble, le coeur de votre armée d'Italie.'[38] 'Votre' because Gina then is the widow of one of Napoleon's generals, and has been an ornament of the court of the 'aimable Prince Eugène'. Fabrice has been present —one can hardly say more—out of enthusiasm for Napoleon, at the battle of Waterloo. Clélia is 'une petite sectaire du libéralisme',[39] and it is she who exclaims 'O pouvoir absolu, quand cesseras-tu de peser sur l'Italie! O âmes vénales et basses!'[40] Clélia is totally unconcerned with anything that might be termed politics—poetic generalizations and sympathy for the oppressed are as far as she goes towards them—and her love for Fabrice rapidly extinguishes any other consideration.

These three people, the ones whom Mosca prefers, are then the representatives of all that Stendhal most values in life, and they are not merely apolitical but anti-political. And yet politics are irresistible and provide the necessary activity for an active and practical intelligence. Like Stendhal, Mosca inhabits two worlds, and both are enjoyed because each enhances the other; far from being a cause of tension or conflict, they are absolutely essential one to the other. The nearest approach to happiness consists in a life of constant activity and risk, with moments of solitary *rêverie tendre*, and the pleasures of imagining vividly a world elsewhere of noble tranquillity and Palladian harmony. One hour in this world, and the *âme généreuse* is back in the saddle and riding away at full gallop to the problems of daily existence. So Mosca returned to Parma from the duchess's magnificent palace at Vignano. Métilde/Clélia's contempt for the 'prosaïque' is answered by Mosca, and answered in terms made familiar in our time by Anouilh's Créon and Sartre's Hoederer—someone must take action in the present,

38. Ibid., ch. 6, vol. i, p. 179.   39, Ibid., ch. 18, vol. ii, p. 110.
40. Ibid., ch. 15, p. 43.

never mind the noble theories and the visions of the future. So to the sentence that causes most trouble to interpreters of Mosca's character: 'Quant aux soixante et tant de coquins que j'ai fait tuer à coups de balles, lorsqu'ils attaquaient la statue du prince dans les jardins, ils se portent fort bien, seulement ils sont en voyage.'[41] It would be naïve to imagine that Mosca does not realize the enormity of what he is saying here. His style of speech translates all but his deepest thought; his natural instruments are wit and cynicism. His account of the suppression of the revolt needs, like the Ancient Mariner's story, a gloss, but one that Stendhal expects his reader to be able to supply: 'To be involved in politics is to inhabit a world of theories, statistics, and masses, which is inhuman. Once these anonymous members of a mob begin to emerge as individuals with names and personalities, I cease to be able to act; and if I do not act, there will be chaos in Parma and infinitely more than the sixty rebels will die.' As Stendhal could contemplate and describe the sickening carnage at Ebelsberg in 1809[42] only by 'putting a frame round it' and temporarily abandoning all human emotion, so Mosca must see life in Parma in terms of a country house charade. He has, as he says, been termed 'le Cruel' by the liberals; yet he tells the duchess, after Fabrice has put himself into the enemy's power by returning to the Farnese prison instead of to the town jail: 'Depuis que j'ai le pouvoir en ce pays, je n'ai pas fait périr un seul homme, et vous savez que je suis tellement nigaud de ce côté-là, que quelquefois, à la chute du jour, je pense encore à deux espions que je fis fusiller un peu légèrement en Espagne. Eh bien! voulez-vous que je vous défasse de Rassi?' But she refuses—not because she has scruples about political assassination, but because she would not wish Mosca in retirement to have 'des idées noires le soir'.[43] This frequent tendency towards apparent levity is displeasing to some of Stendhal's more serious-minded readers; and it certainly makes the assessment of the work as a political novel more difficult as one proceeds and finds that the complexities and contradictions in attitudes and relationships continually increase. But the great virtue of Stendhal is that he makes nothing clear. The 'profondeurs

41. Ibid., ch. 23, vol. ii, p. 243.   42. *Journal*, pp. 920–2.
43. *La Chartreuse de Parme*, ch. 24, vol. ii, p. 276.

du coeur humain' are impenetrable, love, politics, art, and all
other human preoccupations are inseparable; to achieve anything
worth while in Parma, Mosca must not only maintain his innate
generosity and capacity to love, but maintain a fine balance
between emotion and reason, in a situation which encourages
unbalanced emotion and extreme action, and is impatient of
reason. Mosca seems to share Stendhal's doubts about the republican regime. One might say—though one would undoubtedly
be contradicted—that for Stendhal as for Mosca the real danger
is the fanatic, Ferrante Palla. Stendhal had long ago ceased to be
a Jacobin. His whole work as an artist denies the neat formulas
and dogmatic pronouncements which in certain moods he liked
to copy out, admire, and rely upon. As soon as he reached the
point of saying: 'Les choses qu'il faut aux arts pour prospérer sont
souvent contraires à celles qu'il faut aux nations pour être heureuses. . . . Toutes les âmes généreuses désirent avec ardeur la
résurrection de la Grèce, mais on obtiendrait quelque chose de
semblable aux Etats-Unis d'Amerique, et non le siècle de
Périclès. . . .'[44] he was admitting that, as Sir Isaiah Berlin expresses
it, 'If . . . the ends of men are many, and not all of them are in
principle compatible with each other, then the possibility of
conflict—and of tragedy—can never wholly be eliminated from
human life, either personal or social. The necessity of choosing
between absolute claims is then an inescapable characteristic of
the human condition.'[45] Stendhal came to accept this, but reluct-
antly. It would have been consoling to believe that there was
some absolute truth about liberty and justice towards which
humanity must inevitably progress, and that freedom should
mean something more than freedom to choose by whom one
continued to be oppressed. But attractive as the dogmatism of
others always was to Stendhal, his own intelligence, as revealed
in all his writings, was sceptical and empirical. Mosca is constantly
on guard against his own tendency to believe in a 'final solution'
towards which men can be forced for their own good; his own

44. *Rome, Naples et Florence*, vol. ii, p. 15.
45. *Four Essays on Liberty*, p. 169. A book which Stendhal might greatly have
enjoyed, and from which he would have borrowed freely. The same applies to
Professor M. Cranston's witty *Political Dialogues*.

comment on his conduct towards the young prince shows this more clearly than anything: 'On a persuadé au prince que je me donne des airs de dictateur et de sauveur de la patrie, et que je veux le mener comme un enfant; qui plus est, en parlant de lui, j'aurais prononcé le mot fatal: *cet enfant*. Le fait peut être vrai, j'étais exalté ce jour-là. . . .'[46] How is the last sentence of *La Chartreuse* to be interpreted? 'Les prisons de Parme étaient vides, le comte immensément riche, Ernest V adoré de ses sujets qui comparaient son gouvernement à celui des grands-ducs de Toscane.'[47] As a cynical reminder that 'l'ultracisme, le culte des vieilles idées' has triumphed? But in what does 'progress' consist? In a 'république . . . avec le poète Ferrante Palla pour dictateur', with his mission to 'réveiller les coeurs' and to force them to be free according to his theories of freedom? In this case it is reprehensible that the prince should be 'adoré de ses sujets'. But Mosca had achieved the extraordinary result of a state in which there were no political prisoners; not, presumably, because he had had all the liberals assassinated, but because they were no longer feared? In the end the value of *La Chartreuse* is that it asks innumerable questions that are of enduring importance, and gives no answers to any of them.

46. *La Chartreuse de Parme*, ch. 23, vol. ii, p. 245.
47. Ibid., ch. 28, p. 373.

8 The Journey Continues

Count Mosca in old age: the *âme généreuse* turning towards the past in an attempt to hold his country back from terrors that he knows to be inevitable in the end; ironically aware that he has spent much of his adult life in saving others from the consequences of their own recklessness and stupidity, and shrewd enough to realize that this will have earned him more hatred than gratitude; but accepting this because what he had most cherished and admired in life was this very recklessness and defiance of convention and safety. The moment of joy he experienced when he participated in Fabrice's escape from the Tour Farnese and realized that he was committing high treason, his love for the impulsive Gina; these must be his compensation for refusing to allow Parma to slide towards anarchy. But Stendhal goes on beyond Mosca and his Mozartian distinction, to the cacophanies of Dr. Sansfin, the intelligent, ambitious, vindictive hunchback of the unfinished novel *Lamiel*. *Lamiel* carries the weight of the artist's resentment of the middle-aged caution and the 'juste milieu' materialism that made him admire and respect the achievements of the July Monarchy. The Tourist's nostalgia for the 'heroic age' of the Girondins and the sublime poetic distances of the imagination, here find relief in the expression of a mood in which he could have blown up the whole complacent, money-loving, anti-poetic society, with its Citizen King, its smug bourgeoisie, and its corrupt bureaucracy, where the Blifils always seemed to triumph; this society of which he himself was the representative in Civita-Vecchia. He had always regarded it as part of the duty of a novelist to portray his own times. But he could not, as an artist, endure the world that Balzac observed with such gusto. Stendhal could have observed a Marneffe;[1] he might have started to write about him; but it is impossible to imagine his writing more than a page. A society obsessed with money and material possessions, where the 'liberals' had at last succeeded in wresting power from the

1. Balzac, *La Cousine Bette*.

'ultras'; from this the return to Italy was still a return in time, to a place where liberalism still meant the struggle against tyranny, the liberating and unifying of a country long subjected and divided.

Lamiel is important as an attempt to explore an underworld of the imagination, both personal and collective. The mysterious element that creates a feeling of uneasiness and depression in certain sections of *Mémoires d'un touriste*, is very much stronger here. The personal disappointments and resentments which lie behind Sansfin, the frustrated ambitions, as well as the literary origins of the character, have often been examined—but there is more. There is a deliberate effort here to study a subject that had long ago become inevitable in connection with the *âme généreuse*, and which he had only touched upon in the great novels—the subject of the *âme basse* intelligent and sensitive enough to know that he is one, and that there are dimensions of experience forever closed to him, and that he is like a man with a double-bass forced by some mysterious compulsion to waste his time trying to reach the high notes of a violin. When the reaction to this knowledge is hatred and resentment for beauty, talent or good fortune in others, then all hell is possible, if the *âme basse* is intelligent enough to become powerful. Two sentences from the *Mémoires* give a clue; the one about Alfieri 'qui . . . abhorrait tout ce qui était plus haut placé que lui dans l'échelle sociale';[2] and 'Les âmes basses qui se trouvent réunis à beaucoup d'esprit ne font que rendre le poison plus subtil. . . .'[3] the 'poison' being the effect upon Stendhal's mind of contact with characters of this kind. But there is more still. *Lamiel* has more than a little of the nightmare nature of the fairy tales of the brothers Grimm. Even the language has at times a familiar naïveté: 'Il faut convenir, se dit Fédor, que voilà un bossu bien laid; mais l'on dit que de ce vilain bossu et de cette petite fille si singulière dépend toute la volonté de ma mère. Tâchons de leur faire la cour afin d'obtenir d'elle qu'elle veuille bien me laisser retourner à Paris.'[4] The characters are no longer quite human, that is the disquieting aspect of *Lamiel*; they are attitudes, abstractions. On the surface, the novel is firmly rooted in a time—France at the end of the Restoration, with the

---

2. *Mémoires d'un touriste*, vol. ii, p. 465.   3. Ibid., vol. i, p. 311.
4. *Lamiel*, ch., 7, p. 956.

July revolution of 1830 leading to the beginning of the July Monarchy; and in a place, the village of Carville in Normandy. But time and place seem unimportant; the selfishness and malevolence that pervade the book create an ambiance of their own. Lamiel, the orphan of unknown parentage, adopted by two worthy villagers, to be useful to them and care for them in their old age, has the intelligence, generosity, and liveliness of other heroes and heroines of Stendhal; the influences upon her encourage her to be heartless and self-absorbed. The local doctor, the hunchback Sansfin, vain and ambitious, bitterly resentful of his deformity, sets out to corrupt her by his cynical reasoning, in order to use her in his projects for self-advancement; since she has become the companion to the local great lady, her influence is considerable. Madame de Miossens, her son Fédor, the abbé Clément, a naïve young priest; all participate more or less in the education of Lamiel; but her own independence, scepticism, and curiosity are a guarantee that none, not even Sansfin, whose power is greater than that of the others, will succeed in dominating her completely.

Lamiel cannot be judged on the same terms as the other novels—no part of it was finally completed, and hesitations and uncertainties, even about the names of the characters, mark it at every stage. Towards the end Stendhal became obsessed with a character to be called either d'Aubigné or Nerwinde, whom he regarded with fascinated dislike and could not seem to leave. The story ceased to advance; he was still working on it at the time of his death. One of the most interesting of the many plans, sketches, and marginal comments in manuscript, now published in most modern editions, is the one dated 25 November 1839, which begins, hopefully, 'L'intérêt arrivera avec le véritable amour'[5], for Lamiel is an *âme généreuse*, and her curiosity about the nature of 'la partie morale de l'amour' is the mainspring of most of her activity. Her earlier curiosity about 'la partie physique' is satisfied in Chapter 9 when she imperiously pays a docile young villager to instruct her. But according to his plan, Stendhal destines her to love a murderer, the outlaw Valbayre, and to revenge his imprisonment by setting fire to the Palais de Justice and perishing in the flames. It sounds like sensational nonsense, and so it is to a certain extent; but the

5. Ibid., p. 1031.

idea may well be that it is she who will translate into action the
hatred and vindictiveness of Sansfin against society, while he
himself takes care to ingratiate himself with the ruling party after
the 1830 Revolution, and is appointed to a *sous-préfecture*. The last
we see of him is in Chapter 8, where he has celebrated his official
appointment by immediately granting himself leave and returning
to Carville to look after his interests there. Stendhal had plans for
him, but these remained in the form of notes. In Chapter 5 the
nature of his influence over Lamiel is stated: 'Toute son âme était
rempli du bonheur d'avoir réduit la jeune fille à l'état de *complice*.
Il l'eut engagée aux plus grands crimes qu'elle n'eût pas été
davantage sa complice. Le chemin était tracé dans cette âme si
jeune, c'était là le point essentiel. Un second avantage, non moins
important, qu'il avait obtenu en appliquant *la terreur*, c'est que la
jeune fille allait acquérir l'habitude de la discrétion.'[6] In a sketch
of Sansfin, dated 6 March 1841, Stendhal wonders 'Dominique
aura-t-il assez d'esprit pour avilir comme il faut Sansfin?'[7] It is
as though the creation of this character is a duty that he has
imposed on himself. He at first intended the work to be a comedy;
but it is too bitter and sinister. In any case, the comedy that he
achieved quite effortlessly in his main works could never be
achieved by deliberate effort. He never realized this; all his life he
seems to have persisted in that most laughter-killing enterprise,
the solemn attempt to analyse laughter.

There is no doubt that he was aware of the anarchical forces
always waiting to disrupt the civilization he valued. *Lamiel* appears
as a kind of morality, with allegorical characters; it is rather as
Chateaubriand must have seen his times when he referred to
Talleyrand and Fouché in old age as 'le vice appuyé sur le bras du
crime, M. de Talleyrand marchant soutenu par M. Fouché; la
vision infernale passe lentement devant moi . . .'[8] Perhaps Stendhal
saw that protracted wars produced as their aftermath a regression
to savagery. At times *Lamiel* seems like a confused nightmare in
a state of madness—youth moving inexorably towards lawless-
ness and death. This incomplete, at times grotesque and complex
work has for a twentieth-century reader a sinister fascination far

6. Ibid., ch. 5, p. 927.   7. Ibid., p. 1037.
8. *Mémoires d' outre-tombe*, Pléïade, vol. i, p. 984.

beyond Stendhal's apparent intentions. He seems to be in touch with the fears of a future beyond his reckoning. But he has not found a new form that might fit the new and strange content of the work; *Lamiel* is throttled in the traditional structure of the novel.

Yet however much of Sansfin there may have been in Stendhal himself—and there was probably a good deal—and however much he may have shared and desired to exploit the Romantic attraction towards horror, erotic fantasies, and violence, the fact remained that these things were not his element. 'L'*ignoble* ferme le robinet de mon imagination et de ma sensibilité *which makes all my pleasures.*'9 The remark is not an expression of pious self-righteousness; it is a simple statement of fact. In certain moods he would have seen this ironically: the Egotist, compelled by the mysterious requirements of his Muse to be the chronicler of the *âme généreuse* in its aspirations; to evoke visions of the most serene beauty in art and landscape, of courage in adversity, and fidelity in love; unable to remain long in the *aria cattiva* of life, but seeking another reality in higher regions. But, lest the reader should be too carried away by so much nobility, there is always *Souvenirs d'égotisme.* Or Sansfin. . . .

Stendhal seldom finished a work; or if he did, it was rarely without leaving among his manuscripts, plans for other possible developments of it. And in writing of him, one never reaches a conclusion; there is always the possibility of setting off again in a different direction. The journey that he began seems still to be going on, as in every generation the *chasse au bonheur* takes its myriad different forms, liberalism must be redefined, the validity of his idea of the *âme généreuse* re-examined, his notion of *amour-passion* accepted by some or mocked by others.

The works I have chosen to write about here are some of those which seemed to mark in Stendhal's life pauses of the kind that occur in the lives of his characters—Julien in the mountains, or Fabrice by the lake or in the belfry of the abbé Blanès' church—when they gather up their store of experiences and reflect upon them, before proceeding on their journey. Each of the works of non-fiction might be compared to one of the long 'interior

9. *Mélanges intimes et Marginalia*, vol. i, p. 218.

monologues' that reveal the heart of the character; here, the revelation is that of the artist's slow development. But the revelation is never complete, something is always kept in reserve, as when, in his long *Journal*, he warns the reader that he has left out the record of his most important experiences—'ce qui en vaut le mieux, ce qui a été senti aux sons de la musique de Mozart, en lisant le Tasse, en étant réveillé par un orgue des rues, en donnant le bras à ma maîtresse du moment, ne s'y trouve pas. . . .'[10] One cannot long have the illusion that one knows Stendhal. Perhaps it was the cavalry officer, M. de Stendhal, who invented Henri Beyle, and the child Henry Brulard. . . . The many different names with which he signed his letters, his other aliases—Philippe L., Bombet —are perhaps an acknowledgement that the writer has the identities that innumerable individual readers give to him, and cannot have one final identity. He reflects a world of constant change. To read the works written in journal form after reading the novels may be to discover that a great portrait painter was also a great landscape artist, capturing effects of light that at any moment may change, are indeed already changing. His titles—*Histoire de la peinture en Italie, Rome, Naples et Florence, Promenades dans Rome* —open up great perspectives, against which to see the novels. The faults of these works of non-fiction fade out on recollection, as did the miseries and disappointments of their writer's life when he created these works, leaving an impression of freedom and of those moments of joy that were the more precious because of the infinite difficulty of living. The last chapter of *Henry Brulard* is perhaps the place in all his work where he succeeds best in finding the form to express gradations of pleasure, from the pleasure of food to the spiritual ecstasy of the *âme généreuse*; that chapter which begins 'Un matin en entrant à Milan par une charmante matinée de printemps . . .' and ends 'On gâte des sentiments si tendres à les raconter en détail'; and in which he succeeds both in experiencing the mental and physical discomforts of the present: 'Je suis très froid aujourd'hui, le temps est gris, je souffre un peu' and in evoking a past forever freed from physical limitations, the imperishable past of the imagination. And it is this chapter that contains the sentence which many Stendhalians like best to

10. *Journal* (Note to the entry for 19 mai 1810), p. 962.

remember: 'Je passerais dans d'horribles douleurs, les cinq, dix, vingt ou trente ans qui me restent à vivre qu'en mourant je ne dirais pas: Je ne veux pas recommencer.' That as many as possible of his fellow human beings may share this feeling in the course of their own lives, is perhaps the supreme hope of the *âme généreuse*.

Bibliography

EDITIONS USED IN FOOTNOTE REFERENCES

Several volumes of the *Oeuvres Complètes* in the Cercle du Bibliophile edition which is being published under the direction of MM. Victor Del Litto and Ernest Abravenel had not appeared at the time of writing. This admirable critical edition completes and revises the earlier Champion edition, adding much new material; the prefaces and the bibliographical and critical introductions to the Champion volumes, by different writers and scholars, have been kept. I have used this edition where possible, and my footnotes for *Histoire de la peinture en Italie, Rome, Naples et Florence, Armance, Promenades dans Rome, Le Rouge et le Noir, Lucien Leuwen* (in which vol. i reproduces 'Le Chasseur Vert', the first version of the novel), *Mémoires d'un touriste*, and *La Chartreuse de Parme*, refer to it. But as this book is intended less for Stendhal specialists than for general readers, it seemed more practical to use the single volume *Oeuvres Intimes* of the Pléiade edition for *Henry Brulard*, the *Journal*, and *Souvenirs d'égotisme*; and the Pléiade *Romans et Nouvelles*, vol. ii, for *Lamiel*. There remained the question of the many marginal notes, essays, and drafts in manuscript, first published by M. Henri Martineau in the *Mélanges* volumes of his Divan edition. This edition is inevitably being in some measure superseded by the work of recent scholars; corrections, augmentations and rearrangements of material are being made. The volumes of the new Cercle du Bibliophile/ Champion edition that deal with this material represent a remarkable achievement. But while admiring them, I suspect that certain readers may continue to cherish the little volumes of the Divan *Mélanges* in which they first discovered to their delight new aspects of Stendhal. So I have referred to the Divan edition for *Mélanges intimes et Marginalia*, *Mélanges de littérature, Courrier anglais, Théâtre*, and *Napoléon*.

SELECTED GENERAL WORKS

Alain, *Stendhal*. Paris, Presses Universitaires de France, 1959.
Arbelet, P., *La Jeunesse de Stendhal*. Paris, Champion, 1919. (2 vols.)
Bardèche, M., *Stendhal romancier*. Paris, Table Ronde, 1947.
Blin, G., *Stendhal et les problèmes de la personnalité*. Paris, J. Corti, 1958.

Bonfantini, M., *Stendhal e il realismo* (saggio sul romanzo ottocentesco). Milan, Feltrinelli, 1958.

Brombert, V., *Stendhal: Fiction and the Themes of Freedom*. New York, Random House, 1968.

Del Litto, V., *La Vie intellectuelle de Stendhal. Genèse et évolution de ses idées (1802–1821)*. Paris, P.U.F., 1959.

— *Bibliographie stendhalienne*. Lausanne, Grand-Chêne, 1947 onwards.

— *En Marge des manuscrits de Stendhal. Compléments et fragments inédits (1803–1820) suivis d'un courrier italien*. Paris, P.U.F., 1955.

Hemmings, F. W. J., *Stendhal: a study of his novels*. London, Oxford University Press, 1964.

Jourda, P., *Stendhal, l'homme et l'oeuvre*. Paris, Desclée, 1934.

Martineau, H., *L'Oeuvre de Stendhal: histoire de ses livres et de sa pensée*. Paris, A. Michel, 1951.

— *Le Coeur de Stendhal: histoire de sa vie et de ses sentiments*. Paris, A. Michel, 1952. (2 vols.)

Michel, F., *Etudes stendhaliennes*. Paris, Mercure de France, 1957.

Pincherle, B., *In Compagnia di Stendhal*. Milan, Pesce d'Oro, 1967.

Prévost, J., *La Création chez Stendhal* (essai sur le métier d'écrire et la psychologie de l'écrivain). Paris, Mercure de France, 1967 (reprint).

Richard, J.-P., *Littérature et sensation*. ('Connaissance et tendresse chez Stendhal', pp. 15–116). Paris, Editions du Seuil, 1954.

SELECTED WORKS OF SPECIALIZED INTEREST

Albérès, F. M., *Le Naturel chez Stendhal*. Paris, Nizet, 1956.

— *Stendhal et le sentiment religieux*. Paris, Nizet, 1956.

Alciatore, J., *Stendhal et Helvétius: Les sources de la philosophie de Stendhal*. Geneva, Droz, 1952.

Arbelet, P., *L''Histoire de la peinture en Italie' et les plagiats de Stendhal*. Paris, Calmann-Lévy, 1914.

Benedetto, L. F., *La Parma di Stendhal*. Florence, Sansoni, 1950.

Berlin, Sir I., *Four Essays on Liberty*. London, O.U.P., 1969.

Boppe, R., *Stendhal à Rome. Les débuts d'un consul (1831–1833)*. Paris, Horizons de France, 1944.

Caraccio, A., *Variétés stendhaliennes*. Paris, Arthaud, 1947.

Coe, R., 'Stendhal and the Art of Memory' in *Currents of Thought in French Literature. Essays in memory of G. T. Clapton*. Oxford, Blackwell, 1965.

— 'La Chartreuse de Parme, portrait d'une réaction' in *Aurea Parma*, (Atti del VI° congresso internazionale stendhaliano) Anno LI. Fax. II–III. Maggio-Dicembre 1967. pp. 43–61.

Constant, B., *De l'Esprit de conquête et de l'usurpation dans leurs rapports avec la civilisation européenne. Oeuvres*, Paris, Pléiade, pp. 951–1062.

Cranston, M., *Political Dialogues*. London, B.B.C. Publications, 1968.

Crouzet, M. (ed.), *Stendal: romans abandonnes*. Paris, Jalard, Bibliothèque 10/18, 1968.

Dédéyan, C., *L'Italie dans l'oeuvre romanesque de Stendal*. Paris, Editions de l'Enseignement Supérieur, 1963. (2 vols.)

Del Litto, V., ' "Lamiel". Pages inédites.' *Stendhal Club*, 15 oct. 1958, pp. 3–8.

Destutt de Tracy, A.-L.-C., *Commentaire sur 'De l'Esprit des lois' de Montesquieu*. Paris, Lévi, 1828.

Fox, C. J., *Memorials and Correspondence of Charles James Fox,* ed. Lord John Russell. London, Bentley, 1853. (4 vols.).

Gunnell, D., *Stendhal et l'Angleterre*. Paris, C. Bosse, 1909.

Hazlitt, W., *Complete works*. Centenary edition, vol. 16. (Contributions to the *Edinburgh Review*) London, Dent, 1930–4.

Heisler, M,. *Stendhal et Napoléon*. Paris, Nizet, 1969.

Imbert, H.-F., *Les Métamorphoses de la liberté ou Stendhal devant la restauration et la risorgimento*. Paris, J. Corti, 1967.

Jansse, L., 'Stendhal et les classes sociales'. *Stendhal Club*, 15 oct. 1963, pp. 35–45.

— 'Stendhal et la constitution anglaise'. *Stendhal Club*, 15 juillet 1967, pp. 327–48.

— 'Stendhal et les grandes théories de "L'Esprit des Lois" '. *Stendhal Club*, 15 oct. 1969, pp. 25–48.

Jones, G., *L'Ironie dans les romans de Stendhal*. Lausanne, Grand-Chêne, 1969.

Leroy, M., *Stendhal politique*. Paris, Divan, 1929.

McWatters, K. G., *Stendhal lecteur des romanciers anglais*. Lausanne, Grand-Chêne, 1968.

Parc, Y. du, *Quand Stendhal relisait les Promenades dans Rome. Marginalia inédits*. Lausanne, Grand-Chêne, 1959.

Paupe, A., *La Vie littéraire de Stendhal*. Paris, Champion, 1914.

Ponteil, F., *L'Eveil des nationalités et le mouvement libéral (1815–1848)*. Paris, P.U.F., 1960.

Poulet, G., *Etudes sur le temps humain*, IV, *Mesure de l'instant* ('Stendhal', pp. 227–51). Paris, Plon, 1968.

Rude, F., *Stendhal et la pensée sociale de son temps*. Paris, Plon, 1967.

Seznec, J., 'Stendhal et les peintres bolonais'. *Gazette des Beaux-Arts*, 6ᵉ période, Tome 53, 1959, pp. 167–78.

Trahard, P., *La Sensibilité révolutionnaire (1789–1794)*. Paris, Boivin, 1936.

Trompeo, P. P., *Nell'Italia romantica sulle orme di Stendhal*. Roma, Leonardo da Vinci, 1924.

Trotter, J. B., *Memoirs of the Latter Years of the Right Honourable Charles James Fox*. London, Phillips, 1811.

Turnell, M., *The Novel in France* ('Stendhal', pp. 125–208). London, Hamish Hamilton, 1950.

— *The Art of French Fiction* ('Stendhal's first novel' pp. 63–90). London, Hamish Hamilton, 1959.

Vigneron, R., 'Stendhal et Hazlitt'. *Modern Philology*, vol. 35, May 1938, pp. 375–414.

Vizinczey, S., *The Rules of Chaos* ('One of the very few', pp .147–98). Macmillan, 1969.

Index

Index   157

Printed in Great Britain by
Hazell Watson & Viney Ltd, Aylesbury, Bucks

Colour Craft

Colour Craft

Janet Allen

Book Club Associates
London

This edition published 1980 by
Book Club Associates
By arrangement with
The Hamlyn Publishing Group Limited
London · New York · Sydney · Toronto
Astronaut House, Feltham, Middlesex, England

Filmset in England by Photocomp Limited, Birmingham
in 11 on 12pt Apollo

Printed in Spain

Contents

Introduction

Before reading this book you may have thought that when it came to fabric dyeing, the use of commercial dye was the limit of your capability, and that fabric printing was best left to fabric manufacturers. You may have thought that the equipment used for fabric printing was mysterious, not to mention vastly expensive, and that the use of anything other than the little pots of powdered dye was restricted to professionals with a firm grasp of chemistry. Nothing could be further from the truth. Misconceptions such as these prevent many people from trying out a craft that can prove to be a satisfying hobby when practised by one person, or a rewarding enterprise for several people.

Batik, silk screen and tritik are just a few of the textile arts you will find explained in this book, as well as instructions for using commercial dyes successfully and creatively and how to get the best results from natural dyes.

You may be pleasantly surprised to find that fabric dyeing and printing is really a 'kitchen-table craft', and that so long as you have a large flat surface to work on, a few old wooden spoons and a plastic bucket or bowl you have the basic equipment. The book tells you which fabric dyes or inks to use for each technique, and what fabric is best suited to your purpose.

Because experience is the best teacher, each set of instructions is accompanied by a project. For example, in tritik you are given a pattern for turning a length of tritik-dyed fabric into a cool summer dress; wools coloured with natural dyes can be knitted up into a beautiful cardigan using the pattern chart provided in the chapter on natural dyeing.

But, given all this, why go to all the trouble and expense dyeing or printing fabric? The obvious answer to this is – creative expression. Our everyday way of life is becoming increasingly stereotyped, obliging us more and more to conform. Here is a chance to learn how to do something totally different and to gain the satisfaction of knowing that you, in however modest a way to begin with, are giving expression to your own personal ideas, using the creative ability that all of us possess, and at the same time producing attractive useful items.

Because of the growing disenchantment with the sameness of mass produced articles, many people willingly pay exceedingly high prices for a unique, hand-knitted sweater or a hand-printed scarf, purely to enjoy possessing something unusual. With the methods explained in this book you can create your own totally exclusive designs – it is fun actually doing it, but what is more, you can be proud of the finished results.

So, if you get satisfaction from making your own clothes or even baking your own bread, you have a creative urge, and fabric crafts are an obvious outlet. Artistic ability – being able to draw or paint beautifully – is not a prerequisite to success. This is something that I feel very strongly; that one should not be put off a craft because of preconceived ideas about artistic flair. If you can look at the world about you, you can then translate what you see into a good, and above all, original design. And, if you can read, you can follow simple instructions, thus enjoying a craft that, in one form or another, has been practised all over the world, for generations.

There are many ways to use these techniques, from the recycling of cloth and garments by changing their colour to putting a truly personal design signature on furnishing fabrics, household items, gifts, your own and the children's clothes. Dressmakers can cleverly position a printed or batiked pattern on to the cut out pieces of garment before making it up, and using the simple technique of transfer rubbing, children can put the photograph of their favourite pop star on to a T-shirt or scarf.

Each textile craft possesses its own kind of magic, and the finished result is always an intriguing combination of your own ideas plus the inherent qualities of the technique you have used: you never know exactly how the thing is going to finish up. At some point in the procedure the technique itself seems to take over; you simply can not dictate – there is nothing like the thrill of extracting a garment from the dye because you can never forsee just how the new dye colour will influence the original colours of the printed cloth. When printing fabric, there is always the excitement of seeing what sort of image is going to result. Respect this aspect of the craft, this element of surprise; be conscious of the fact that each method has its own distinct qualities. For example, in your first experiments with batik you will discover that it is the sort of pursuit where spontaneity is all important, on the other hand, certain forms of block printing may be highly organised and controlled.

Thinking about design

You may well be feeling a little disturbed by the word 'design'. Perhaps, because of the emphasis on specialisation these days, you feel you ought to have had a complete training in fine art to be able to even make an attempt at any sort of design. It would appear, though, that people have always had a natural sense of design and an urge to arrange and decorate things, and this intrinsic characteristic constantly manifests itself, however inartistic you may consider yourself to be. In all our activities we appear to have a feeling of what looks good. Take cooking as an example: you would never indiscriminately heap an assortment of potatoes, steak pie, peas and carrots on a plate and then present it at the dinner table. You arrange the meal so that each separate food is seen to advantage, making the meal more appetising. Most cooks will feel aware of the need for colour variety in a dish, even if it is only a garnish of bright green parsley or a couple of slices of tomato and many a dull trifle has been enlivened by the addition of a few red cherries: preoccupation with design is the central activity of interior decorating. People will spend hours agonising over wallpaper patterns and different coloured paints in an attempt to achieve a scheme that is not only attractive, but reflects their personality.

These may be rather minor, but they are nevertheless fundamental examples of our innate interest in arrangement, organisation and the awareness of the visual impact which can be achieved by design. In the more advanced forms of both these pursuits, cooking and interior design, the design urge is given greater scope and encouragement. Think, for instance, of elaborate cake decorations or the fantastic creations of a master pastrycook; of the complex task facing an interior designer when a new hotel has been built and is to be decorated.

So, how can you develop this natural ability? Experimenting is the answer. The more you try out different colour combinations, different arrangements of shapes – playing large against small, group against group – the more you will become aware of design all around you. The whole of nature is one great masterpiece of design and engineering. The sections of a plant, the anatomy of an animal or the interlacing of different geological strata are all sorted out to function with efficiency. Surely this is why the natural world has always inspired artists and designers – flowers and plants have always been especially important to the textile designer. Perhaps this is because we want our man-made environment – our wallpapered and curtained rooms – to imitate the serene background of the natural world.

You can gain further ideas and inspiration from the work of designers and artists. This is, as it were, someone else's interpretation of nature and one step removed from the real thing, but the ways in which other people have portrayed their surroundings can be immensely stimulating to you. Look about you at all the objects that have been designed and decorated – furnishings, the labels on bottles and jars, posters, fancy brickwork, even manhole covers can serve as inspiration.

Some of the techniques in this book are particularly suitable for starting you off on thinking about design and arrangement. For example, tie-dyeing and printing with improvised blocks (that means all manner of odds and ends lying around the house) are both methods of decorating which automatically create their own patterns. So the job is already half done for you. It is just up to you to group or space the pattern shapes in an attractive and suitable way, and to organise the colour scheme.

As soon as you begin you must consider the scale of the pattern you are going to apply in relation to the article being decorated. Clearly a pale-complexioned diminutive person is not going to appear to best advantage in a dress that is covered in gargantuan tie-dye sunbursts in brilliant contrasting colours. Watch the positioning of motifs also: two sunbursts side by side on the bust and one big one on the stomach is something to be avoided.

The scale of the applied pattern must also be adjusted to suit the type of fabric you are using. An intricate, delicate design with lots of fine lines will not work successfully on a coarsely woven material; a more pronounced design would be better.

Do always bear in mind that you are producing work done by hand; you are not competing with a machine. A machine can do many things far better than you can – like repeating a printed shape in precisely the same way *ad infinitum*. Why try to emulate the machine? Leave it to do its own job while you make use of all the advantages available to the hand craftsman. You, because you are not a machine, are at liberty to suddenly change a colour if you want to; to completely rearrange a group of motifs or to turn them all upside-down, or to add an extra row of dots in an outrageous shade of pink, should you feel so inclined.

You will find that with many of the techniques designs and patterns will evolve on their own out of the method itself. So, rather than feeling you must invent a really original shape as a motif, see what an amazing number of pattern combinations you can achieve from groupings of identical triangles or rectangles. Many cultures, notably the Arabic, developed the arrangement of repeated simple geometric shapes in myriad ways. Get ideas from art history books in your local library. Extract and use, in your own way, motifs and shapes from any and every source. As soon as you start you will begin noticing relevant factors, such as the way someone has solved the problem of finishing off the corner of a tiled floor, or how the pattern on the border of dinner plate, elaborate at first sight, turns out to be a simple motif, cleverly repeated.

You will find you want to analyse and pinpoint just which colours constitute a particularly successful scheme in a vase of

flowers, a picture or the decor of a room so that you can translate that success in your own terms and apply it to your own uses.

A few practical considerations
There are several important points to note before you start work on any of the fabric crafts.

Make sure that in adition to a suitable working surface, you have ample space in which to leave the work to dry out. There is little point in spending considerable time and effort over something that is then ruined because the wet colours have touched and marked the fabric in the wrong places. The best methods for drying the different types of work are given with each.

Get into the habit of saving old newspapers, rags and useful sizes of jars. Have two rag boxes, one for clean and one for dirtier, but still usable rags for cleaning up. That way the supply will last longer.

Although it is boring when you are anxious to get started on something new, do be sure to read the instructions and recommendations on the use of dyes and inks thoroughly. Also, read through the instructions just as you would read through a recipe before beginning, noting special procedures and the materials required.

Test the colour of a fabric dye paste or a printing ink by lightly dabbing a little on the fabric to be printed. This gives you a good idea of what the finished printed colour will be. Colours in the tube or jar can be very misleading as their density alters the appearance of the colour.

Do test the various techniques on small scraps of the fabric you will be using. Apart from making you familiar with a new method, this enables you to check that everything is working properly – that dyes suit fabric etc. These test pieces can later be used for fancy patches or even to make an interesting patchwork, so it is worth saving them.

Janet Allen

Chapter 1

Plain Dyeing

Dyeing fabrics

Colour is one aspect of the world around us that appears to influence our senses more than anything else. Colours have immensely emotive properties associated with them making us feel elated or depressed. Azure blue skies and golden sands, together with a deep bronze tan, instantly create the feeling of luxury and pleasure; whereas grey Monday morning drizzle immediately and forcibly means quite the reverse.

By using dyes you can take advantage of this aspect of colour and introduce your own choice of colours to completely transform your clothing, co-ordinate household linens and alter soft furnishings or just simply for the fun of it.

With fabric dyes you can revive all those dismal things you feel you can't throw away because they are still in such good condition or give last year's wardrobe a new lease of life – introduce some really brilliant colours or go for cleverly matching subtle shades. Brighten up the children's T-shirts, dungarees and dresses and re-vitalise sad-looking woollens, shirts and dreary underwear. Dye ill-assorted accessories, gloves, scarves, tights, etc., to create elegantly co-ordinated new fashions. Effecting these stunning transformations costs very little and it is all surprisingly easy to do. There are just a few basic facts to grasp first to avoid disappointment later.

Choosing the correct dye

Chemical dyes as opposed to natural dyes (see page 25) are available in hardware shops, chain and department stores and some craft shops. There are a number of different types of chemical dyes on the market, each being suited to a different kind of fabric. This may appear somewhat confusing so, rather than wandering aimlessly about the shop, equip yourself beforehand with all the necessary information, then you will know what to buy.

You need to know what material the items you intend to dye are made from. In many instances the label will tell you this. All natural fibre fabrics will readily accept any type of dye. Natural fibre fabrics are cotton, wool, silk, linen and viscose rayon.

Viscose rayon, which is made from cellulose, is marketed under the following trade names: Darelle, Delustra, Evlan, Raycelon, Sarille and Vincel.

Most fabrics that can be washed can be dyed at home, but there are a few exceptions. These include anything with a specially treated permanent finish – flame-proofing, drip dry, water-proofing or glazing – and acrylic fabrics. Trade names for acrylic fabrics are Acrilan, Cashmilon, Courtelle, Dralon, Leacril, Neo-spun, Orlon and Sayelle. Fibreglass and plastic-backed fabrics are unsuitable for home dyeing also. Certain polyesters may accept the dye colour only in a reduced form thus giving pale colours, and some polyester-cotton mixtures may dye in an even but all-over mottled effect. This is because there are cotton fibres in the material that will absorb more dye than the polyester fibres.

Sort the items to be dyed into groups according to fabric type, then weigh each group and record the weight. Weigh them when dry; this is most important as the weight determines the amount of dye used. The dye manufacturer's colour chart will indicate the quantity of dye needed for your weight of fabric. If you cannot establish from which material an article is made, the safest approach is to cut off a small piece and test dye it with your other items rather than risk spoiling the whole thing.

Some buckles, buttons and so on will accept dye, but there is no way of knowing this until you try dyeing the garment they are attached to, so they may have to be replaced with new ones. Alternatively, what about painting them with nail varnish or model maker's enamel paint?

Doing the dyeing

There are two basic types of commercial dye suitable for home dyeing; one using cold water, the other hot water. Dylon Ltd. produce a good range of each and also provide adequate, clear instructions. Obviously, to obtain satisfactory results, you must follow the manufacturer's recommendations.

When you come to the dye mixing stage, the following is worth noting: most probably you will be using cold water dye as it is particularly good for cotton. You may not need to use all the dye in the tin because you have only a small amount of fabric to dye. With cold water dye it is possible to store any extra dye solution. Simply dissolve the dye powder in warm water as usual but *do not* add any fix. Then put that amount of the solution that you don't require at present into a screw-topped jar to store it. In this state, mixed with *water only*, not salt, fix or soda, it will keep for some weeks, preferably in a dark place.

COLD WATER DYES. These are only suitable for natural fibre fabrics but, with the exception of woollens, they give excellent strength

Commercially prepared dyes are no doubt the easiest way to colour fabric. But because these dyes are transparent, one must have a basic understanding of how colours work in combination – when these dyes are used over a coloured fabric, they can produce some surprising changes.

In the chart below, blue and orange were used to alter the fabric samples. Notice how, where two primaries combine, a secondary colour results; use the colour circle, right, to work out other combinations.

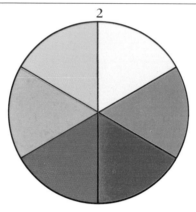

2

On the other hand, the sweaters, right, illustrate the use of a secondary colour over a primary. The boy's sweater is the original colour, the girl's has been dyed in a shade of lilac. See how the yellow stripes have turned a greyish non-colour.

The use of commercial dyes and their colour properties are discussed fully in Chapter 1.

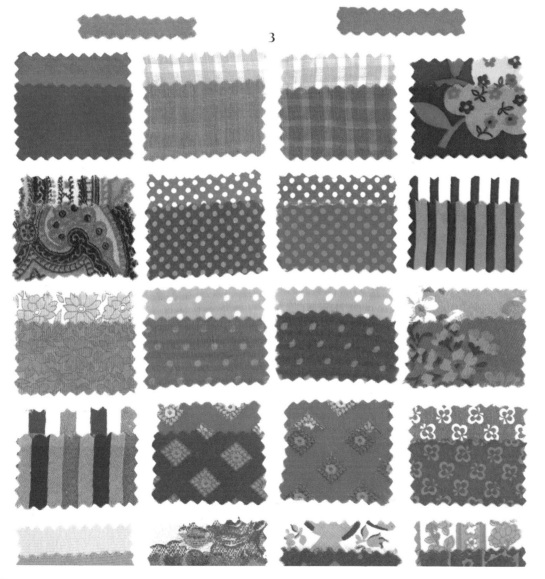

3

18

of colour and will withstand frequent washing. They are ideal for bed linen, curtains, towels, tablecloths or clothes made from any of the natural fibres. Wool can be dyed with cold water dye but only a pale version of the colour will result. Check the manufacturer's instructions as the procedure for dyeing wool with cold water dyes is slightly different to that for other fabrics. When buying your dye be sure to see what, if any, other additives are required. These may be a special (inexpensive) dye fix, salt, washing soda or vinegar.

You will definitely need a pair of rubber gloves (cold water dyes leave a lasting stain on hands), a clean stick or an old wooden spoon, and a container large enough to take your dye mixture and the fabric and to allow ample room to stir it all around. This could be the sink, provided it isn't chipped or scratched, a plastic bucket or a dustbin. Afterwards any dye stains can be removed with scouring powder or diluted bleach. Large articles can be dyed with cold water dyes in a washing machine if the machine will run a cold cycle. It is sensible to wear old clothes when doing dyeing and to cover working surfaces with plastic or newspaper.

HOT WATER DYES. These will dye both natural and synthetic fibre fabrics (except those already mentioned). These dyes are a little less colour and light fast than the cold water dyes. Here you will need a large heat-proof container – a big saucepan, preserving pan or metal bucket – on top of the cooker, and a stick or old wooden spoon with which to keep the fabric constantly moving. Hot water dyes may also be used in a washing machine.

Especially intended for dyeing large items easily, a bedspread, for instance, a special dye and detergent blend such as Dylon Wash 'n Dye will obviate the pre-washing. It cleans and dyes simultaneously in a washing machine. These blends will dye all natural fibres and, as explained on the colour charts, many synthetics.

Wools and yarns for knitting, embroidery and weaving may be dyed (this can save money). As usual, a dye that is correct for the fibre must be used. (An economy hint – wool from hand-knitted garments can be successfully recycled. Unpick the garment and wind the wool into skeins. At this point it will be very crinkled but washing will straighten it out.) Any wool, old or new, should be washed prior to dyeing. To do this, loosely tie a string around each skein at three equally spaced points, winding the string in a figure-of-eight as shown in fig. 1, so that it doesn't all come unravelled in the water. Hand wash it in warm water using a mild soap. Keep it in the skeins and dye it as you would a fabric. However, don't allow a hot water dye to heat up to simmering point – you wouldn't simmer a woollen sweater. Certain cold

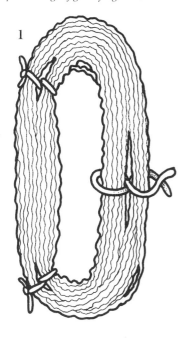

1 Wool that is to be dyed should be wound into skeins and tied in three places using a figure-of-eight knot.

water dyes give special instructions on using *warm* water for wool – just to confuse! Dye the total amount of wool required for an article all at the same time to be sure the skeins match.

IMPORTANT: whichever type of dye you are using, always make sure there is plenty of room in your dye mixture container for the fabric to move around freely. If not, the dyeing will be streaky or patchy. If you are using a washing machine for dyeing, dye items which altogether weigh, when dry, only half of the weight of a normal, full washing load. When the dyeing session is finished and you've removed the articles, run the machine through a complete cycle with detergent and bleach to clean it thoroughly.

At the end of the dyeing procedure always rinse the items over and over again before hanging them up to dry. Let them dry naturally with plenty of air circulating around them. When the time comes for you to wash a dyed article wash it separately just in case any of the dye should run at this first washing.

Articles must be clean before they are dyed. It's no good expecting the dye to conceal stains or faded areas. They will, unfortunately, just be repeated in a new colour scheme! There are colour removing preparations, such as Dygon, on the market but they are not successful on all ready-dyed fabrics. It is best to check the results by running your own tests on small pieces cut from a seam allowance before attempting to strip the colour out of a complete article. Remember, when fabric is wet it always appears some shades darker than it will when it is dry.

What colour will you choose?

Obviously there are thousands of variations of colours, but any one dye colour can look quite different on two different fabrics because of the contrast in texture: think of the difference in appearance between a piece of blue velvet and a piece of canvas in the same blue. Dyes are more like ink than they are like paint. That is, whilst being coloured they are also transparent and will only stain; a paint, if sufficient coats are applied, will obliterate the colour underneath it. So when dyeing you must remember that the final result will be strongly influenced by the original colour of the article. For example, a light blue dress dyed rose red will not come out rose red but will turn purple. You can only dye to a colour which is darker than the original colour of the item. However, because of the staining, as opposed to covering properties of dye, you can have a lot of fun trying out different colour combinations on both plain, single-coloured fabrics and on multi-coloured patterned materials.

A white fabric can be dyed to any colour, but a pale-coloured

Although commercial dyes may be the easiest to use, there is enormous pleasure to be found in using dyes obtained from plants that you have gathered yourself. But most pleasurable of all are the colours these plants will yield, for they are as soft and subtle as the natural fibres they must be used with, as natural dyes will not successfully colour synthetics.

Elderberries, blackberries, ivy, lichen, onion skins and certain tree barks and weeds are just a few of the organic colouring agents that can be gathered from field and forest.

Dyeing wool for knitting is a good place to start: in the photograph, left, the small sweater was coloured with onion skin dye and the leggings with blackberry dye. The wool for the hat was dyed in various strengths of elderberry dye, and the sweater is being knitted with a variety of naturally dyed wools – from onion skin dye for the golds to cochineal for the pinks.

The basket in the photograph above holds a selection of wools dyed with organic substances. As a rough guide, the bright pink is dye from cochineal, dusty pink from sloes, brownish red from beetroot, bright yellow from saffron, light yellow from goldenrod and turmeric, ginger and gold from onion skins, beige from tea, pale cream from apple skins, purples and blues from blackberries and elderberries.

Instructions for making your own dyes from nature begin on page 25.

23

fabric may influence the new dyed colour, depending upon how intense the original colour is: a pale grey vest dyed cream will become a pale greyish-cream vest; a much better idea would be to use a strong red or a blue.

Any colour can be dyed to black, but don't expect a selection of different coloured items to come out all looking the same black. Some may appear bluish-black, others brownish-black, some a very dark grey.

UNDERSTANDING COLOUR. Red, blue and yellow are known as the *primary* colours. They are the colours from which all other colours can, in theory, be mixed. If equal amounts of red, blue and yellow are mixed together the result is a 'non-colour', supposedly black, but really a dark grey. Manufacturers of dyes and paints find it impossible to produce a pure red that has no trace of yellow or blue (the other two primaries) in it, likewise a pure blue, containing absolutely no red or yellow, and a pure yellow, containing neither red nor blue. Consequently the theory does not stand up in practice! However, it is a useful guide through the otherwise totally confusing maze of colours.

Pairs of primary colours mixed together produce the three *secondary* colours as follows: red+blue=*purple*; blue +yellow= *green*; yellow+red=*orange*. This mixing applies when you are dyeing an article from one colour to another, i.e. as when the dye colour stains over the original colour, blending with it, or when you mix the dyes themselves. Mixing dyes is perfectly possible. Do not feel bound all the time by the colours on the colour chart, make up your own if you want to. Do, however, remember the dry weight of fabric to quantity of dye ratio.

Primary and secondary colours are pretty straightforward. The problems arise when the original colour of an item is an inbetween: a 'sort of greeny-blue' or 'beige with a touch of purple, or even khaki'. Here the resulting colour when you dye will be difficult, not to say impossible, to foresee, although you can discern if the original colour is something like one of the three primaries or the three secondaries. This will help you to predict and thus control, to some degree, what will happen.

Remember that the three primaries when combined make black (or dark grey), and that the secondaries are comprised of pairs of primaries. You will be combining all the primaries if you add red to green (green being blue+yellow) and therefore making a colour that tends towards black, away from a bright colour. In fact, in such a combination there is a far greater proportion of one of the primaries, in this case red. This will influence the final result which will be brown – that is, red being pulled towards a non-colour.

The colours that are shown opposite one another on the colour circle, fig. 2, page 18, are those that, when mixed, produce a non-colour. They are the most contrasting they can be, like red and green.

The chart, fig. 3, page 18, is a guide to what happens when one transparent colour goes over another. The original fabric colour and the dye colour are both interchangeable – the final result is the same.

Making your own dyes from nature

Extracting dyes from the natural materials found in the countryside and the garden can be a fascinating adventure. But first a few words of warning. It is a slow and sometimes rather laborious process, and for home dyeing, commercially produced chemical dyes are definitely less trouble to use than natural dyes. Dyeing wool only is recommended as other fibres are more difficult to dye, whereas chemical dyes will dye fabrics made from many different fibres too (see page 17). In chemical dyes the colour is highly concentrated; to achieve deep colours with natural dyeing, the dye-producing material must be collected, often in bulk. Some, such as bark or nettle leaves, can be large or otherwise inconvenient to handle. In chemical dyes the necessary additives are either already incorporated in the dye mixture when you buy it or are simple to use; in some natural dyes they can be a bit more complicated. In chemical dyes the colours are constant – number 63 will always come out the same number 63 colour, but with natural dyes the resultant colour is influenced by the time of year, the part of the country where the material was gathered, and the very nature of the season, whether it was rainy or dry.

With all these dire warnings why does anyone ever embark upon the pursuit of natural dyeing? Probably because it is so unpredictable, and it is remarkable that some parts of virtually every plant will yield a dye colour when simmered. The colours have a quality all their own too and even a delicious, and in some cases a lasting, open-air country fragrance. Surprisingly the dye colour is often quite unlike the colour of the plant. Purple heather, for example, makes a yellow dye.

Both adults and children can gain a great deal of enjoyment in the preparation and use of these dyes. First there is the foray into the countryside, the garden or the park to collect materials. (With the latter you must obviously check with the park keeper before removing any bark or leaves from trees, etc.) Then comes the sorcery; the mixing and boiling of strange potions, resulting in the most subtle and lovely colours.

Chemical dyestuffs were developed in the middle of the nineteenth century. Prior to that all dyeing and fabric printing was done with natural materials, specific dye-producing plants

Both of the garments and the bedspread shown here were patterned with tie-dye, which is probably the best known fabric colouring craft. It is extremely easy to get attractive results with this technique, and experimenting with the ways in which the fabric can be knotted, tied, wrapped with string or stitched to produce the characteristic cobweb-like patterns can become quite obsessive.

The bedspread, right, is made up from handkerchieves which were tie-dye experiments (see page 39). Strips of white cotton sheeting were used to frame each square.

Fabric for the suit, above, was tie-dyed after cutting out so that the tie-dye motifs could be placed exactly where desired, around hems and so on.

Alternatively, a length of fabric may be given an all-over tie-dye patterning before cutting out, as for the kaftan in the photograph, right. (Pattern and instructions for the kaftan begin on page 48.)

being cultivated as crops. Much study and experiment went into making natural dyes colourfast. Plants are the prime dye source, but certain minerals and insects produce particular colours too. All over the world indigenous plants were used to produce distinctive dyes; the many different colours in woollen Scottish tartans were all originally dyed with local raw materials, certain lichens particular to that country being used for browns and reds. Persian carpets were originally made from wools coloured by dyestuffs native to the area.

Nowadays commercial dyeing in the west is done with chemicals, but there has been an interesting widespread revival of the use of indigo to dye denim fabric to the familiar blue which will fade. (Scientists spent many years trying to perfect blue dyes that would not fade!) Indigo dye comes from a shrub which grows in semi-tropical countries.

What to dye?

For the beginner working at home the most practical approach is to dye small quantities of white or light cream woollen yarn in skeins as a first project. The different dye recipes will all demand different proportions of raw material to wool, but in many cases quite a large gathering of material may still produce only a small amount of dye; it could be very awkward finding enough of a particular wild plant to dye a complete garment. Also, it is most difficult to dye a piece of woollen cloth evenly with a natural dye. The fabric fibres need to be prepared beforehand in various ways, depending upon what dye is being used, and this is a very long-winded procedure. In some instances, as explained later, woollen yarn must also be somewhat elaborately prepared, but then the chances of success will be greater.

Natural dyes cannot be used on man-made fibre fabrics. They may be used on natural fibre fabrics or yarns other than wool but, once again, the involved preparation makes this unsuitable as a home pursuit.

Natural dyed wools are ideal for use in knitting, crochet, weaving or embroidery – and the colours are, of course, unique. Working with small quantities you will be able to experiment with a variety of dyes on an easy-to-handle scale, using lots of different substances; all the dyes come from plant material.

The equipment

You should not need any special equipment for dyeing, all you require will be found in the house. A pocket knife, scissors, and a number of small polythene bags in which to segregate different plants inside a large carryall or rucksack, are necessary for gathering the raw material.

You will need a receptacle in which to do the dyeing. This must be heatproof, must not leak and should be as large as possible. Suggestions are a preserving pan (aluminium, stainless steel or enamel, providing it is not chipped), a very big saucepan or a metal bucket. As some of the plants may be poisonous, vessels which are used for food should not be used for dyeing. Also required are some small containers, such as old tins (they need to withstand hot water) for mixing up the additives; a selection of sturdy sticks stripped of bark or lengths of dowelling for stirring; some muslin or similar fine cloth (old tights might be handy here); kitchen weighing scales; a sharp knife; a chopping board; a sieve and a pair of rubber gloves. Some form of heating is needed. This can be a ring on the cooker or a camping stove.

IMPORTANT: Because heat and sharp knives are used, and as some of the plants may be poisonous, children must be supervised.

Natural dyes work very much better in soft water, so do try to obtain some. This could mean using water from a lake or stream. Why not make a back-to-nature day of it, boiling the dyes over a camp fire? Or, with foresight, you could put out containers to collect rainwater. If natural soft water is unobtainable, you could add some water softener to ordinary tap water.

The different types of dyes

There are two different kinds of natural dye. One type, known as *substantive* dye, needs no additives. In this instance the dye extracted from the plant material will adhere successfully to the wool and remain relatively fast. (Some substantive dyes are much more fast than others.) Examples of substantive dyes are those produced by onion skins, lichens and sloes.

The other type of dye is called *mordant* dye. Here the extracted colour will not adhere properly to the wool or be fast unless the wool is treated with a chemical solution. This process, which is explained in detail later is not difficult, but it must be done carefully to ensure even dyeing. There are several different chemical mordants which have the effect of producing different coloured dyes from the same plant. The majority of plants need to be used in conjunction with a mordant – in this case, alum.

Nothing in natural dyeing can be categorically laid down. There is an infinite number of variables, so the whole thing must be viewed as an adventure into the somewhat unknown. The proportions of mordant solution to wool quantity can be fairly standardised although the quality of the wool itself differs so much. An extremely rough guide to the amount of vegetable dyeing matter required is to have three times the dry weight of

These delightful summer dresses and the circular tablecloth overleaf were patterned with tritik – a method of tie-dyeing in which the design is traced on the fabric with lines of running stitch which are then pulled up tightly. The cloth is immersed in the dye bath, and where the stitching is gathered the dye does not penetrate, producing a delicate tracery of lines. This technique is particularly useful for producing images such as flower shapes, stars and so on.

For tritik instructions turn to page 50; directions for making the dresses begin on page 52.

the wool in plant material, i.e. 300g berries, bark, leaves or whatever to 100g wool (or 3oz to 1oz). This cannot, however, be taken as an absolute guide because the colour is more concentrated in some plants than in others.

With the dye recipes it is a good idea to keep a notebook. Glue in an example of the finished yarn alongside a piece in its pre-dyed state. List the proportions of the ingredients, where and when they were gathered, the method of preparation, the time taken to simmer plus any other useful comments. (This could turn into a really interesting diary, linking nature and craft studies.)

Preparing the wool for dyeing
You can use new or recycled wool. The latter should be from a handknitted item that has hand-sewn seams, because it is extremely difficult to unpick machine-sewn seams and still retain a continuous thread. To unpick a knitted article, first undo all the seams. Unravel from the point where the piece was cast off, winding the wool around a chair back into a skein. The wool will be very crimped when it is first unravelled, but it will straighten out when it is washed. Washing is an important prerequisite of dyeing. Dirt and grease must be removed from recycled wool, and any sort of finish removed from new wool. New wool, if it is not already so, must also be wound into skeins.

Make each skein a size that will fit reasonably into your dye container so that it can be stirred easily. Wind the wool around a book to make a small skein. The two ends of each skein must be tied together to prevent its coming undone and turning into a hopeless tangle during both the washing and the dyeing processes. In addition, tie short lengths of string, not too tightly, around the skein at three evenly distributed points as shown in fig. 1, page 20. String is recommended because, at the end of the dyeing you should be able to distinguish it from the wool when you wish to undo it. Don't use a coloured string in case the colour is not fast, it would run into the wool and discolour it in patches. Be sure to tie these strings around fairly loosely. If they are tight you will be, in effect, tie-dyeing by preventing the dye reaching the tied sections.

The wool, whether it is new or old, must be thoroughly washed before dyeing. Hand wash it in a soap or detergent specifically intended for wool, in lukewarm soft water. Gently squeeze out the suds, rinse and wash again. Then rinse repeatedly, making sure the water is lukewarm at all times, until all trace of soap is gone. As when washing woollen clothing, the water temperature should remain the same throughout the washing and the rinsing. Wool when wet, in whatever form, should never be wrung out, sharply squeezed or over-handled and never allowed to boil. (Bear this in mind when actually dyeing.) Harsh treatment such as this will cause the fibres to *felt*, that is, to become hard and matted (this, in fact, is the method by which the material called felt is made from wool).

Using substantive dyes

These, if you recall, are the dyes that do not require a mordant. Onion skin dye is a good one to start with, producing some fine golden orange colours. Use just the outer brown skins of the onions. Because of the quantity of skins required, you could ask neighbours to collect them for you, or a local greengrocer to save the skins when clearing out the bins in his shop. Search out recipes which require lots of onions – for example French onion soup – although it will take longer to collect them yourself and you may get exceedingly tired of onions!

Put the onion skins in the large dye container and cover them with soft water. Bring the water up to simmering point and allow the concoction to simmer for half an hour or so. Then strain the liquid off through a sieve into another receptacle. Discard the skins and return the liquid to the dye container. Heat it up again to simmering point. If you have washed and rinsed the wool, place it in the dye. If it has dried after washing, re-wet it thoroughly in warm water and then transfer it to the dye.

Allow the dye to simmer gently but do not let it boil. Use a clean stick to turn the wool over in the dye occasionally, but don't keep agitating it. Wool left in for a few minutes will dye to a yellow. Left for longer it will turn to orange or ginger. Remember that when the wool is in the dye, it will look a much darker colour than when it has been rinsed and dried. Also, wools of different quality and texture accept the dye in different ways. The baby's jacket in the photograph was dyed in the same dye, for the same length of time, as the darkest of these examples. Because it is made from soft, fine baby wool the jacket has absorbed more colour.

When you think your colour is right use the stick to lift the wool out of the dye. Wearing rubber gloves, very gently press the excess dye out of the wool and then put it into a bowl of clean warm water. Rinse it repeatedly until the rinsing water is colourless and then hang it up to dry. The wool when wet but fully rinsed will still appear stronger and darker in colour than when it's dry. Any onion smells will soon disappear if you hang it out in the open air.

Because it is extremely difficult to judge and match colours, dye all the wool you want of one colour in the same dye bath. (The dye container must, of course, be amply big enough.) It is often more practical – and more interesting – to dye small quantities in a number of different colours.

Do confine the mixing stick to its own colour. The colour is all too easily transferred from a stick stained with one colour on to wool being dyed another colour. It is advisable, particularly if you are using several different dyes at the same time, to attach a label to each skein giving details of what the dyestuff was, how long the wool was in the dye, etc.

Two other dyes to try that will work without mordanting can be found in a delicatessen. They are cochineal – for pinks and rose reds – and turmeric, a powdered root used in curry, which gives lovely orangey-yellows. Here you just add the dyestuff to a pan of soft water and simmer it for about a quarter of an hour before putting in the warm wet wool. Let the dye continue simmering until the wool is the colour you want.

Other substantive dyes are obtained from sloes (dusty pinks), lichens (different species produce different colours), fresh green walnuts for browns (use the entire nut, shell and outer husk included), and whortleberries or bilberries, a moorland shrub whose berries yield a bluish dye. Where possible cut up or crush the dye-making substance before simmering it in soft water. Then strain off the dye liquid through a sieve or muslin. Some of the harder, tougher materials may require longer simmering time to release their colour.

Using mordant dyes

As already mentioned, alum is the mordant which was used on all those wools in the photographs which were mordanted. Although both the alum and the dye substance will dissolve separately in water, when the two are combined on the wool they form an insoluble colour. The mordanting process with all these examples was done prior to the dyeing. There are other methods and other mineral salts used as mordants in natural dyeing, and these influence the resulting colours in different ways. However, the pre-dyeing alum method is easiest for the beginner and the clearest introduction to the craft. A rich range of colours can be achieved with it and, as well as making the dye fast, alum tends to brighten the colour. As and when you wish to study the subject in more depth, visit your local library to find books dealing solely with natural dyestuffs.

To do pre-dyeing mordanting with alum you will need 40g (1½oz) alum and 15g (½oz) cream of tartar to 225g (8oz) wool (weigh the wool dry). Cream of tartar and alum are sold at chemist shops. If you intend to divide your white wool up into batches, each to be dyed with a different colour, you can first mordant all the wool together. You'll need a container large enough so that all the wool can be moved around freely inside. Fill this container with soft water and heat it up. Mix the alum and cream of tartar in a cupful of the warm water. When these have dissolved completely, stir the solution into the remainder of the water, mixing thoroughly. Now add the pre-washed, wet skeins of wool. Allow the mixture to simmer for about forty-five minutes, or an hour if your wool is heavy and coarse. Occasionally turn the skeins over gently with a clean stick to make sure the liquid reaches all parts of the wool equally. Don't stir it briskly or otherwise agitate the simmering wool and do not let it come to the boil.

Remove the wool and gently press out the excess liquid, don't wring it out. Do not rinse the wool, it can be dyed straight away or, as many professional dyers recommend, rolled up in a cloth or towel and left for a day or two before dyeing.

Keep to the given proportions of alum and cream of tartar to wool. If you use too much alum it spoils the texture of the wool and can make it all sticky. It's the mordanting that largely makes or breaks the final dyed result. So mordant with care, watching that the wool simmers continually and that there is ample room in the pan so that the liquid can penetrate all of it.

Whilst the mordanting is taking place you can be preparing your various dyes. After the mordanting the dyeing process is the same as explained for substantive dyes. Alum mordanting may also be used in conjunction with a dye material like onion skins, which will make a substantive dye. It helps the fastness and, in some cases, alters the colour.

Here is a guide to some of the different colours you can get using alum mordanted wool:

> Yellows, ranging through light greeny-lemon to rich orange-gold: apple skins, golden rod flowers, saffron (from a delicatessen), the flowers of ling (the heather *Calluna vulgaris*, other heather species make yellows too), marigold flowers, young bracken shoots.
>
> Greens: chopped up elder leaves, ivy berries when they've turned black, young common reeds (*Phragmites communis*).
>
> Pinks, lilacs and purples: sloes, blackberries, elderberries, beetroot.
>
> Browns: onion skins, larch needles, tea, chopped up oak bark.
>
> Black: the chopped roots of common yellow iris.

Do experiment with other plant materials to find new dye colours for yourself. To see what kind of a colour a new material will make, put a short length of washed wool into the water and plant mixture whilst you are simmering it to extract the dye.

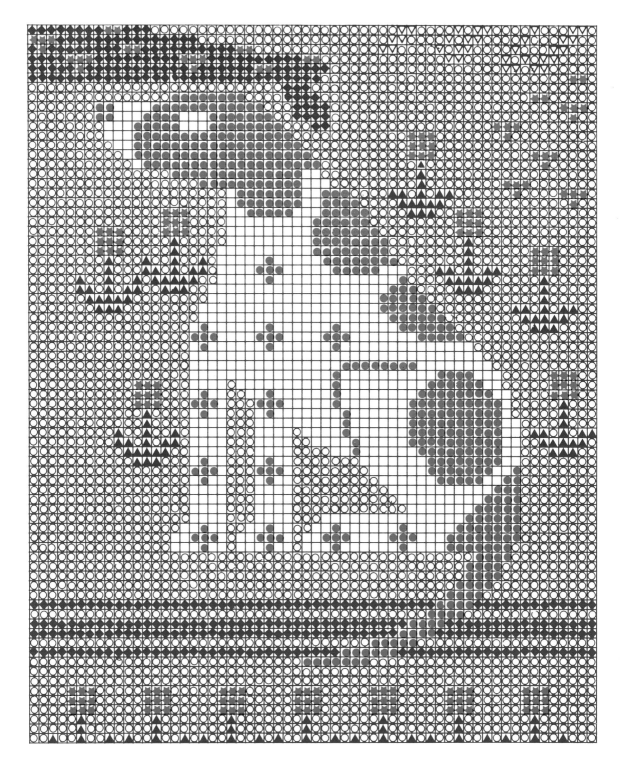

Dyeing garments

You can natural dye garments made of wool. The baby's jacket is knitted out of pure wool and has taken onion skin dye very successfully. The leggings are made from a wool and synthetic mixture yarn. The wool has accepted the elderberry dye fully but the synthetic has dyed to a lighter shade. Providing a mixed yarn has a high proportion of pure wool, good results can be achieved, and the lighter coloured synthetic threads will produce an even all-over flecking. The important points about dyeing garments are to make sure your dye container is big enough and that you have plenty of the raw material from which to make sufficient dye.

After a dyeing session the dye liquid will retain some of its colour. This semi-exhausted dye will give some lovely delicate tints. Natural dyes will keep for several weeks if stored in the fridge.

Use this chart to knit a sweater with motifs similar to those shown on page 22, using wool you have coloured with natural dyes.

Chapter 2
Tie-Dye and Tritik

Tie-dye

Tie-dyeing is an intriguing craft that enables you to create unique designs on fabric. It is a relatively easy craft too; you need no artistic ability to produce the abstract, slightly dreamlike patterns characteristic of this technique. The method is quite direct and so tie-dye is especially suited to children. The quilt in the photograph on page 27 is made from lots of handkerchieves, all tie-dyed in different ways and then sewn together like patchwork. Everyone in the family can enjoy joining in a project such as this.

The basic idea in tie-dying is to isolate parts of the fabric so that when you immerse the material in the liquid dye, the dye colour cannot penetrate those isolated parts. It's done by tying up little bunches of the fabric very tightly; the string protects the fabric from the dye. The different ways in which you tie up the bunches of fabric produce different shaped motifs and patterns.

The tied-up parts of the material remain the original colour, where the dye has been prevented from penetrating. The remainder of the fabric is dyed all over. As with plain dyeing, you can only dye to a colour that is darker than the original fabric colour. Thus it is best to use fabrics that are white or fairly light in colour so that the tie-dyed patterns will show up well. If the colour change is too subtle, many of the intricacies of the patterning will be lost.

Use lightweight, closely woven fabrics as these are easiest to handle when you are actually tying them up, also you will get more clearly defined patterns than on coarse cloth. Fine cotton poplin or batiste is recommended, and tie-dyed lightweight silk is exquisite. Don't forget that, as with any kind of dyeing, you must always use a dye that is appropriate to the fabric fibre.

Start off by doing a few tie-dyeing experiments on small items, getting to know the technique and how to obtain different patterns. Pure cotton handkerchieves are excellent for this. Keep them just as handkerchieves, use them as headscarves or join them together to make larger things like the quilt: several handkerchieves (or odd squares of cloth) can be joined to make cushion covers, a skirt or a top.

Once you have grasped the skills, tackle some larger articles: re-vitalise ready-made clothes like shirts, T-shirts, lightweight dresses, jeans and jackets that have become rather boring. Household linens can be given a new lease of life – tie-dye curtains, towels or sheets.

Innovate with tie-dye in dressmaking too, by cutting out the pieces for a garment and then tie-dyeing them before making up. The positioning of the tie-dye motifs can be well controlled, so you can plan your over-all design with motifs running up the sleeves, around the skirt hem – or wherever you wish. Alternatively, when the pieces are cut out, consider tie-dyeing some of the smaller features of the garment: introduce tie-dye patterning on the collar, the yoke, the cuffs or pockets and, using the same dye colour mixture, plain dye the larger pieces of the garment. In this way you can give clothing a truly personal finish.

Handkerchief experiments

For your first test pieces you will need several plain, pure cotton men's handkerchieves in white or plain light colours, or squares of fabric measuring approximately 45cm × 45cm (18in × 18in); these could be cut from an old cotton sheet. As with any type of dyeing, the fabric must be washed first. This also applies to brand new fabrics which generally contain a dressing or finish. The washing process removes it, thereby allowing the dye to penetrate the cloth completely. Iron the squares before tying so that any creases that do appear and form part of the dyed pattern are ones you put there, not just accidents.

The tying part of this craft's name means either tying knots in the actual fabric itself or tightly binding up sections of it. For the latter use various types of thread and string which are *waterproof*. This is important, otherwise the dye will go through the binding thread. Using threads of different thickness gives a wide variety of results. Nylon and plastic string and thread are fine, as well as elastic bands and plastic covered wire. Clips of varied types produce other patterns, so gather up some clothes pegs and bulldog stationery clips. Another interesting approach is to tie little objects into the fabric – small (clean) stones, buttons, dried beans, in fact anything that won't disintegrate in the dye, will all make their own individual designs. The uncommonly dextrous (and patient) can create gorgeous delicate spotty patterns by tying-in grains of rice – one by one!

Tying the fabric

Get together the washed and ironed fabric, all the binding and clipping materials, and some pointed scissors (clippers may be necessary for wire). Work out how much dye you are going to need in relation to the dry weight of your material. Don't prepare the dye yet, but assemble all the components. All the details on dyeing in Chapter 1 apply here too.

Tie all the pieces of fabric in their various ways first and dye them all together. Try tying some with the fabric dry but dampen others before you tie them. For certain methods, especially where flat creasing is involved, damp cloth is easier to control.

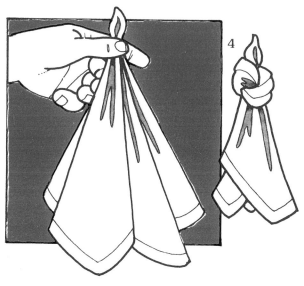

4 *The simplest way to produce a circular motif is to tie the fabric into a knot.*

KNOTTING. Perhaps the simplest approach is to lift up the centre of a handkerchief, twist the material round and tie it into a knot. Pull the knot nice and tight (fig. 4). This produces a circular motif. Try knotting each corner in the same way too. Knotting like this gives a design shaped rather like a flower. If the fabric is very fine, rather than having one large motif only in the centre, you will be able to lift the material and knot it in a number of places. It is a good idea to mark lightly in chalk where you want the motifs to appear whilst the square of cloth is still smooth and untouched. Just mark the point you need to lift up to start the knot, i.e. the centre of the motif. Ordinary school chalk or tailor's chalk are recommended as they can be rubbed off easily before dyeing. Avoid pencil and certainly ballpoint pen as the lines might prove permanent. Lightly indicating the positions of the motifs is worthwhile; as soon as you tie the first knot the fabric square becomes crumpled and distorted and it is surprisingly difficult to judge which bit lies where. This also applies when you are binding up sections of material.

Another way of knotting is to first fold the handkerchief into narrow accordion pleats to form a long thin rectangle. Use clothes pegs to hold it together temporarily. (See fig. 5.) Then tie knots

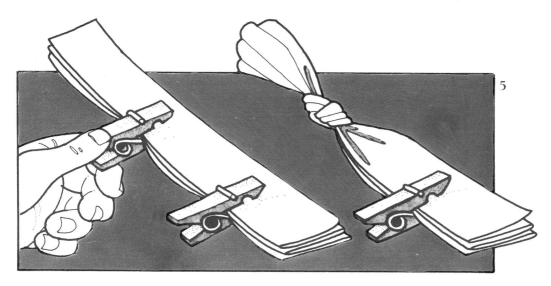

5

along the length of the piece. This will produce irregular striping. A variation on this method is to first fold the pleats diagonally over the square rather than straight across.

The tie-dye process produces its own distinctive type of design. There is always an element of excitement as you never know until the final undoing just how the design is going to turn out. It is essential to remember that tie-dye is not a totally neat, tidy ordered craft – the technique really seems to have a secret power of its own, so don't try to over-organise it. By all means use the experimental sessions to begin to familiarise yourself with the likely results of any action you take, but thereafter continue to let the element of chance play its part.

Circles and sunbursts

Experiment on one of the handkerchieves with irregular concentric circle patterns. The method is to lift up part of the fabric, twist it to form a point and then bind it tightly round. The thickness of the thread you use and the space between the threads as they go round the fabric will all affect the final pattern (see fig. 6 for some examples of binding). Remember that where the thread goes, the dye doesn't penetrate. So if you leave quite a large peak of unbound material, your circular design will be a fairly big dye-coloured circle. If you bind just the tip of the peak with a thin thread you'll get some spidery undyed circles. Play around with thread and string of different thicknesses, and also vary the spaces between the bindings. Wrap some of the threads round many, many times over; space others out much more; criss-cross some of them. Each time you start binding leave a length of thread loose so that you will be able to tie it to the other end when

5 By first pleating and then knotting the fabric you will achieve more interesting tie-die results. Use clothes pegs to hold the pleats in place while you are knotting the fabric.

6 Two ways of binding the fabric with string: left, wrap the string around the fabric at evenly spaced intervals, increasing the number of wraps at each; right, use varying thicknesses of string for each wrap.

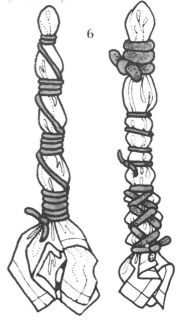

6

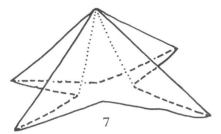

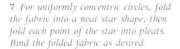

7 For uniformly concentric circles, fold the fabric into a neat star shape, then fold each point of the star into pleats. Bind the folded fabric as desired.

the binding is completed. Always bind the thread round tightly all the way and knot it very securely.

Contrast big, bold circles with delicate ones like spider's webs. To make one of the latter, lift up a peak of material with a needle and use a very fine thread to bind it, leaving spaces between each 'wrap-round' of the thread.

To make a more regular and controlled design of concentric circles, fold your handkerchief as shown in fig. 7 prior to binding it. Notice that this method of folding means that each facet of the pyramid of cloth is exposed to the dye equally. Just folding the handkerchief diagonally over and over again to form a pyramid doesn't work. Some areas are very open to the dye, others become enclosed. The resulting pattern would be very uneven.

TYING IN OBJECTS. Enclosing objects in the material will produce other kinds of motif based roughly on a circle. The final pattern depends upon the shape of the object being used. You may like to use two of your handkerchieves for this project; one to create a design on quite a large scale, the other for a smaller, more intricate type of decoration.

For a large scale pattern, select a pebble about the size of a tennis ball (or use an old tennis ball, provided you don't object to its changing colour) and four smaller ones, approximately ping-pong ball size. Lightly mark the centre of the handkerchief square in chalk and also four equidistant points, say 15cm (6in) in on the diagonal from each of the corners. These are where the smaller objects will go. Place the large object in the centre of the handkerchief, pull the cloth up around it and bind it round with string, securing it tightly. Enclose the other smaller objects in the same way. The cloth that is stretched over the object is, obviously, exposed to the dye. The way in which the binding thread causes the fabric to pucker up and resist the dye can create some very unexpected patterns. Different shaped objects will produce widely differing designs (see fig. 8). Experiment with things like corks, coins, buttons, lengths of wood, bottles or cans.

Another fascinating idea is to enclose a coloured item that is not dye fast with the intention of allowing its colour to seep out into the fabric during the dyeing process. This will produce a different

8 By tying different objects into the fabric you can make widely varied tie-dye designs.

coloured centre to the motif. Many objects that have this property are not bulky enough in themselves to act as the tie-in object, so enclose these with the stone, cork, or whatever is being used. Certain of the plants mentioned in Chapter 1 will yield up their colour in this localised way if you are using a hot water dyeing method. Some brilliantly coloured cloths and felts used in display work are not fast to water, so use small pieces of these to wrap the objects in before you bind them into your material. Similarly, coloured tissue paper and crêpe paper are not normally colourfast; it is easy to test the paper in a little water. (As tissue paper is so thin use several layers when wrapping up an object.)

For a small scale design you will need a number of little objects: grains of rice, dried peas, lentils or chick peas; a slender needle, some fine nylon thread and a degree of patience. Each tiny object will produce a minute, irregular star-like motif. These can be used very effectively to outline a design, making a kind of dotted line, or can be the main design. In this case, when deciding on a design, choose one which is not too complicated. You could do a geometric pattern, a heart shape or a bird – but keep it simple. Chalk it on to the fabric and then tie-in the objects.

Because little objects such as rice really are too fiddly to tie into the material individually, it is much easier to sew them in. Like embroidery, it is a very relaxing and satisfying pursuit. Thread a needle, and tie a knot in the thread about 10cm (4in) from the end. Pass the needle through the fabric from the wrong to the right side, so that the knot and the trailing end are underneath. Hold a rice grain in position on the wrong (or underside) of the material and lightly bind the thread round it a number of times on the right side. Then, right next to the grain, insert the needle, bringing it out again where you want the next grain to be. (See fig. 9.) Continue all the way round your design like this. Don't space the grains too far apart because then the design won't read as a dotted line, only as some dots spotted randomly around. If it helps, you could mark each interval at which a grain must be inserted with little cross lines. Finish off by tightly knotting the thread to the trailing end left at the beginning.

9 For an intricate, small-scale design, sew grains of rice into the fabric, either randomly or following a pattern. See the photograph above for an example of this technique.

Rice grains, seeds or similar minute objects can be massed together to form exciting textured areas as part of a larger design. They can be gathered together in a formal, regular way, in parallel lines, for instance, or assembled in a random fashion. The Nigerians excel in this craft, so visit your local museum and ask to see any examples of this technique they might have.

9

Squares and stripes
The tie-dye technique does not permit absolutely regular straight

10

10 *To make a square border decoration, fold the fabric as shown and bind it round where you want a light band.*

lines. However, there are ways of treating the fabric to achieve patterns which are based on straight line designs.

Here's how to make a square border decoration for one of the handkerchieves. Fold the square into the same sort of pyramid as shown in stage 1, fig. 7 for making a regular circle. Then, holding the pyramid by its left apex, pleat each triangular section of the material as evenly as you can all the way around and bind it in isolated sections. (See fig. 10.) Each bound section represents a light band on the border. Use thicker string for the lower binding to make a wider outside band.

To produce a striped handkerchief, first crease the fabric into neat accordion pleats right across; dampened material will be easier to control. Then tie around the resulting long narrow piece at whatever intervals you choose. For a more fluid sort of linear pattern, form the cloth into even gathers, rather than pleats, before tying it. The intervals at which you tie will determine the type of design. You could, for example, bind the fabric in evenly distributed groups of three sets of ties; or tie one section with

11 *For a striped effect, pleat the fabric first, then bind it.*

12 *Paper clips, instead of binding will make small rectangles along the folded edges of the fabric.*

11

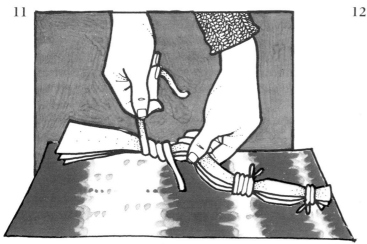

12

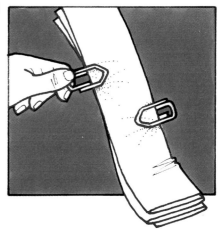

very thick string, many times round, the next two with lightweight thread, back to thick string, and so on (see fig. 11).

To obtain a pattern of small rectangular shapes use paper clips instead of binding on the pleated piece (see fig. 12). Try arranging the clips in different ways too.

Marble patterns
The finely veined pattern of marbling is very easy to achieve. Simply crumple up the fabric into a rough ball shape and bind it round in different directions as shown in fig. 13. To marble a large piece of material it may be necessary to put an object inside, otherwise the fabric in the centre of the ball might not receive any dye at all.

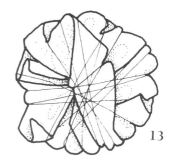

13 *Marbled effects can be achieved by crumpling the fabric into a ball and then binding it round several times with thin string.*

Doing the dyeing
Having tied up or clipped together all the handkerchieves in their different ways you are now ready to dye the fabric. Prepare the dye following the instructions and first wet and then dye these funny little lumpy objects in just the same way as you would dye any other fabric. When stirring the pieces take care with the clipped ones, moving them gently in case the clips should spring off.

After the fabric has been in the dye for the correct length of time remove it and rinse it thoroughly and repeatedly. This is important because you don't want any unwanted dye to flow into the intentionally undyed areas when you release the ties. When the rinsing water is clear you can cut the threads or remove the clips, open out the material and see what patterns you have made. Be very careful not to cut the fabric by mistake. Hang the tie-dye up to dry.

Fold and dip
Another way of producing dyed patterns with a quality different from that of tie-dye is called fold and dip. Cold water dye solution is used, and you will need a large shallow container in which to put it, such as a big washing-up bowl or a photographic developing tray. Before you begin, put up a clothes line on which to hang the dyed items; when you first hang one up it will be dripping dye, so either do this outside – somewhere where dye splashes don't matter – or spread plastic or newspaper liberally on the floor. With the fold and dip method the fabric is folded up and clipped to hold it all together, just the very edges of the folds are dipped into the dye.

For your first test piece (one of the handkerchieves would be ideal), accordion pleat the fabric. Do this on dry fabric this time, using the iron to make the pleating easier. Clip the piece together along the top edge: use six or so clothes pegs on a man's handkerchief. Quickly dip just the bottom folded edges into the dye. Don't leave it in there more than a moment as the dye will immediately start to creep upwards. Hang it up by the clipped edge with the dyed edge dripping until the dye has dried. When it is dry you can unclip it and rinse it. (See fig. 14.)

The pattern which results from this method of folding is one of uneven parallel stripes. You can imagine that if you then accordion pleated the cloth in the other direction, at right angles to the first, you would achieve a check. You can experiment with different kinds of diagonal folding too.

If you dampen the cloth prior to dipping, the dye will flow rapidly across it. This can produce some delicate, pale shading effects. Folding and dipping can never, anyway, give a really strong colour because you cannot leave the fabric in the dye for more than a second or two as it spreads exceedingly rapidly.

Introducing more colours

All the techniques discussed so far use only one colour, and this is advisable when you are just getting the hang of a particular method. Once you have grasped it, go on to explore the richer effects that additional colours can create; there are a number of ways in which they can be applied. You will develop your own

14 *For fold and dip, hold the fabric in pleats with clothes pegs and then dip the other edges very quickly into the dye.*

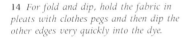

procedures as you experiment, but here are two suggested approaches – neither method is superior to the other, simply different.

In the first method you do not untie the cloth at the end of each dyeing. You add more binding and then re-dye. Imagine you are working on a piece of white fabric with a big stone tied up inside it, and it is now a strong yellow colour after the first dyeing. Add some more binding, using fairly thick thread or string; tie in a few smaller pebbles too in various places around the central one. Now dye the piece scarlet red. The yellow and the scarlet will blend to make orange. When this second dyeing is finished untie all the binding threads; the rings in the centre part of the cloth will have remained white. These were bound up at the beginning beneath the big stone and the original thread stayed there during both dyeings. The new bindings which were added after the cloth had been dyed yellow have protected it from the scarlet dye, producing yellow rings on an orange background.

In the second method you untie the fabric after you have dyed it in the first colour. Say, for example, you have at this point achieved a pattern of stripes in various grades of yellow on the white material. Re-tie the fabric in another fashion to make a circular pattern. Now dye it in the scarlet. When you undo it, small areas of white will still remain (they have not been dyed at all); some parts are still yellow, having been isolated from the scarlet dye by the second lot of binding threads; other bits are pure scarlet where the scarlet has dyed over white fabric; further sections are orange-yellow combined with scarlet.

DESIGN HINTS FOR TIE-DYE. When you have become more proficient in the technique of tie-dyeing you will want to exercise more control over designs. If a design uses the contrast of large and small motifs, as, for example, by tying-in pebbles and grains of rice, you will find it better to tie all the small sections first. The smaller ties distort the fabric less, so you can see the general layout for a longer time.

A proprietary colour and stain remover like Dygon can be used to create reverse tie-dye effects. For example, instead of a white pattern being isolated on white cloth and the rest of the fabric being dyed, say, blue, the result of using blue cloth and colour remover is a blue pattern on a white fabric. First of all you must ascertain that the colour remover will work by testing a sample of the fabric, as some dyes cannot be stripped. Fabric which you have dyed yourself in *hot water dye* will be suitable for reverse tie-dyeing. Binding, clipping, etc. is exactly the same as for tie-dyeing. The actual stripping is simple and all explained on the pack.

15

15 *Wool may be tie-dyed by winding it into skeins and then binding round at intervals. Loop it over a wooden spoon to dip it into the dye bath.*

Wool and yarn can also be tie-dyed. When knitted up it forms curious, unpredictable patterns. It may also be used in weaving. Tie-dye all the wool or yarn you will need for a garment in one session to avoid any colour matching problems. Wind it into thinnish skeins and bind them round securely at intervals as when binding cloth (see fig. 15). More than one colour of dye may be used, or course. Dipping, as explained in fold and dip on page 46 can be employed on wool and yarn for pale colours too.

How to use tie-dye designs

The various tie-dye patterns lend themselves to different uses. Large circles and sunbursts are appropriate to flowing items on a big scale. In the home these might be curtains – with a smaller scale version in a matching colour scheme used as cushion covers, or on a bedspread. Garments such as long flowing wrap-around skirts and kaftans can take these bold circular designs or pleated stripes beautifully too. The simpler the shape of the garment, the more effective the tie-dyeing. The more delicate rice grain type of pattern suits lightweight blouses and children's wear, whilst marbling would be better for masculine clothing. The square border technique would look good on the two front pieces of a jacket, maybe repeated on patch pockets. Delicate, misty fold and dip would enhance a beautiful, floating summer evening dress.

Tie-dye Kaftan

The kaftan on page 27 is based on a simple-to-make traditional pattern. The two-colour tie-dye design was done on the cut out pieces prior to making up. The marbling in pale grey was done first, then the pleating in yellow ochre.

The loose shape of the garment fits virtually anyone. The kaftan takes 5m (5½yd) of good quality lightweight cotton 90cm (36in) wide (an old sheet will do). The pattern pieces, with the exception of the neck, are simple, straight sided shapes; you can draw them straight on to the fabric with tailor's chalk and a ruler. If you are either very tiny or very large it's easy to adjust such a straightforward pattern to your size by altering the length of the body. Also extend or reduce the sleeves on the longest side.

You will need 5m (5½yd) of 12mm (½in) wide bias binding in either a matching or contrasting colour, and additional decorative trimming as and where you like it. (See page 84 for some ideas for printing your own fancy trimmings.)

First cut out the pattern pieces and then apply your chosen method of tie-dyeing. If the design is such that a motif needs to continue smoothly from one piece to another, for example a sunburst going across from the shoulder down part of the sleeve,

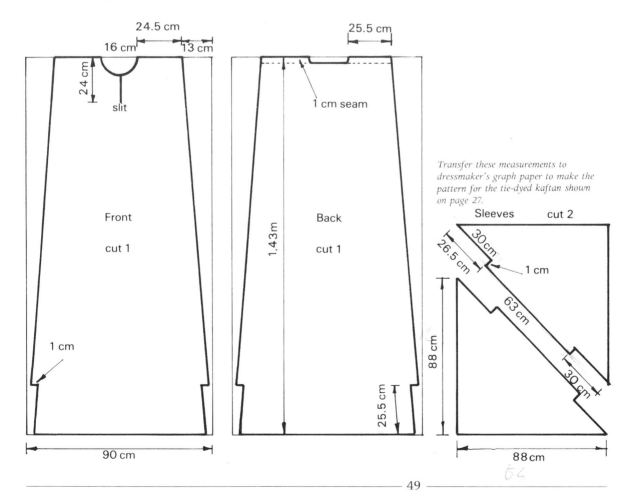

Transfer these measurements to dressmaker's graph paper to make the pattern for the tie-dyed kaftan shown on page 27.

it will be necessary to tack the pieces together securely along the seam lines before tie-dyeing.

To make up the kaftan, first sew the shoulder seams. Then bias bind right around the neck and the edges of the sleeves as shown on the drawing.

Line up the centre point of the sleeve armhole edge with the shoulder seam and join the sleeve to the body with a 2cm ($\frac{5}{8}$in) seam. Join the side seams beginning at the armhole and sew down to the slits at the hem. The underarm sleeve seams are left open. Bias bind the hem and the slits. Attach a fastening at the neck such as ties or a suitably delicate button and loop.

Tritik

Tritik is another version of tie-dyeing. Here, instead of isolating areas of cloth by tying it up at selected points to prevent the dye from penetrating it, you run lines of gathering stitches and draw them up tightly. The area of cloth pulled up with the gathering stitches is isolated from the dye. This method allows you to exercise considerable control over the tie-dyed design.

As with other forms of tie-dye, use lightweight, closely woven fabrics like cotton lawn. To start, it is a good idea to make a sampler so that you can try out different ways of stitching and so discover the effects which can be achieved.

In addition to the fabric and the dye, you will need a needle, some pointed scissors and some strong thread (it needs to be strong to withstand the strain when you gather up the sewing but not too thick, as this would leave holes in the fabric). Be sure to use a thread that is colourfast, as you don't want the colour of the thread to bleed accidentally into your work. Transparent nylon, as used for bead threading, linen carpet or button thread are all suitable.

All the sewing is completed before any gathering up is done. Begin by knotting the thread about 15cm (6in) from one end. Sew a straight line of small running stitches along the top edge of the square of material; if you need a guide, rule a line with tailor's chalk first, however, the stitching need not be fantastically straight and even. Cut the thread, leaving an end of about 10cm (4in).

Leaving a gap below the first line of stitching, sew two parallel lines of running stitches, quite close together. Try making the stitches in these two lines a little longer than the previous ones and line them up so that they form pairs, one above the other. Next do a band of four rows of running stitches. This time group them so that they are not lined up vertically, but staggered. These different arrangements will influence the way in which the pattern gathers form.

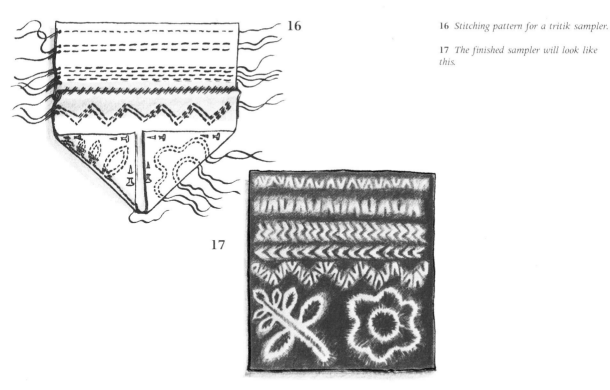

16

16 *Stitching pattern for a tritik sampler.*

17 *The finished sampler will look like this.*

17

Now take a small tuck across the square and oversew this with slanting stitches. Below the tuck, chalk a zigzag line and run two rows of running stitch along it. For a floral motif, turn back the bottom right hand corner of the fabric and pin it down at the edges. On this triangle draw half a flower – when it is finally opened out it will read as a complete flower. Trace round a circular object like a cup if you need a guide to the outer perimeter; a wavy line drawn inside this will make the petals. See fig. 16. For the centre you can draw round smaller circular objects. Run double rows of running stitches round these lines through both thicknesses of fabric. Remove the pins.

Next turn the bottom left-hand corner of the square back and pin it down. Work one half of a stalk and leaves design on here. Keep the line of stitches that draws the stalk close to the fold; otherwise you'll end up with an ugly fat stalk. When the tritik is finished this will open out to form a symetrical sprig with six leaves. Try further experimental stitching of your own if there is any room left.

Now that all the sewing is finished, carefully gather the fabric up by pulling on the unknotted long ends. Make each gathering as tight as possible and knot together the threads from either end, the result will be an odd little bundle.

Dampen and then dye it. Be sure to rinse it very thoroughly after dyeing. Finally, carefully cut the threads and extract them, flatten out the cloth and see the curious lacy patterns. See fig. 17. If you are satisfied with the results, why not hem the raw edges and frame the sampler for an unusual wall hanging?

A tritik patterned summer dress

The dresses in the photograph on page 30 use tritik for individual designs, and both are extremely simple to make. The woman's dress is to fit sizes 10 to 14. The little girl's dress fits a 55cm to 65cm (22in to 26in) chest. As shown in the drawing, each dress is made out of a single rectangle. The bodice is ruched with narrow elastic. For the adult's dress you will need 2·70m (3yd) of 110cm (48in) wide fabric, 12m (13yd) of narrow, soft knicker elastic and 29·5m (33yd) of 12mm ($\frac{1}{2}$in) wide straight tape. The child's dress requires 56cm (22in) of 150cm (54in) wide fabric, 5·5m (5$\frac{1}{2}$yd) of elastic and 11m (12yd) of 12mm ($\frac{1}{2}$in) wide straight tape. Use a fine fabric like cotton lawn or sea island cotton as these will both tritik and ruche well.

In tailor's chalk, sketch the tritik design on to the fabric rectangle. Stitch, gather and dye the piece.

To make up the dress, first pin a single 4cm (1$\frac{1}{2}$in) turning to the wrong side along the top edge, then pin a length of straight tape over the raw edge. Machine stitch the tape in place along both long edges, creating a hem and also a channel through which the elastic will be threaded. Do not stitch the ends. Carry on by

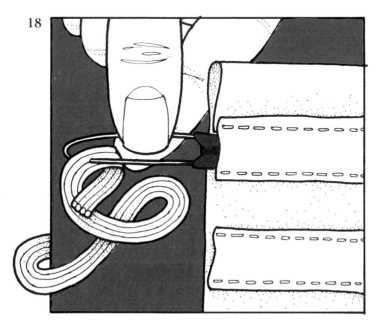

18 *The bodices of the tritik-patterned dresses on page 30 are ruched by elastic threaded through channels as shown here.*

stitching parallel bands of tape at 12mm ($\frac{1}{2}$in) intervals: the woman's dress takes eleven bands; the child's seven.

Now thread lengths of elastic through each channel. The woman's dress has lengths of elastic approximately 105cm (40in) long and for the child 80cm (32in) long. Thread elastic on a bodkin or safety pin and ease it through the channels (fig. 18), gathering up the fabric as you go. At each end secure the elastic with pins as you finish. When you've threaded elastic through all the channels, run a double line of machining down one pinned edge. Now adjust the ruching by pulling up the fabric on each length of elastic so that the fabric of the bodice is evenly gathered up. On the woman's dress this should now be reduced to 85cm (34in) wide: the child's 60cm (24in). Remember, it's now stretchy if you think it looks rather small. Sew up the centre back seam with a double line of stitching taking a 2cm ($\frac{5}{8}$in) seam. Hem the skirt with a 3cm ($1\frac{1}{4}$in) double turning. Add halter or straight shoulder straps, made in either the same material as the dress or in a contrasting braid or ribbon – the more daring may prefer to go strapless.

Chapter 3

Batik

Batik

Batik is another way of creating patterns on cloth that have their own distinct quality. The craft of batik rests entirely on the resist principle: a substance that will resist dye, usually hot liquid wax, is applied to the cloth before dyeing. Imagine a star shape of hot wax painted on to a piece of white fabric. The fabric is then dyed blue, and afterwards the wax is removed. A white star is revealed on a blue background (fig. 19). The wax has formed a protective barrier and has prevented the dye penetrating that star-shaped area on the cloth.

The craft of batik is extremely ancient. Where it actually originated is uncertain, although it is considered to have been in the Far East. Batik is still used in several oriental countries as well as Africa.

The word *batik* is Javanese, and the island of Java is renowned for its fine work. The craftsmen's traditional skills and designs are continuously passed from one generation to the next. Indigenous

A typical example of Javanese batik patterning; its colours are brown, indigo and white.

plants are used to make the dyes and Javanese batiks are traditionally produced in a range of blues and browns. However, do remember that the meticulous designs of Java are done by professionals, steeped in the tradition of the craft, possessing a high degree of skill. Don't let this put you off. That is only one approach, admittedly probably the best-known, but you can find a lot of pleasure in doing your own personal version of batik. The results may be a bit less sophisticated, but you'll be really intrigued by the process.

Materials for Batik

DYES. To start doing batik, cold water dyes are essential; hot water dyes would obviously melt the waxed areas, ruining everything.

FABRICS. Cold water dyes work only on natural fabrics, and for batik plain cotton is the ideal. Silk and linen are also suitable, but as they are expensive don't use them for your first efforts. Viscose rayon too may be batik patterned. Wool, although it is a natural fibre fabric, is not suitable because at the final stage of removing the wax the fabric must be boiled. Don't use synthetic fabrics because the cold water dye will not take on them. For your first attempts a piece of white cotton is best so that you can keep control over the colour blending that will automatically occur when you dye one colour over another. Starting off with a coloured fabric would mean that all subsequent dye colours were influenced and altered by the original colour of the fabric, as explained in the section on dyes. The fabric must be thoroughly washed and ironed before you start your batik. This applies

19 *Where wax is painted on the fabric, in this case the star motif, dye does not penetrate. Thus, white fabric dyed in a blue would leave a white star.*

19

particularly to new material as it is necessary to remove any finish that may be present in the fabric.

RESISTS. Although substances other than wax may be employed as a resist, begin by using wax (other methods are discussed later on). A prepared batik wax can be obtained from craft shops, or you can mix together beeswax and paraffin wax which can be purchased from do-it-yourself shops. Alternatively, you can melt down ordinary candles which are made of paraffin wax (remember to remove the wicks after the candles are melted). Paraffin wax is cheaper than beeswax but it doesn't adhere to the material as well, so a mixture of the two is advisable. The proportion of one type of wax to the other is largely a matter of what type of effect you wish to achieve. 'Crackle', that is, fine spidery lines over the waxed areas, is a feature of batik and is produced by the brittle quality of the paraffin wax in the resist mixture. Start off with one part of beeswax to two parts of paraffin wax; by experiment you will decide upon the proportions that suit your kind of work best.

Wax may be removed from brushes and other equipment with either petrol or benzine. As these solvents are inflammable (and smelly) it's best to use them out of doors, and away from a naked flame.

Artist's charcoal will be useful for lightly tracing in the design on the fabric prior to waxing.

The equipment
To heat and melt the wax you need either a ring on a cooker or a freestanding camping stove, Bunsen-burner or hotplate. As a

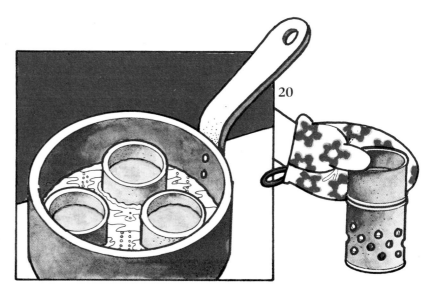

20 *Small, individual pots of wax can be provided by using small tins holding wax, each set over its own 'stove' made from another small tin.*

receptacle an old double-boiler saucepan is ideal, but some type of container for the wax which won't itself melt, placed in water inside a saucepan will be fine (a tin can, for example). Don't melt the wax just in a single saucepan. This is too dangerous, the container of wax must stand in water. At all times great care must be taken as hot wax can ignite in the same way as cooking fat when deep-frying. *Never leave it unattended.* The hot wax must be next to the work. It is clearly inadvisable to walk about with a brushful of wax dripping everywhere; also the process doesn't work if the wax cools, which it would do as you made your dangerous progress across the room.

In a classroom or a situation where several people are doing batik together, a number of wax pots can be provided in the following way. To make each one take a small tin can and punch some holes in the sides. You can do this with a can opener. Place a slow-burning little candle used for a night-light in it – the holes will allow air in so that the candle flame doesn't go out. Put some water in a large saucepan. In this place a number of tin cans, each containing some wax. Heat it all up in the manner explained in the batik project section. When the wax is ready, carefully, using an oven glove, transfer each can on to its miniature nightlight stove. The small amount of heat from the nightlight should keep the wax in workable condition. Fig. 20 shows how to use this small stove.

It is best to work with the fabric stretched out over some kind of frame. If it were placed flat on the tabletop the wax would stick it to the table. You can buy a special batik frame or use an old picture frame, a stretcher frame as used for stretching artist's canvas or an easily made frame of square or rectangular section timber – no need to bother about mitring the corners. Whatever you choose to stretch the fabric, attach the material to the frame with drawing pins; it only needs to be held taut.

The liquid wax may be applied with a brush. Here you can experiment with a variety of brush shapes, ranging from small watercolour to paste or decorator's brushes. The delicately drawn patterns of Javanese batik are made by using a tool called a *tjanting*. The tjanting is a small metal cup with a spout (or sometimes spouts) attached to a handle (see fig. 21). These can be bought in craft shops selling batik equipment, but you may, however, like to make an experiment with some home-made versions. Obviously the material from which you make your tjanting must be heat-proof and you'll need a handle that isn't going to get hot. It must be possible for the home-made tjanting to scoop up hot wax successfully and you must be able to hold it comfortably when drawing with it. Metal icing funnels, which are made in different shapes, can be attached by wire to a wooden or bamboo holder. Try squashing a small foil freezer dish into a cone.

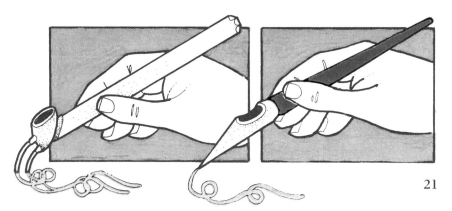

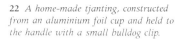

21

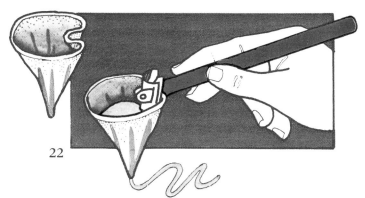

22

21 *Left, a double-spout tjanting; right, a single-spout tjanting. Wax is poured into the cup and the tool is held at a slight angle to fabric.*

22 *A home-made tjanting, constructed from an aluminium foil cup and held to the handle with a small bulldog clip.*

Snip the end off it to make the spout and attach it to the holder with a bulldog clip as shown in fig. 22.

For the cold water dyeing part of the craft you will need a dye container, mixing sticks and rubber gloves. Have plenty of old newspapers handy to spread on the work surface, and wear overalls or old clothing. Some old rags will be useful too.

Arrange your work area so that the heat source is conveniently near to hand. The wax pot needs to be positioned rather as an ink bottle would be; you want as little distance as possible between it and the work because the wax cools so quickly.

A first batik project

To get the feel of the technique try making an abstract-patterned sampler in batik, experimenting to see how many different effects you can get. If you work in this way you'll be able to concentrate purely on the technique without worrying about whether or not you can cope with drawing a particular shape. Just such an experimental piece of batik produced the wall hanging shown on page 66, and a smaller version would make an interesting cushion cover.

Two separate applications of dye are used so that you can become familiar with the effect of one colour over another. Choose two dye colours which when combined will make a third colour. In the sampler shown here a rose pink and a sea-green were used. Where they combine a purple-grey results. Wax is applied in different ways to white cloth which is then dyed (in this case) rose pink. After that all the wax is removed. At this stage the fabric is pink and white. New waxing is added, some over the existing white areas, some over the pink parts. Then the cloth is dyed green. This green will dye any white sections green and will overdye any pink sections to a purple-grey colour.

Stretch the washed and ironed fabric over the frame, just so it is held smoothly and evenly. Now, with faint charcoal lines, divide the whole area within the border into smaller sections. These dividing lines can be straight, curved, zigzag or wiggly. Now you have a series of small spaces and you can try out a different batik method in each one.

Heat the wax so that it just shows a very slight whiff of smoke. Then reduce the heat right down to keep the wax in that liquid condition. Don't forget to keep an eye on the water level in the saucepan; it must not boil dry.

Start by using a biggish brush to fill in one of the areas completely. Hold the brush in the melted wax for a moment or two and let it take up the wax. Carefully wipe it on the side of the wax container and, holding a rag under it to catch any drips, bring the brush to the fabric. Paint the wax on. With a little practice you'll find out how much wax the brush will comfortably accept and how much pressure is needed as you paint. The wax must penetrate right through the fabric; if not, when it is immersed in the dye, colour will be able to get in from the back of the work. The wax should look transparent on the cloth, like a grease stain. If it looks opaque, it is not penetrating correctly but merely lying on the surface. Wax will lie on the surface if it is too cool. This could be because it has not been heated up enough or because you are dithering about as you transfer the brush from wax to cloth. Batik is essentially a free, flowing technique because of this very reason – the rapid cooling. So you must be confident, willing to take the plunge and get on with it. Paint quickly otherwise it will not work. Accept this and you'll very soon develop an easy rhythm of dipping and painting.

On a large waxed area, such as this first one, it is advisable, after you've wax painted the top side of the fabric, to turn the whole frame over the wax the corresponding area on the back to be sure the fabric is thoroughly covered.

When you have done that and the wax is dry (it dries hard rapidly), unpin as much of the edging as you need to enable you to get hold of the waxed area. Now crumple the area in your hand so that the wax cracks all over. The dye will seep into these cracks to produce a delicate marble veining which is a main characteristic of batik work. This is the *crackle*. The colder the wax is the more defined the crackle will be. On a hot day the wax will remain pliable and may refuse to crackle, if so, pop it in the refrigerator for ten minutes or so.

Repin the cloth to the frame and move to another section of the fabric to try out a different variation of the crackle effect. Select a space that is some distance from the original one. This is because you are going to crease the second one in another way. This time, after you have released the fabric from the frame, fold the waxed section into pleats so that the coating cracks in parallel lines. Then pleat it again at right angles to the first creases. Return the fabric to the frame.

Next try some stripes: these will end up multicoloured. If you're working on quite a large scale the big brush will do, if not, scale down accordingly and use a smaller brush. Choose an area and paint a stripe, leave a stripe, paint a stripe, and so on. If they are broad stripes, paint the other side also to be sure the fabric is well protected. To get another crackle variation, crumple up the waxed stripes less severely than the first area you did.

In the remaining sections see what different kinds of marks you can get the brushes to make – a new approach in a new section. You can try out the brush marks on scrap cloth or newspaper first. Make lines, dots and dashes with the tip of a soft pointed brush; then try splodging the brush down repeatedly to produce a fan-like pattern. Contrast these effects with those made by a stiff brush.

After a few brief preliminary experiments on scrap material, try using newspaper to mask all but a selected area of the design. Then let wax drip and trail off the brush on to the exposed area. Also try gently flicking the brush to get a spatter of wax.

Having filled approximately half the sections in the design with experimental brushwork, try using the tjanting. This will give you a more free and flowing line than the brush. You'll find it is rather like a pen, and a relaxed linear technique similar to writing is just what you should aim for. Try a practice session on scrap material first of all. Hold the metal cup of the tjanting in the hot wax for a few moments to warm it. Then scoop up half a cupful of wax and, holding it sloping backwards a little to prevent it spilling, lift it over to your work. (Hold a rag underneath during this movement.)

Place the spout on the material, tip the tjanting up a little to let the wax flow out, and start drawing (see fig. 23). You can change the thickness of the line by altering the slope at which you hold

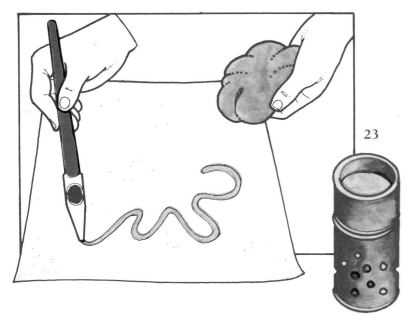

the tool. If the spout clogs up with solidified wax but there is still liquid wax in the cup, dip the tjanting into the hot wax to warm it and free the blockage. Refill as you need to do so.

Once you've got the feel of it start filling in the blank areas on your finished work. Try a series of parallel lines, some lines criss-crossing and some wavy lines. With a free writing motion create a pattern out of repeated circles overlapping one another. In line, echo the outside shape of one of the areas, taking the line gradually from the outside into the centre. If you have more than one tjanting, see how many other different patterns you can invent. Leave one or two sections blank so that they will be dyed a plain solid colour in contrast to all the textures and patterns.

Doing the dyeing

The fabric is now ready for the first dyeing – pink in the case of the photographed example. Prepare the pink cold water dye and dye the waxed fabric following the instructions given in Chapter 1. It is now necessary to remove the wax from the fabric. Iron the piece of cloth between sheets of clean brown paper. Then boil the piece of cloth in a pan of plain water for about three minutes. After this, pour the water into a container. When it has cooled you can remove the set wax. Allow it to dry out thoroughly and it may be re-used. *DON'T* pour hot water containing liquid wax down the sink as it will probably block the drain.

Now wash the fabric in a solution of liquid detergent and very hot water. Rinse it well and dry the fabric. Wax residue from the detergent wash cannot be used again. At this stage your batik will look something like the example shown, a design in pink and white.

Iron the fabric and repin it to the frame for the second waxing. In this second application the wax will form a barrier against the second dye colour – in the example, green. If you now paint the wax over a white area it will remain white. Neither the pink nor the green dye is able to reach the fabric. If you wax over a pink area it will stay pink, protected from the green dye. So all the exposed un-waxed places will dye green. An exposed area that is white at present will turn green as shown in the photograph of the wall-hanging; an area that is pink at present will be overdyed in green and come out purple-grey. Many more subtle and exciting variations will occur throughout the design where pink and green textures and patterns combine.

ADDING MORE COLOURS. You can go on to add more colours. However, as with all the dyeing and printing techniques, plan your approach sensibly so that you get as much use as possible out of each colour and the way in which the colours will combine. A well thought-out design in two colours can appear much more lively than a thoughtless one in eight.

Here is another two-colour method which is quicker than that already shown, but which will not give you three colours – pink, green and purple-grey – in the end.

After you have waxed and dyed the fabric once, let it dry thoroughly without removing the wax. Imagine you have dyed the material pink (it will resemble the photograph on page 67). When it is dry apply additional wax. The original wax is still there, still protecting the white fabric from any dye. The new waxing will go over the pink areas of the design, so these pink areas will be protected from the next dye colour; say this is green. The green dye cannot get to any of the white areas because they are sealed off by the first waxing, so it will just over-dye any exposed pink areas, turning them purple-grey. When all the wax is removed the finished batik will be in pink, white and purple-grey – no green.

Removing stubborn wax

If, after washing, your batik still retains some wax stains, try sandwiching it inside layers of scrap paper and ironing it, changing the paper as it becomes greasy. Follow this with another detergent wash.

Dry cleaning (use the local launderette) is an excellent way of removing persistent wax.

Starch paste batik

For their batik work the Nigerians use a flour paste instead of wax to act as a resist to the dye. Although the flour they use (which is also used in bread-making) comes from the root of the cassava plant, our own wheat flour makes a good dye resist. This technique does not use heat, so it is especially suitable for children. Starch paste batik cannot be as refined as the wax type, but lots of different kinds of line and texture are possible.

In batik, wax penetrates the fabric completely sealing both the front and the back of it against the dye. Starch paste lies only on the surface of the cloth, so the back is not sealed. You cannot immerse a piece of fabric painted with starch paste in a liquid dye because the dye would seep in at the back of the cloth and spoil the design, also the liquid dye would dissolve the paste. Therefore, fabric dye paste (see pages 80-82) is used, applied either with a brush or a sponge.

Remember some fabric dye pastes will only work properly on natural fibres; check this before you select your fabric. (Dylon Colorfun dye paste is suitable for use on both synthetic and natural fibre fabrics.) Use a white or light-coloured material because the design shows up as light against dark. First wash and iron the fabric and some scrap pieces for experimenting on. Tape them down on to a working surface which can easily be wiped clean afterwards.

Make up the resist paste by blending together approximately three parts of flour to two parts of cold water, making a stiffish batter; make sure there are no lumps. This you apply to the fabric. Try out different methods of application on the scrap pieces first: use large and small brushes; spread it on larger areas with a knife; make a forcing bag out of a polythene bag with a tiny corner snipped off and pipe the paste (fig. 24). While a large area is still damp you can scrape patterns across it with a blunt penknife or a comb cut from cardboard (fig. 25). This technique produced the giant 'fingerprints' in the Nigerian example shown on page 65. Wash the brushes in cold water as soon as you've finished or the flour paste will turn them to stone.

You may find the white paste rather difficult to see on a white fabric background. If so, colour the paste slightly by adding a little watercolour or poster paint, but before you add the colour, just check that it will wash out completely by applying it to a piece of the cloth. A successful extension of this idea is to colour the paste with a dye that will deliberately stain the fabric. Mix in a small quantity of dye powder or a natural, highly staining substance like turmeric powder. When your batik is finished the painted paste shapes will be in a light colour, rather than white, against a dark background.

24

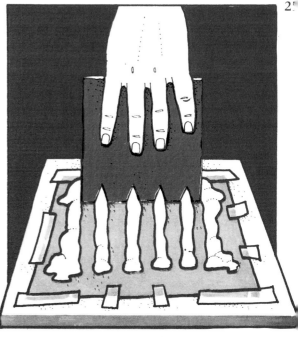

2

24 Starch paste patterning for batik may be applied with a polythene forcing bag.

25 Large areas may be decorated using a cardboard comb to scrape patterns into the starch paste.

When you've finished applying the flour paste, leave your batik overnight so that it can dry thoroughly. It should be kept flat while drying. As it dries the paste contracts, causing the material to pucker up. When it's completely dry stretch and screw up the material on some of the larger areas to create a crackle. Now paint or sponge fabric dye paste over the pasted side of the cloth. Make sure you work the colour right down into the material. More than one colour can be used at this stage if you wish.

Allow the dyed batik to dry out. When it is absolutely dry you must iron it in order to fix the dye. Lay a thin scrap of cotton cloth over the work and iron it for as long as the dye manufacturer's instructions recommend. Be sure all of the fabric gets the right amount of heat treatment.

Put the batik in a bowl of cold water; this will start to lift the paste off. You can help it along by scraping it gently with the back of a knife. Rinse the piece again to remove any paste residue. Let it dry out and then iron it.

The principles about the order of colours used applies to starch paste batik in the same way as to wax batik.

Using batik fabrics
Batik is a technique that can be used both on clothing and in the home by adjusting the scale of your design to the size of the

article. A co-ordinated scheme for a bedroom, for instance, might use quite a large, bold design on the curtains. The same motif or motifs could be reduced on the edging of sheets and pillowcases and a lampshade. Use the technique to give an overall pattern to roller blinds, and cushion covers. The craft is especially suited to dressmaking; batik on to the cut out pieces for border patterns or on to a complete dress length for overall decoration. You can also apply batik designs to ready-made garments, providing the article can be stretched out over a frame for the waxing process.

Batik rubbings

As a child you probably made rubbings of coins on paper with a pencil or crayon. This same principle can be applied to fabric batik. The rubbing, done with a block of colourless batik wax or a candle, forms a resist to the dye. When the fabric is dyed only the wax-free areas will accept the colour. The result gives a reversal of the coin and crayon technique.

   Choose an object (or objects) with an interesting pattern or

This contemporary fabric from Nigeria has been stencil and resist printed. The 'fingerprint' patterns are produced by combing the design into the resist paste.

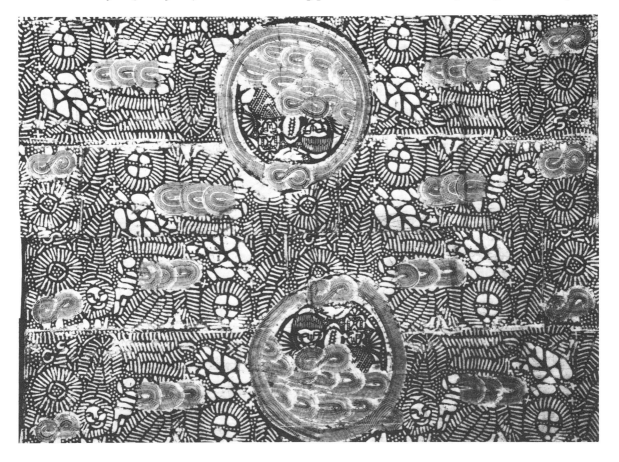

Left. *The wall-hanging was made as a first project in batik to discover the properties of the wax resist and also to see the kinds of marks that can be made using brushes and tjantings to apply the wax to the cloth.*

The sampler is dyed in two colours, and the result of the first dyeing session is shown above.

Full instructions for making a similar sampler begin on page 58.

The decorative trim on the neckline of the silk shirt in the same photograph was printed with a twisted pipe cleaner. See pages 94-96 for more ideas for simple blocks.

Marbled fabrics such as the ribbon above are extremely easy to make; the results are completely unpredictable, and children especially enjoy this interesting technique, explained on page 162.

design in low relief. This could be an embossed metal article – a container, a badge or a cast iron grating or manhole cover. Also, look at carved wooden furniture and panelling or stonework (churches and churchyards are both rich sources). There are many possible sources, but the most beautiful batik panels are made from rubbings taken from antique brass memorial plaques such as those found on medieval tombs. Because so many church brasses are deteriorating due to the popular interest in brass rubbing, there are now several centres at which you can make rubbings from facsimiles.

In the usual kind of brass rubbing a black crayon is used on white paper, and only the raised areas of the design are picked up by the crayon. Any recesses, for instance, the carved grooves that make up the features of a face, don't pick up the crayon and so come out as white lines. In a batik rubbing, colourless wax takes the place of the black crayon. Once again the incised lines of the features receive no wax, but when the material is dyed those unwaxed features will appear as coloured lines.

Use a firm, closely-woven lightweight cloth like good quality sea island cotton in white or a light colour. Wash and iron the fabric first. (Roll it round a cardboard tube to prevent it getting creased when in transit.)

Attach the cloth to the surface to be rubbed with masking or freezer tape. (These are stronger than ordinary adhesive tapes, and will not harm the surface.) The cloth must be securely taped all round as you do not want it to move at all. Now all you need is patience. You must systematically rub all over the selected area, making sure you apply a good, thick coating of wax. Because the cloth is inclined to move it helps to hold a small section of the fabric very firmly down against the object. Rub that part really thoroughly and then go on to the next section, holding this down firmly in turn.

After this, cover the waxed side of the material with fabric dye paste applied with either a brush or a sponge. Use a strong, darkish colour as this will define the design clearly. Allow it time to dry out completely, and then fix the dye by ironing.

At the same time you can remove the wax. Lay down a pad of newspaper with a sheet of clean unprinted scrap paper on top. Spread out the fabric on this and then cover it with another sheet of unprinted paper and a couple of layers of newspaper. Unprinted paper is recommended right next to the fabric because newsprint or other printed matter might come off on to your work – use shelf or lining paper for this job. As you iron, the dye gets hot and therefore becomes fixed and, simultaneously, the wax melts out of the fabric and into the paper. You may need to change the paper as it absorbs the wax.

Printed batik

In the last century, following a great increase in the demand for their fabrics, the Javanese developed a speedier method of producing batik although they still continued to make fine hand-painted fabrics. A metal block for printing the wax, called a *tjap*, was introduced. The design, instead of being drawn on in wax, is printed in repeat with wax. These wax impressions will resist the dye, leaving the print the original colour of the cloth. The tjap blocks, still in use today, are often of a very intricate design. They are made out of metal strips soldered together with a handle at the back.

A copper tjap from Java. Blocks like this are used to print designs in wax on to cloth, a much quicker batik process than drawing with a tjanting.

You can make your own relief printing blocks for this technique, and many of the methods suggested in Chapter 4 are applicable. Whatever materials you use to make the tjap it obviously must be able to stand up to immersion in hot liquid wax. Metal things are fine, either hold them in a pair of pliers or fix them to a convenient handle. Pipe cleaners make excellent tjaps too (see page 96 fig. 47).

Use a light-coloured natural fibre fabric (cold water dyes are used remember). Wash and iron it, and also a scrap piece for preliminary experiments. Attach a piece of the scrap fabric to a frame and prepare the wax as explained on page 57.

You need only a small quantity of wax for this dipping technique, but it must be about 1cm ($\frac{1}{4}$in) deep in the receptacle. Dip the tjap into the liquid wax, and, with a rag held underneath to catch any drips, quickly transfer it to the fabric. Press it carefully down to print. When all the printing is completed the cloth is dyed in cold water dye and the wax removed (see page 62), leaving the motifs in the colour of the cloth against the dyed

The most elementary approach to block printing is the use of everyday objects for the blocks. Anything from screwheads to leaves can be used, which is how the jacket in the photograph, left, was patterned with its cheerful bouquet of flowers. The leaves that make up the design were carefully painted with fabric dye paste and then pressed on to the cut out fabric pieces before the jacket was assembled. The appliqué hand holding the bouquet was also applied before sewing. Instructions for making this jacket begin on page 87.

Fabric shoes like those above are perhaps an unusual place to apply printed designs, and the results can be just as unusual, cheering up dull footwear. The matching sneakers and socks were hand painted with bouncy polka dots using fabric dye paste and the method explained on page 162.

Like the jacket opposite, the espadrille tapes were printed with a 'ready-made' block, in this case a screwhead, following the instructions on page 83 for making the repeating border patterns. An attractive extension to this idea would be to decorate the hem of a skirt with a matching pattern.

background. Subsequent colour may be added by more wax printing and dyeing.

This process allows you to exploit all the different possibilities in repeating patterns. The final results are really a reverse of block printing, i.e. light on dark. Follow the suggestions on page 97 for marking out guidelines to help you position the wax-printed motifs.

STARCH PASTE TJAP. Earlier in this chapter the use of starch paste as a dye resist is discussed as an alternative to wax. In addition to the various painting techniques, this paste may also be applied to cloth with suitable printing blocks; the general details outlined in Chapter 4 are relevant here too. The consistency of the starch paste is similar to that of fabric dye paste or fabric paint, but you can adjust the proportion of flour to water if you wish to make it a little stiffer. Starch paste works successfully with potato cuts and most of the different types of relief printing blocks mentioned in the chapter on block printing.

Liquid dye is not suitable for this technique so you should use a fabric dye paste. A fine, closely woven material will give the best results. Make sure that the textile fibre of your cloth is correct for the brand of fabric dye paste you are using.

After you have printed the cloth with fairly liberally applied starch paste allow it to dry out overnight. Then coat the material with fabric dye paste and proceed as previously explained for starch paste batik.

Stencilling too can be done with starch paste. The Nigerian example on page 65 combines the use of painting, combing and stencilling. (For more on stencils see Chapter 5.)

Chapter 4
Block Printing

Block printing

So far all the techniques described for making designs on cloth have worked on the principle of isolating an area, or areas, of the fabric – by tie-dye, batik, etc. – and then colouring the surrounding material by dyeing it. If the material started life white, those techniques produce white motifs on coloured backgrounds. Now, with block printing, the reverse takes place. It is like drawing or painting on a blank sheet of white paper. You create a design by arranging coloured motifs on the white background.

Block printing on fabric, like all the textile crafts, is a pursuit that can be highly complex and sophisticated, yet designs can also be most effective when they really are extremely simple. The beginner can take up block printing and immediately find enjoyment in the technique itself and satisfaction in the results produced. Once again the ability to draw is not necessary, the pattern and design are contained in the printing block itself, you simply arrange and print it!

Improvised printing blocks

What can you use to begin block printing? All sorts of things that you will find in the house, the garden or the shed will serve as ready-made blocks. They are just sitting there ready and waiting to be used; you don't have to do anything to them! The idea is the same as the standard type of date stamp on which the numbers stand up in relief, away from the background. When the date stamp is pressed on to the ink pad only the raised numbers make contact with the inky surface. The date stamp is then stamped on to the paper, transferring the ink from the inky numbers on to the paper. This type of printing is known as relief printing. Bearing this in mind, many commonplace items, when you look at them now as possible printing blocks, will assume an entirely new dimension.

Some craft suppliers and toy shops sell ready-made printing blocks intended primarily for children. With a little imagination these can produce some amusing and attractive results.

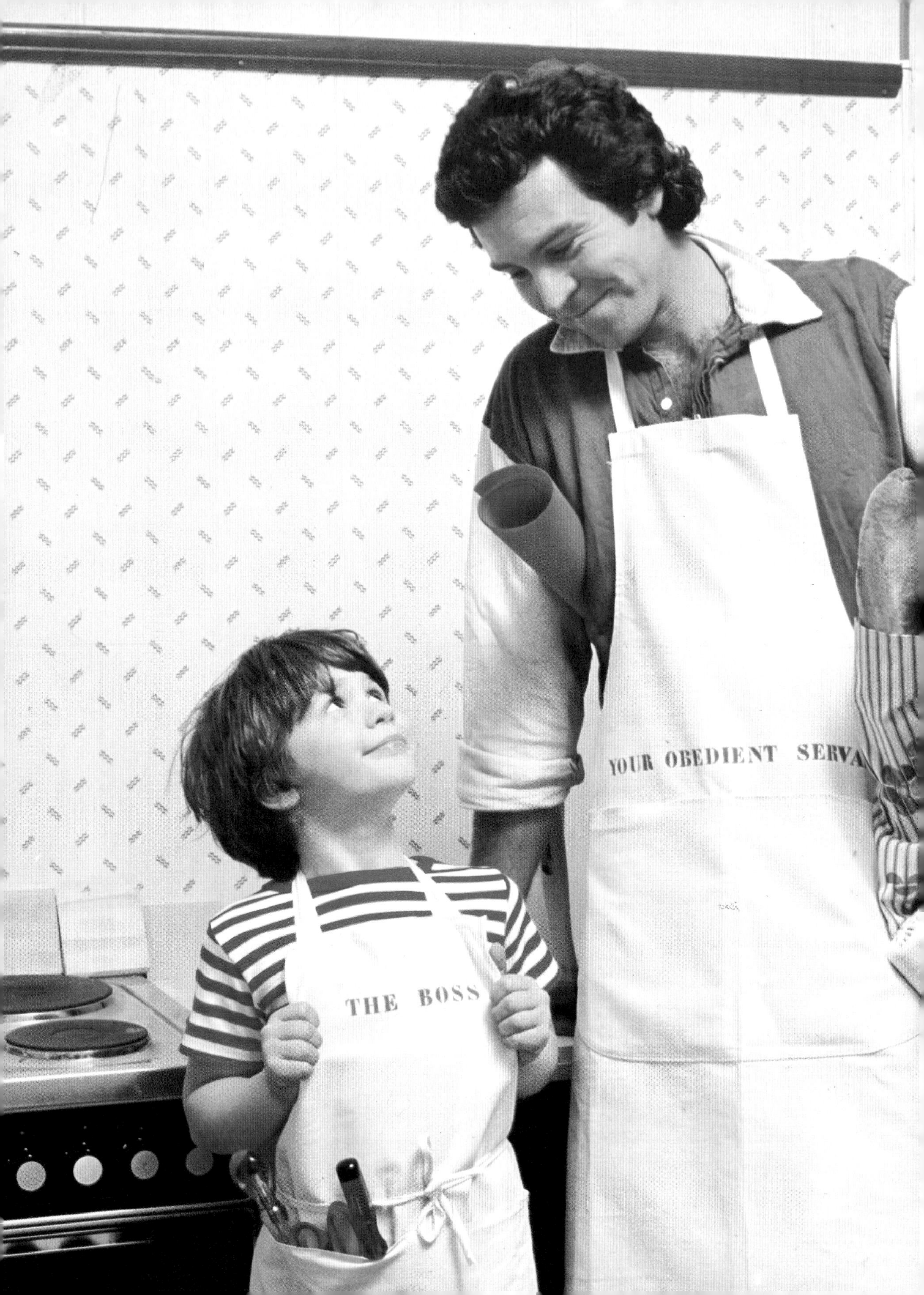

YOUR OBEDIENT SERVA
THE BOSS

The stencils which can be bought from stationery supply stores and craft shops may be used with fabric dye paste to print motifs such as flowers, birds or boats on to ready-made clothing. An alphabet stencil and the methods described on pages 121-125 were used to print the amusing titles on the carpenter's aprons shown left.

The carry-all in the photograph has been printed with a cork using the lines of ticking as part of the finished design. Instructions for making the bag are on pages 93-94.

Above. Potatoes may be used as printing blocks following the instructions beginning on page 99. This method of block printing is ideal for children who could make a set of table mats, or even decorate their own clothes with colourful designs.

A late 19th-century multicoloured wood block printed fabric by the English designer, William Morris. The clearly defined shapes of his textile designs were ideally suited to block printing.

What to print with

FABRIC PRINTING INK. The consistency of the colour used for block printing must be much thicker than that used for dyeing; it has to be gooey enough to stick to the block. There are a number of different types of printing preparations on the market, all possessing different qualities, all intended for different purposes. In the art shop this can be very confusing, so it is important to grasp the essential differences before you purchase. Two types of preparation are used for block printing on cloth. Firstly, there is *fabric printing ink*. This is an oil-bound ink available in a good range of colours, plus a colourless substance named either *reducing medium* or *extender base*, used for making tints, i.e. lighter, transparent versions of the colours. (Fabric printing ink suppliers are listed on page 168.) Artist's oil paints are not suitable for printing on fabric – the consistency is wrong and they are also too expensive – but you can add a touch of oil paint to fabric printing ink to mix a particular colour, and this may save you having to buy a complete tube. Don't confuse fabric printing ink with the oil-bound ink intended for printing on paper. This is called printing ink or proofing ink and although similar to fabric printing ink, it is not always washable. Fabric printing inks are fast to gentle hand-washing in mild soap or detergent. Do not, however, scrub or rub them. These inks work satisfactorily on paper too, so they can be very useful for making your own stationery, greeting cards, etc.

To add to the confusion you may also see block printing watercolour inks on the market. These are suitable only for printing on paper as, obviously, being watercolour they would wash out if you were to use them on cloth.

Closely-woven, natural fibre materials, with the exception of wool, are recommended as a ground for fabric printing inks. The ink will make the material a little stiffer so something like a firm cotton is best. Flimsy chiffon would be unsuited to this rather heavy type of printing, where the colour always remains on the surface of the fabric and does not penetrate the fibres. The first wash (a gentle hand-wash, remember) will improve the feel – or 'handle' as it is called in the textile world – of the printed cloth. Always give any fabric a thorough wash before printing it. It's a very good idea to have some scrap material to practise on, preferably the same type of fabric as you are using for your finished article. Wash the scraps too prior to printing.

Suede takes fabric printing ink well so you might think about making some previously unco-ordinated belts or bags co-ordinate by printing them with a motif taken from a piece of clothing.

APPLYING THE INK. The ink may be applied to the block with either a brush, or a roller. A small, inexpensive paste brush or a flat oil painting brush is best for inking objects that it would be difficult to roll ink on to, for example, grasses, the seeds of which would all stick to the roller; or for tiny, fiddly things like the ends of matchsticks. The brush-on technique enables you to apply a thicker layer of a slightly more runny printing ink (see below). This may be necessary to achieve a strong printed impression if the fabric is very absorbent or somewhat textured.

As the ink is rather sticky straight from the tube you will need to thin it with a small quantity of boiled linseed oil, prepared thinning oil or white spirit (which is also used to clean brushes etc). Have ready a piece of glass, Formica or a similar non-porous flat surface to use as a mixing palette. Squeeze out a little ink on to the palette and, with a palette knife or an old dinner knife, blend in some of the thinning additive to produce a creamy mixture.

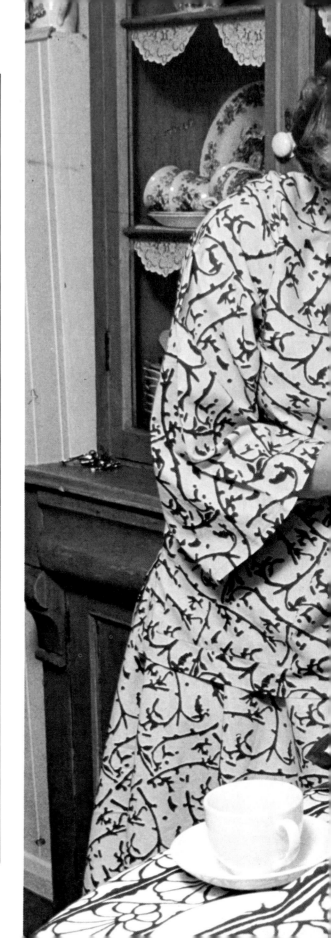

Linoleum is a very good material to use for making printing blocks. It is soft enough to cut (special cutting tools are available), yet firm enough to retain the cut image through a prolonged printing session. Lino may be left untreated for use with fabric printing ink, as it was to print the badge above (see page 107), or the surface may be specially prepared with flocking so that fabric dye paste can be used. All the fabrics in the photograph left were printed in this way by the crafts people at Yately Industries, Camberley, Surrey, using techniques similar to those described in Chapter 4, beginning on page 114.

Although block printing an all-over pattern on fabric may seem a chore, flocked lino block printing is a much more direct approach than silk screen printing, and is certainly a great deal less restrictive. A random pattern like that on the woman's blouse and skirt is the most spontaneous to create, while a repeating motif follows a definite scheme. For how to use border patterns and repeating designs see Chapter 4 pages 83-93.

A printing roller of the type used for printing lino cuts and sold in craft shops should be used for larger flat objects. You will also need an inking slab, again, a piece of glass will suit. (Bevelled edges are recommended on glass, otherwise it can be dangerous.)

Squeeze out a line of ink that is the same length as the roller on to the inking slab. Roll the ink out into an even layer on the slab, rolling out an area just sufficient for the roller to revolve completely; a larger area is wasteful. Roll the ink in different directions on the slab to distribute it evenly before applying it to the object.

Place the object on newspaper and roll ink on to it, again rolling in several different directions. After a little practice you'll get to know the right thickness of ink and how much rolling is required. Keep recharging the slab as the ink is used up. Some inks may be too stiff straight from the tube to roll out satisfactorily. If so, blend in a little of one of the thinners mentioned above. Mixing of any sort, adding thinners or colour blending, should always be done thoroughly with a knife on the edge of the slab prior to rolling out. It is hopeless endeavouring to mix colours by rolling them together.

When the printing session is over, roller, slab, knife (and hands) must be cleaned with white spirit and rags. Never leave them as the dry ink is absolutely permanent.

Fabric printing ink will work successfully on improvised blocks like corks, buttons, offcuts of wood, feathers or leaves.

FABRIC DYE PASTES. Because it is oil bound, fabric printing ink won't adhere properly to anything moist like an apple cut in half or an absorbent surface like felt; fabric dye paste (or paint) is what you need here. This is a dye made into a paste-like consistency. Dylon Colour-fun Fabric Paint is readily available and has the great advantage of being fast on both natural and synthetic fibre fabrics. For small quantities of different colours, for example to decorate clothing, these little jars are ideal. However, if you require a larger amount, perhaps to print a big expanse of curtain fabric, it may be more economical to buy the pigment (the concentrated dye colour) and the binder (the transparent base which gives the paste-like quality) separately and mix up your colours: these are available from most craft suppliers. When mixing your own dye paste, the strength of a colour depends upon how much pigment you add to the binder; the manufacturer's instructions should give a guide. To mix the paint, put some binder in a jar and add the dye to the binder, not vice versa.

Fabric dye paste colours and fabric printing inks are transparent, so if you use a coloured background the printed colour will be influenced by the colour of the background. To obtain an opaque, non-transparent colour you must add white, which means that opaque colours will be light in tone. The white can, of course, be used as a colour on its own as well.

Here is an important point which applies when mixing up light-tone colours, whether they be opaque or transparent, in any kind of paint or dye. Always put a blob of the transparent base or the white on your mixing palette first, then gradually add the colour to it. If you do it the other way round, by adding light to dark, you could find you've mixed up a whole jar of white and your longed-for delicate shell pink still remains a determined strong red.

As well as enabling you to print things like half apples, fabric dye paste is suitable for printing most other objects, although because it is less sticky than fabric printing ink, and very much like poster paint or watercolour in a tube, it will not adhere successfully to anything too shiny. The printed image is not generally as clearly defined as that which can be achieved with fabric printing ink. This does vary, though, according to the texture, or lack of it, in the cloth being printed. However, the handle of fabrics printed with fabric dye paste is softer.

Use a brush to paint the dye paste on to the object being printed. You can wash the brush, palette and so on in water. An alternative way of applying the paste is to make a stamping pad. This is particularly suitable for printing something like a cork. It's fun for younger children too, who might have difficulty in controlling a brush. Make the pad out of a small piece of very thick felt or a layer of plastic sponge. Place it in something waterproof like a tin lid or saucer and spread some dye paste on it. Press the cork on to the pad so that it will pick up the colour. Then print with it.

FIXING THE COLOUR. Material printed with fabric dye paste should be allowed to dry thoroughly. Then you must fix the colour to make it fast to washing; this is done with heat. Cover the printed area with a thin cotton cloth and iron it for several minutes with the iron set at as high a temperature as the cloth can safely take. Full instructions are given by the manufacturers and these should be carefully followed. Fabric printing inks, on the other hand, do not require any sort of fixing process.

You cannot mix inks and dyes together, just as you would not attempt to combine oil and emulsion paints.

You can use artists' acrylic paints for fabric printing. They do make the cloth feel stiff but they are suited to a heavy material which is stiff anyway. The disadvantage of using acrylic paints for printing is that they dry rapidly – so you have to work fast or else no impression will come off the block. There is, however, a retarder available (from art supply shops) which when mixed in with the colour will slow down the drying rate without altering the consistency. The stamping pad technique would be unsatisfactory because the paint would dry on the pad, so a brush must be used. This can be cleaned in water – but do make sure you don't let the paint dry and harden on the brush because you won't be able to remove it. Acrylic paints on fabric do not have to be fixed and they will withstand gentle hand-washing. As there are preparations especially made for printing on to materials it seems sensible to use these in most cases in preference to acrylic paint. The use of paint could be applicable in the theatre, perhaps for printing soft furnishings or scenery.

The printing table

Whichever type of printing colour you are using you will need the same basic working arrangement. The work surface must be slightly resilient, so cover the table with an old, uncreased blanket. Wrap the edges of the blanket around under the table. Use sticky tape or drawing pins (if it's an old table and nobody objects) to secure the edges of the blanket to the underside of the table so that it is stretched out flat. (See fig. 26.)

Iron your already-washed fabric or garment – dampen it if necessary – and for experiments, scrap pieces. To keep the fabric taut pin it along the edges to the blanket. Insert the pins as shown in fig. 27 so that they pull against one another. Before pinning out a garment like a T-shirt, put a piece of paper inside to be sure that the colour cannot go through on to the back by mistake.

First do some practice printing on the pieces of scrap material. This will enable you to decide how thick a layer of colour to apply to the object and how hard to press it down on to the fabric. Press

26 *The printing table should be padded with a blanket on to which the fabric to be printed is pinned.*

27 *When securing fabric to the printing table, place pins directly opposite each other, and at right angles to the edges of the fabric.*

26
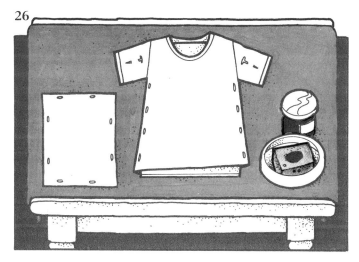

27
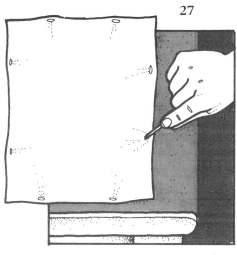

28

down gently, don't stamp it down fiercely.

To keep all the prints the same strength of colour you need to apply more of the colour to the block after each print, ready for the next one. This is called 'inking up'. Do also see what results you get by sometimes not inking up between prints, thus producing a lighter toned print. You could build up a design from a deliberate arrangement of full strength and lighter toned impressions.

Making repeat border patterns

The espadrilles shown on page 71 are printed with fabric printing ink using the head of a screw. Borders and designs like this which follow a line are a useful starting point for block printing. Having made the first print you have only to decide which way up and how much further along the line the next one is to be, and so on. To work out how to organise the repeated printed motif into a successful design you may find it helpful to do some trial prints on scrap paper. You can cut these prints up and juggle them around until you like the arrangement. If you need any guidelines to help you to position the design on the fabric, draw very lightly in tailor's chalk or use masking tape markers, see fig. 28. Masking tape is especially good for making temporary straight guidelines, you just pull it off when it has served its purpose.

There are endless variations on the border theme. Here are some ideas you can adapt yourself, using the printing objects you have found. The first eight lines use the same single motif. See how an additional colour makes another design element available to you (and that's only one additional colour, think of the permutations using three or four). In fig. 29, each motif touches the adjacent one, all the same way up. In fig. 30 they are all the same way up but spaced apart. In fig. 31, alternate motifs are upside down; spaced slightly apart.

Fig. 32 is the same as fig. 31, but unspaced. The motif is turned on its side in fig. 33. Note how the white spaces between assume a clear shape. In fig. 34, the motifs are alternately turned to one side and then the other side. The white space now formed is even more apparent. Fig. 35 is the same, but spaced into pairs. A new butterfly-like motif emerges. Fig. 36 shows some combinations of the above arrangements. Another motif is introduced in fig. 37.

Decorative patterned ribbons and trimmings can really enhance a garment but they are costly. So why not print and dye your own? Inexpensive coloured fabric tape looks terrific when printed and you can deliberately match articles to one another. Wash and iron the tape first. In the case of the espadrilles this is not practical but it doesn't matter as they don't need to be fast to washing. Pin the tape out, making sure that the pins aren't in the way of the design to be printed. If it's a long piece, just work your way along gradually. If you need to space your motifs at particular intervals, mark these in chalk before you print.

Pin a section down and print it. Then release it and either let it hang down off the end of the table, or if it's very long, loop it up over something to dry. Wet fabric printing ink remains sticky for some time, so make sure your work won't flap around in the breeze picking up tacky ink marks in the wrong places and spoiling the design.

To print the toe area of a shoe stuff it first with newspaper to give a firm support.

29-35 *Ideas for making different repeating border patterns using one motif.*

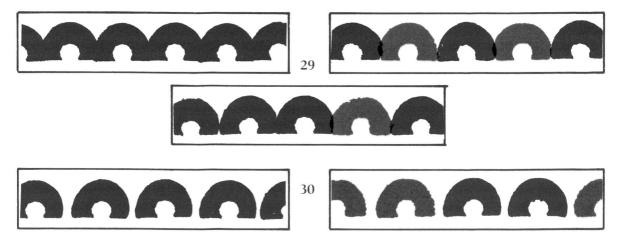

29

30

31

32

33

34

35

36

37

36 A few of the many variations to be achieved for border patterns using one motif.

37 The introduction of a second motif expands greatly the number of border designs possible.

Doing the printing

To print with something fairly flat, like a leaf or a piece of corrugated cardboard, coat it with colour and gently position it, face down, on the fabric. Place a sheet of scrap paper over it (pages torn from an old magazine are handy here) and carefully press your hand all over the object through the paper. Then remove the paper and peel the now printed object away from the fabric.

The quilted jacket, shown on page 70 was printed in this way. All the printing and heat fixing was done before the garment was made up. Real leaves create the flowers and foliage and the hand is an appliquéd shape in another fabric. It is a very easy-to-sew design, and instructions for making it are given here.

To print fabric for making your own version, first wash and iron the outer fabric. With tailor's chalk draw the pattern pieces on to the right side of the material. Fabric dye paste colours were used to print this example; notice how the sage green background colour has influenced all the other colours. Fabric printing inks would do but the slight stiffness that they give the material could make the subsequent quilting less satisfactory. An informal kind of printed design like this permits you to build up as you go along. It is very much akin to painting a picture, you can use whatever colours you wish, blending them as you like. As shown on the flowers (which are made up out of printed leaves, not actual flowers) more than one colour can be brushed on to the object being printed.

These flower shapes show the importance of the shape of an article when it becomes a printing block. The silhouette is all important. What the article actually is in its normal context, what purpose it serves and what its usual colour is are no longer relevant.

You may want to protect a certain printed section so that you can print another colour around it; to print a blue leaf behind a pink flower, for example. To do this make a tracing of the flower. Cut it out of the tracing paper. Pin the tracing paper flower shape exactly over the printed flower shape. Print the leaf in blue in the usual way. Remove it and then unpin and remove the tracing paper shape. The result is an untouched pink flower against a blue background. See fig. 38.

Making up the quilted jacket

Following the preceding directions, the fabric for the jacket is printed first, then quilted and finally made up. For a medium sized jacket (up to 90cm (36in) bust – it's a loose fitting garment) you require 2m (2¼yd) of 90cm (36in) wide fabric for the outer layer. This should be a lightweight, closely woven cotton or synthetic (if your fabric dye paste is suitable for synthetic fibre fabric). You'll also need 2m (2¼yd) of bias binding 2·5cm (1in) wide, lightweight lining, 6·5m (7yd) of bias binding 2·5cm (1in) wide, 1·5m (60in) of 12mm (½in) wide straight tape the same colour as the binding for the tie fastenings, and thread in two colours, one to match the outer fabric; the other for the binding.

38 *To print a second colour without overlapping, protect the first colour by covering it with paper cut to match the shape.*

38

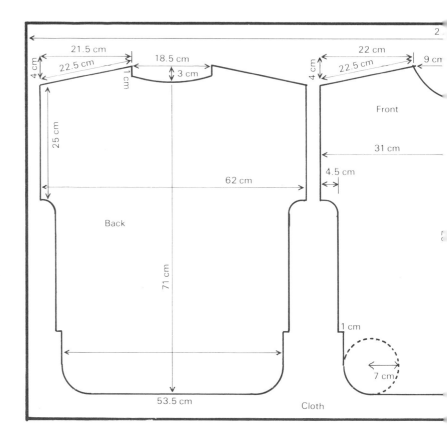

Cut out the pattern shapes in newspaper following fig. 39 and lay them on the outer fabric. There is a 1cm (⅜in) turning allowance. Draw round the shapes in tailor's chalk. Cut out each piece allowing an extra 5cm (2in) around all edges. This is ease to allow for the quilting.

Print your design and fix the dye.

Cut out corresponding shapes, all approximately 5cm (2in) larger than the pattern, in the wadding and the lining. The pockets are not quilted, so do not cut wadding for these.

On the right side of the outer fabric, very lightly chalk vertical lines 5cm (2in) apart as a guide for the machine-stitched quilting. Now sandwich each piece of wadding between its appropriate outer fabric and lining shapes. Tack the three layers together working from the centre out to the corners and then to the edges. Machine-stitch along the guidelines through the three layers, *always* stitching in the same direction. When the quilting is finished pin the pattern shapes on and cut out.

Zigzag stitch or oversew all the edges to finish. This makes binding easier as it holds the three layers together. It also finishes

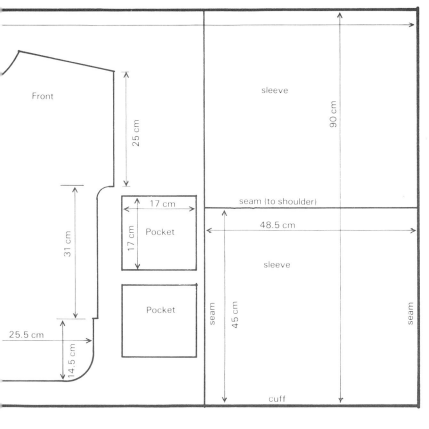

39 *Transfer the measurements given here to dressmaker's graph paper to make a pattern for the quilted jacket shown on page 70.*

any exposed seams, as at the sides of the jacket.

Sew the shoulder seams together. To attach the sleeves first mark the centre point of the sleeve; place this at the shoulder seam, pin and sew. Bind the centre fronts, the bottom edges of the two fronts, the back and the cuffs. The piece of binding at the neck also forms the neck tie-fastening; allow 22cm (9in) of loose binding at each side of the neck opening for this. Pin the binding around the neck. Fold the 22cm (9in) tie length on one side in half lengthwise. Sew along it, around the neck and along the remaining folded tie length.

Turn the jacket inside out. Pin side and underarm seam and sew as one seam. Repeat with other side seam. Bind the raw edge of the pockets and sew in place. Then apply the other six straight tape tie-fastenings – each 22cm (9in) long. These are placed at 10cm (4in) intervals. Finally, lightly press the completed jacket.

Easy-to-make printing blocks

With an improvised ready-made printing block you accept the inherent shape of a printed impression of the object. The designing aspect comes in when you start to arrange groups of the printed shape (or shapes) into a pattern. The next logical stage is to create your own shape and to arrange prints of that into a design.

After you have experimented in printing with ready-made objects, try making your own blocks. Lots of commonplace materials can be used for this very economical form of textile decoration and many of the techniques are ideal for children. The surfaces of practically all the materials described in this section will readily accept either fabric printing ink or fabric dye paste. The exceptions in the case of ink are as explained earlier: any moist object (oil and water not mixing) and anything made from too absorbent a textile substance like felt or pipe cleaners – with these, although they may be used, the ink is liable to pick up an awful lot of fluff. Dye paste, on the other hand, will not coat any greasy surface properly. The printing procedures outlined in the previous section apply in the same way here. Use whichever method of applying colour that suits the particular block.

Corks make excellent printing blocks. Save used ones or buy beautiful new ones in different sizes from a shop that sells wine-making accessories. A print from an untouched cork will look like the print in fig. 40. There is nothing wrong with that if you want a plain circular motif. However, make a slight alteration and you open up all sorts of possibilities. With a sharp knife cut away some of the surface to make a simple design. In fig. 41, just one quarter of the circle has been removed.

When you are in the act of printing you obviously can't see the surface being printed. So, to know which way up you are holding the block, first make a print on paper (you can use either printing ink or dye for this). Then cut it out and glue it to the non-printing end of the block, lining up the printed impression exactly over the design as shown in the diagram, fig. 42.

40 *The end of a cork used as a printing block produces a print similar to this.*

41 *By cutting away one quarter of the cork you alter the shape of the print.*

42 *To know which way up you are holding the block, glue a printed impression exactly over the cut design.*

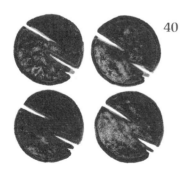 40

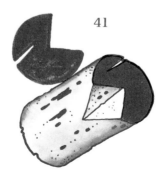 41

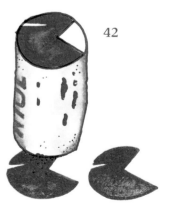 42

Repeating patterns

In printing borders, (see pages 84-86), the motif was repeated from left to right only, forming a line. What happens when you want to print an area – as well as going from left to right you want to go up and down? There is random placing of the design, when you judge by eye where to place each print one after the other, as in fig. 43a. The quilted jacket on page 70 was printed in this way. There, of course, there were many different motifs.

Then there are many, many ways of creating designs based on a grid of squares or rectangles. Try some of these for yourself on paper first. Either rule faint lines or fold the paper so that you have a number of squares, each just the right size for the motif to fit inside. Now start printing.

In example 43b the motif was kept inside the square, each one aligned with its neighbours, both from left to right and up and down. If you now stagger the position of the squares in every other vertical band by dropping them down the distance of half a square you achieve a grid which looks like a brick wall on its side (fig. 43c). This is called a half drop repeat; once again there are lots of permutations. The half drop grid can be turned on its side to become just like a brick wall and any of the grids may be turned to form a diagonal base.

As was shown previously with the repeating border designs, introducing more colours means yet more possibilities, as may be seen in fig. 43d.

Other variations occur when different spaces are left between

43a

43a *A random repeat.*

43b *A one way repeat.*
43c *A half-drop repeat.*

43b

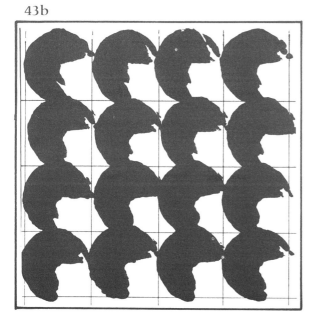

43c

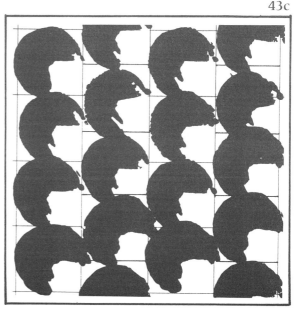

43d **44**

43e **45**

43d *Colour alters the repeating design.*
43e *The space between motifs also changes the pattern.*
44 *A diagonally striped design is an obvious directional pattern.*
45 *A two-way design.*

the motifs as in fig. 43e.

Stripes are another kind of repeating base grid. A striped design, very obviously, is a directional pattern (fig. 44). A one-way design may be used for curtains or wallpaper, and has all the motifs positioned the same way up.

In a two-way design (fig. 45) the material (assuming it has no nap or pile which is itself directional) can be used either way up.

An all-over design has, as the name implies, no specific

direction. This is the most economical form of patterning when pieces are cut and matched together – although, once again, watch out for a nap.

Certain fabrics are woven or printed with regularly repeating checks, stripes or spots. These form an obvious grid. (Spots incidentally, will generally have been distributed according to an underlying rectangular or square grid.) An amusing way of experimenting with printing designs on a grid is to use a length of gingham, ticking or some similarly ready-patterned material as a basis for your personal design. The carryall shown on page 74 is made of printed mattress ticking.

Making the carryall
You will need a piece of material measuring 40cm × 90cm (16in × 36in) and 60cm (24in) of webbing approximately 3cm ($1\frac{1}{4}$in) wide for the handles.

The bag is made by folding the material in half (the fold serves as the bottom edge of the carryall). Two 8cm (3in) turnings are made along the top edges and 4cm ($1\frac{1}{2}$in) is lost in the two side seams. So the area of the finished bag which is to be printed is 36cm (14in) wide and 37cm ($14\frac{1}{2}$in) deep.

Print the design before making up the bag. When the printing is complete and you have heat fixed the dye if necessary, turn each top edge under 1cm ($\frac{3}{8}$in) and stitch. Attach the handles as shown in fig. 46 and then turn the two top edges over a further 7cm ($2\frac{3}{4}$in). Run a line of machine stitching 5mm ($\frac{1}{4}$in) down from the fold. Sew up the side seams taking 2cm ($\frac{5}{8}$in) seams. Iron the bag, and it is finished.

You could print on to a ready-made bag, in which case you must put a sheet of card in the bag to be sure none of the printed colour goes through and spoils the other side.

When planning the design you may find coloured tissue paper a helpful aid, because its transparent quality is very similar to that of printed ink or dye. Concertina-fold a piece and, cutting through all the layers, cut out the shape of your motif. You can try different arrangements of these shapes, and at the same time see how the coloured parts of the patterned fabric will influence the colour of the printed parts. Handle the tissue carefully as it is light and fragile, and avoid working near a draughty window or a constantly opening door – otherwise all your carefully arranged pieces may suddenly fly up into the air!

This moveable cut paper shape method of planning a design is useful in ways other than with ready-patterned cloth. Use it on your own drawn grids or to sort out the placing of the motifs on a garment, etc.

Like a cork, the end of a piece of wood or the sides of a rubber

46 *Attach the handles to the right side of the carryall as shown here. Then fold the top edge of the bag over to the inside. Repeat on the other side.*

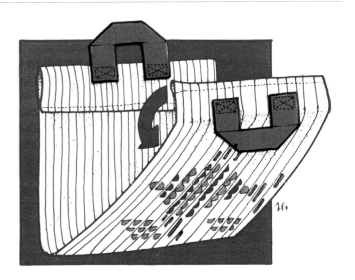

eraser can be carved and cut away to make a relief printing block. A piece of balsa wood is easy to cut into too.

Other simple blocks

A really simple way of producing a printing block is to indent a surface, leaving the parts which will print standing up in relief. Materials suitable for this are plasticine, self-hardening clay (it doesn't have to be fired) or finely-textured expanded polystyrene. All three are sold by craft suppliers, the last in packets of sheets roughly 30cm (12in) square which are intended for use either as a printing or model-making medium. However, you can recycle polystyrene trays of the type in which meat is sold in supermarkets. These will, naturally, give a smaller area to work with than the bought material. You can cut expanded polystyrene sheets or packs with scissors. As no sharp knives or tools are used this method of block making is especially suitable for young children.

The polystyrene is ready for use, but plasticine or self-hardening clay should be moulded first into a rough ball. This ball is then slapped down on to a smooth table top to make one perfectly flat side to be the printing surface. The flat surface of either material may be indented with a pencil, ballpoint pen, or any other similar instrument. You can also press in an article like a key to leave its complete impression. Plasticine and polystyrene blocks can be printed immediately. Use either printing inks or dye paste. For children printing on paper, or when the print does not have to be fast to washing, poster or powder paints are fine.

Obviously, a plasticine block, because it always remains pliable, must be handled with some care, especially during the actual printing. Don't apply heavy pressure because the design will be squashed flat and disappear. If you treat it gently a plasticine block can be printed repeatedly without deteriorating. A block made from self-hardening clay should be allowed to dry out before being printed, and when dry makes a durable substance. Use either ink or dye on it. (Don't forget to seal up the remaining unused clay in its packet – although your printing block may seem to take ages to dry, it's amazing how rapidly the stuff hardens when you don't want it to.)

ADDING BLOCKS. A relief printing block can be made by adding raised areas to a surface, as opposed to the methods mentioned already. All of those methods removed some parts but left standing other parts of the original surface to produce the printed impression. For the 'adding' approach you will need something to form the base. This can be a block of wood, or a piece of hardboard or thick card. A circular base can be made out of the end of a cotton reel or the lid of a tin or jar – make sure it is completely flat, without a raised rim (should there be a paper label, remove it by soaking). Adhesive sticks best to a slightly rough surface, and tin lids are very smooth – it is a good idea to roughen them a little with sandpaper first.

GLUE BLOCKS. Adhesive itself will make one kind of raised printable design. You actually make a design out of lines of dried glue. Use a glue which dries quickly and comes in a container with a nozzle, such as Evo-stik Resin W (woodworking glue). To create the raised lines that will print just trail the adhesive on to the prepared base. It's like piping cake icing; do a free pattern first of all, not attempting to follow a design, to familiarise yourself with the medium. You might then try following a design which you have first sketched on the base. This technique is rather similar to batik – you need a somewhat happy-go-lucky attitude towards it. You have to work fast so don't try to be over-fastidious. When the trail-drawing is complete, put the block in a safe place to dry. Don't attempt to ink it up and print until it is thoroughly dried out.

COLLAGE BLOCKS. Using the same kind of bases and adhesive as already discussed try making collage printing blocks (collage means things glued on to a background). Anything that will create an interesting raised shape can be used – but don't have too great a difference in the height of the glued-on articles, or else only the highest will print. Try sticking on dried vegetables – lentils, beans, pearl barley and rice grains. Pieces of various kinds of textured cloth will produce unusual prints – corduroy, tweed, lace and knitting. Crumpling a light cloth like net before sticking it

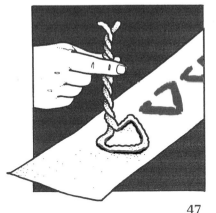

47 *A pipe cleaner, bent into a decorative shape and with the ends twisted to form a handle, makes a good printing block. Pipe cleaners can also be used in this way for printed batik (see page 69).*

47

down will give an interesting result. The collage block can incorporate all sorts of everyday things like paper clips, safety pins, matchsticks and buttons. (For metal objects use a stronger clear adhesive like Bostik 1.)

Rope, smooth string, hairy string, plastic twine, in fact any sort of string has exciting possibilities as collage block material. Coat the surface of the base with adhesive and then 'draw' with the string directly on to this sticky background. Carefully press it all down, weighting it if necessary, and leave it to dry completely before printing.

Both stout cardboard and thick felt are excellent materials for glueing on to a base. Cut out your shapes and stick them on. It's advisable to varnish a card block as cardboard is so absorbent, particularly if you are printing with dye paste. If the card were to become sodden the pieces could disintegrate. Felt, on the contrary, prints very well with dye – the more it soaks up, the better it prints.

You may discover other materials that you would like to try printing. Scraps of cork and vinyl tiles and different types of plastic will all print with their own particular qualities and textures. Try combining some of the materials in a more elaborate collage block – but don't forget to keep the raised areas all more or less of similar thickness.

Pipe cleaners (you can get extra long ones from craft suppliers) are very easy to bend into printing block shapes. Leave the ends standing up at right angles to the table so that you can twist them together and hold them as a handle (fig. 47). As they are absorbent use dye paste rather than printing ink.

NAIL-HEAD BLOCKS. During the eighteenth and nineteenth centuries textile printers developed the type of relief printing block which was made by hammering strips of metal, edge on, and nails into a wooden base. You could make your own version of this by hammering nails, to follow a design, into a wooden block. Use nails with different shaped heads; each one will take up colour and print as a little spot. It's important to have all the nails driven in to end up the same height – aim for 15mm ($\frac{3}{4}$in). When they are all embedded in the base place a flat piece of wood over all the nail heads and hammer on this too to even them up.

The shape and nature of some blocks, such as those made of plasticine, may make it impossible to attach a paper print to the back as a guide as recommended earlier. If so mark, on the reverse of the block, the centre top point of the design with a T; the centre bottom point with a B.

Don't throw away the block-making and repeat pattern trial prints you've made, they can give you ideas for future projects.

Making finished prints

To make final prints be sure to design your repeating motif so that it will fit correctly into the area to be printed. For example, if the printed area is to be 40cm × 60cm (16in × 24in) for a traycloth, a block 10cm (4in) square will fit four times across and six times down inside this space. There is room for twenty-four prints. Of course, depending on the layout of the repeating pattern, you may not need to print the block twenty-four times. Some of the squares may be left blank intentionally. Remember to allow sufficient fabric at the edges for hemming or fraying into a fringe.

You will need to mark a grid of the appropriate size on the fabric so that you'll know where to place the block for each print. A good way of doing this is shown in fig. 48. First mark the appropriate divisions with tailor's chalk along the edges of the fabric. Then stretch fine sewing threads across the cloth from the chalk mark to chalk mark. Alternatively, insert pins at the division points and wrap either end of the thread around each of these to secure it. This method is fine if you can be sure that no part of the block will print across the thread; a white line results if the thread comes between the block and the fabric. If there is any danger of this then rule lines very lightly with tailor's chalk instead. It brushes off afterwards. Don't use a pencil and certainly not any kind of pen or you'll be stuck with a permanent network of unwanted lines.

If you are printing a half drop design within a given area, for instance a rectangle in the centre of a table mat, and you want a plain, unprinted border, take the precaution of taping newspaper over the required depth of border surrounding the area to be printed. Every other line of the repeat will jut down into the border, and the unwanted part of the prints will go on to the newspaper. When you remove it you'll have a nice clear border. (See fig. 49.)

Some of these block-making methods will produce a design in which the background is a solid printed colour and the motif itself is the non-printed section. This applies particularly to the indented blocks like expanded polystyrene. Think of the key impression idea; the print will show a white key on a coloured background.

When you execute a design where one print abuts the next, the joins between the prints will be apparent. However carefully you print you cannot obtain a continuous, even-coloured background, even machine printing could not do so. Machine printed textile patterns are never designed so that the joins occur in a solid background colour. (For more on this subject refer to page 159.) Printed by hand, slight changes in the depth of the colour from one print to the next are inevitable. Also, a minute overlapping of

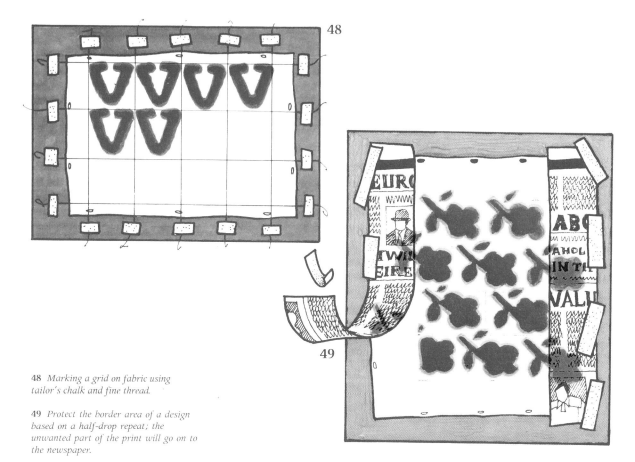

48

49

48 *Marking a grid on fabric using tailor's chalk and fine thread.*

49 *Protect the border area of a design based on a half-drop repeat; the unwanted part of the print will go on to the newspaper.*

the joins will produce a line of dark colour; a minute failure to meet properly will create a white line.

Here are some practical ways around this problem: the most obvious way is to avoid the kind of repeat pattern in which prints abut. Use one with spaces, like a check or alternate diamonds (see fig. 50). The blank spaces could, if you wish, have another isolated motif repeated in them – perhaps in an additional colour as shown in fig. 51.

Another method of disguise makes deliberate use of the join, incorporating it as part of the all-over design. It is achieved by decorating the edges of the background on the block in some way. When the block is printed, with each impression placed slightly apart from its neighbours, a distinct imprinted tracery will emerge. Again, an added colour may help the finished design. See fig. 52 for an example of this type of treatment.

In some cases your finished printed motif may appear a little weak from the point of view of design. It could well be enhanced by the addition of a background area, maybe a patch or a distinct shape. One of the collage block ideas could be useful here, using a textured material like tweed fabric or cork tile, overprinted in a transparent colour.

Hang your finished work up somewhere safe to dry out and never forget to apply the appropriate fixing process to dye-printed cloth when it is quite dry.

Potato cuts

You may well have youthful memories of wild, uncontrolled messes made by printing with potatoes. Unfortunately, this association may make it difficult to take a potato cut seriously. Nevertheless, the potato is a very worthwhile block material for the fabric printer: it is extremely easy to cut and it prints particularly well on cloth with fabric dye paste. You can get repeatedly good, consistent prints, so this makes it an excellent medium for experimenting with different repeating patterns. As new design ideas suggest themselves to you, you'll have no compunction in cutting another block, for a potato is so cheap and the cutting technique is so simple. Clearly the size of the printing area is somewhat influenced by the size of potato you can obtain, but as a quick way of getting results it's hard to beat.

Potato printing can save you much time and effort when planning a project on a larger scale. There is no need to draw a pattern out painstakingly in repeat. Instead, print a quick potato version to see how the motifs will look when organised into

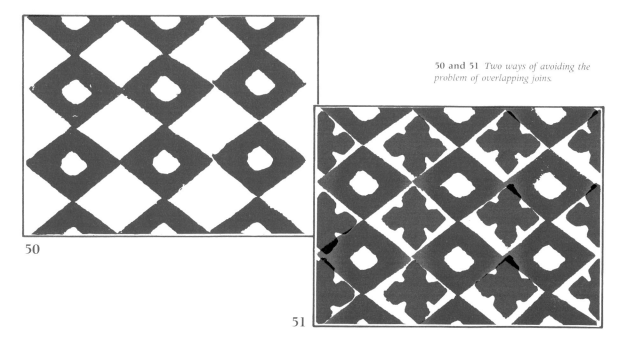

50 and 51 *Two ways of avoiding the problem of overlapping joins.*

50

51

52

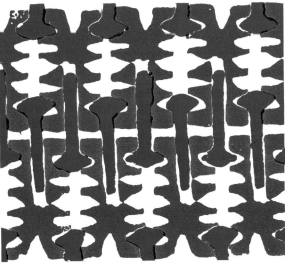

52 *A more elaborate solution to disguising joins is to decorate the edges of the block. The result can be enhanced with the introduction of a second colour.*

various patterns. However, the potato cut isn't just a design short cut, it can hold its own as a printing technique.

To make several blocks all you need is a few potatoes and a small, pointed kitchen knife. Lino cutting gouges or small wood carving tools are useful too if you have them, but not essential. Use either the brush-on or stamping pad (page 120) method to apply the fabric printing dye to the block. The fabric and the table are prepared in the usual way (page 82). Keep some rags handy for cleaning up, with a special clean one kept on one side for wiping away the moisture that comes out of the potato. Too much of this moisture will dilute the dye colour and make the printing surface very slippery.

Wash and dry the potato but don't peel it – the skin helps to hold the whole thing together. Using a careful sawing motion cut the potato in half. Aim for as straight a cut as possible as this cut surface is what you print. Dry the cut surface with a clean rag. The print from half a potato is shown in fig. 53.

You can incise a pattern into this oval shape by making V-shaped cuts with your knife, lifting out the wedges with the point. Lightly indent the design with a pencil first. (See fig. 54).

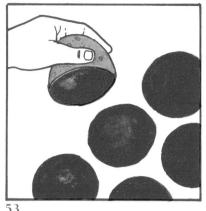

53　　　　　　　　　　　**54**　　　　　　　　　　　**55**

Alternatively, you can leave a motif standing up 5mm ($\frac{1}{4}$in) or so in relief by cutting away the surrounding background (see fig. 55). These different approaches may all be combined in a design. The solid, uncut oval makes a useful background shape.

Adopting a different approach, the potato can be cut up into rectangular oblongs, cylinders, half cylinders and wedge shapes. Prints from these sections are then assembled in a design, rather as a mosaic pattern is developed. Geometric shapes like this will make limitless combinations (see fig. 56). So that you know which way up the design is when the block is held face-down mark the back as explained on page 90.

After a day or so the potato block will shrivel up and become useless, so it is a good plan to do all the printing in one session. Although a potato block will last well for quite a number of prints, you may wish to print the same motif a great many times, on a dressmaking length of material, for instance. Then the block would start to deteriorate and lose its definition. If so, cut a duplicate using the *offset* method. This means you take a print on a piece of paper and then press a new half potato down on to the still wet print. The image will be transferred (offset) on to the new block and you can cut around this, making a replica of the original

53 A potato makes a useful block, and the print from a potato half is a simple oval.

54 A design cut into the potato leaves a pattern in circle of colour.

55 Cutting away the potato makes a relief block.

56

56 Pieces of potato cut into geometric shapes will combine to make attractive designs when printed.

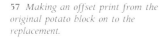

57 *Making an offset print from the original potato block on to the replacement.*

block (see fig. 57). This method is useful too in other forms of block making. Note that if you were to print the original block straight on to the new blank one the design would be in reverse.

With potato printing you can fully exploit the many different forms of repeat pattern-making discussed earlier in the chapter. In addition to printing a rectangular area think how you can treat other shapes like the circular design in the photograph on page 75. It's a good idea to make some prints on paper, cut them out and arrange them around the circle. This will give you an idea of how many prints are going to be required and how far apart you should space them. When you have decided what looks best, make a guide for the placing. This can be done in two different ways. If the fabric on which you are printing is thin enough to see through, you can draw out a plan in heavy black lines on white paper and place it under the fabric. Use a drawing material that is waterproof so that it will not run into the wet dye paste – Indian ink or a waterproof felt-tip marker will do. The circle has to be divided up by the number of motifs required; each motif is positioned on the point of a star, as it were. Here a protractor may be necessary. First draw a diameter across the circle. Then divide the number of motifs into 360° and with the protractor measure that number of degrees up from the diameter at the centre of the circle (see fig. 58). Repeat that measurement all the way round and draw in the appropriate guidelines.

If your fabric is too heavy to see through, cut out your paper circle and place it in the correct position on the material. Using tailor's chalk, lightly mark the motif points on the fabric all around the edge of the circle.

To print a curved border, as for example around a wide boat neck, locate the centre first. Use the cut out paper print method to see how the motifs should be distributed and then mark the positions with the aid of a paper guide.

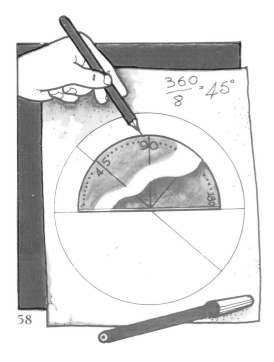

Think how potato cuts can be used either as borders or shapes built up out of grouped prints to decorate cuffs, collars and pockets. Accessories like belts and scarves can be printed to complement and co-ordinate your wardrobe.

PRINTING A BORDER. Depending on the nature of the printed motif, there are two ways to print a straight border which has right angled corners. In either case you first mark the guidelines for the

58 *For a circular pattern, as shown on the boy's overalls in the photograph on page 75, use a protractor to divide the design area into the number of motifs required.*

59 *Lengths of masking tape marked into the number of motifs for a border will help you to position them evenly.*

60 *Mitring the corners of a border design to accommodate a motif that would otherwise fit neatly into the space.*

61 *When the newspaper is removed a new motif is revealed.*

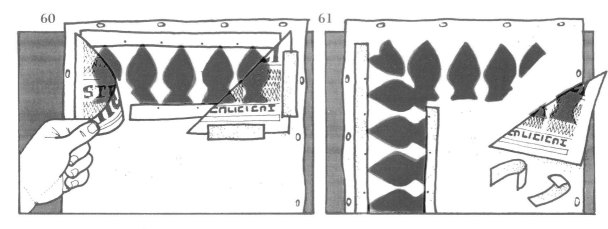

placing of the motifs. A simple method for a border is to use masking tape marked off in divisions the size of each repeated print as shown in fig. 59. This is easily removed when the printing is finished. If the motif is a shape that will fit into a square turning the corner presents no problems. However, if the motif is based on an oblong print, mitre the corners. To do this you need to have ready some sheets of scrap paper cut or folded into 45° triangles. Start with the top line of your border. Tape a paper triangle at either end of the border. Line up the right angles of the paper with the right angles of the cloth so that the 45° edge runs straight through the corner, as shown in fig. 60. Print the top line. Part of the corner motifs will print on to the paper, leaving the cloth blank. Repeat the procedure as you work your way round the border. This same principle can be applied when assembling a non-square motif into a square block (see fig. 61). An entirely

62

62 *Another solution to the corner problem is to design a different motif especially for the purpose.*

different solution to the corner problem is to create a distinct new corner motif. This is shown in fig. 62.

Try experimenting with other vegetable printing blocks; swedes and turnips for larger designs, carrots and celery stalks for small ones. Their textures are different from that of the potato and will produce more varied patterns.

Lino block

In rather the same way as the potato cut, lino cutting has acquired something of a poor image as a craft. Admittedly, some extremely dreary work has been produced, and you may well recall seemingly endless afternoons picking away at an unresponsive, tedious brown surface. This is a great pity because lino cutting can be a really vibrant, versatile medium, and whilst it is eminently suitable for older children, it is certainly not confined to the classroom. Artists such as Picasso, Matisse and Raoul Dufy have used the lino cut as a creditable technique, exploiting its own special qualities; Dufy in particular produced some exciting and complex textile designs using this craft.

The earliest form of fabric printing was done using wooden blocks, carved with designs left standing in relief. Such printed textiles are thought to have existed in Egypt as early as 2500 BC. The early block printers used the resist method (Chapter 3) employing various types of starch paste with which to print first and then colouring the fabric with natural dye. Subsequently the cloth was washed, leaving the design in the original colour of the material, while the surrounding background took the dyed colour. Later the direct printing method was introduced – the application of coloured dye paste to the block for printing.

Lino is easier to cut than wood and the modern fabric dye pastes, paints and printing inks that are readily available, make it possible to do this kind of block printing at home or in school without a lot of expense or elaborate equipment.

Lino is, naturally, a much longer lasting substance than many of the block printing materials previously discussed. Also it allows you far greater control, and therefore much more scope, in designing. Your design can be a simple silhouette shape or an intricate composition with finely cut lines and a variety of patterns and textures.

THE MATERIALS. Use the old-fashioned thick kind of linoleum which has a canvas backing. A few flooring specialists still stock this, or you can buy pieces cut to various sizes in an art shop. (Providing it is not too pitted or scarred, you can use old lino which has been removed from the floor.) Cut the lino to the size you require with a sharp craft knife against a metal ruler. If you

Two examples of block printed fabric, designed by Raoul Dufy in the 1920s. Lino has been a popular printing medium for many years.

first cut through the canvas backing and then score the lino along the cutting line it will snap easily in the hands, along the scored line.

There are two distinctly different ways of printing a finished lino block. In one method the printing surface of the cut block is left as it is. Lino in its natural state is a non-absorbent material, so for this method sticky fabric printing ink and a roller are required. The normal lino surface would repel fabric dye paste, which is too runny to apply with a roller, anyway. You will also need some white spirit for cleaning up the printing ink.

The other method of printing does use dye paste. This means you have to treat the surface of the lino so that it can absorb the dye. This is done by a process called *flocking*. It means glueing fine, dust-like powdered fabric fibre to the printing surface, thus creating a coating which will take up the dye – as felt does. Flocking is explained in more detail further on in this chapter. For more information on the particular qualities of fabric printing ink and fabric dye paste, see Chapter 4.

THE EQUIPMENT. The lino is engraved with small gouges, which look rather like pen nibs. Inexpensive sets of these are available from arts and crafts stores. They are supplied with a handle, and the little gouges are interchangeable in this handle. There are various sized V and U shapes and a flat cutting blade (see fig. 63), The disadvantage of these cheaper interchangeable cutters is that they are not as strong or as easy to sharpen as the better quality gouges. These stouter lino tools (which are also used for cutting wood blocks) are sold by the more specialist artists' suppliers. Each steel gouge is set in its own handle, and a wide range of V and U shapes is available. These cutters are easily sharpened on a fine carborundum stone, lubricated with a drop of oil.

To print by the first method using fabric printing ink you will need a lino roller; a flat impervious surface, such as a sheet of formica, glass, or something similar to act as an inking slab and a knife – preferably a palette knife, but an old dinner knife will suffice. The equipment required for the flocking method is a sieve to apply the flocking powder and a roller for the flocking adhesive and, for the printing process, a stamping pad. For either method the arrangement of the padded printing table is as given on page 82.

Making printed patch-badges
To learn lino-block printing it is best to start off by doing something fairly simple using the fabric printing ink method. Small sew-on fabric patch-badges are an ideal initial project, using odd scraps of cloth to make the patches.

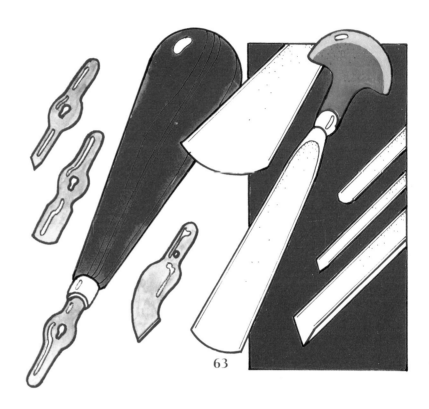

63 *Examples of the lino-cutting tools available: left, holder with interchangeable cutters; right, cutters fixed into their own handles.*

Before you start on your design try out the different cutters on a small piece of lino. This will show the kind of marks they can make best and help you to get used to the actual cutting. Lino is easier to gouge and cut if it is slightly warmed, perhaps on a radiator. This makes it softer and less rigid. Just in case the tool should slip, always take the precaution of keeping the hand that holds the piece of lino behind the hand doing the cutting as shown in fig. 64; then you won't cut yourself.

Experiment with as many cutting techniques as you can devise. Then try continuous straight and curved lines of different widths – you may find it easier to move the block rather than the cutter for curves. Try short sharp stabs with the different shaped tools to create textures; produce zigzag lines by rocking a v-shaped tool as you cut; make crisscross grooves in different combinations and cut away around a shape, leaving it isolated. Fig. 65 shows the wide variety of lines and marks which can be made.

Gouge away so that you always leave the sides of a raised section sloping inwards towards the top printing surface, like miniature ranges of flat-topped hills. If an area is undercut the edges will break down.

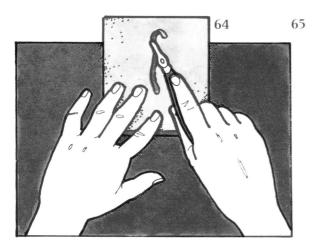

Printing with fabric printing ink

Pin out some previously washed scrap fabric on the printing table. Roll out some ink and ink-up your trial lino cut following the procedure explained on page 80. When the lino block is thoroughly and evenly inked-up place it face down on the fabric; be very careful not to move it once it's down or you will get a blurred image.

Lay a small piece of newspaper over the back of the block to keep the surrounding fabric clean. Now, holding it steady, apply firm pressure through the newspaper by moving your fingers all over the back of the block. Remove the newspaper and gently peel back a corner of the lino, holding the rest of the block in position. If the print is good and clear lift off the lino. If it is not, it may mean that more pressure must be applied or that there was too little ink rolled on to the block.

Odd, unprinted spots on the print are generally specs of dust or dirt that have got into the ink. Always make sure you do any actual lino cutting well away from the ink slab: little slivers of lino are extremely difficult to extricate from the ink. Also, always be careful to leave the inky roller either on the ink slab, or, if it's the type intended to do so, standing up on its back with the roller itself in mid-air. Never lay an inky roller down on the table top, it will instantly pick up fluff and dirt. When you ink it up, place the lino block on a newspaper or magazine so that any stray ink around the block goes on to the paper. Keep renewing the paper as it becomes inky.

Try another print. If your results are persistently pale try dampening the fabric before you pin it down.

After you have got the feel of lino cutting and printing from your experimental block, plan your badge-patch design. Remember that, as with all the relief printing techniques, the

64 *When cutting lino, always cut away from your body and keep your hands behind the cutter.*

65 *An example of the kinds of marks that can be made with lino-cutting tools.*

image will come out in reverse – important if your design includes any letters or numbers. You can draw the design straight on to the lino block or transfer it with carbon paper. To do this, tape your drawing (or tracing) to the lino block to prevent it from moving. Remember to reverse it at this stage if necessary. Slide a piece of carbon paper under the drawing and, with a hard pencil, draw over the design to transfer it on to the lino.

Whether you have drawn straight on to the block in pencil or have used carbon paper you must now go over the lines with a pen and waterproof indian ink or a black waterproof marker. This is necessary, because your hand could accidentally rub the drawing off as you do the cutting. (Another reason for using an impervious drawing ink; the white spirit used for cleaning off the printing ink would also remove any other type of drawing.)

Now cut the design. If you are doing a design that is an isolated pattern without any background, gouge out a groove all around the pattern and cut the unwanted lino away with scissors. Even if you were to clear away the background very thoroughly with the cutters it might still pick up some ink and print. On the other hand, for certain designs a deliberate, restrained cut texture may make a good background.

Take some prints on paper to check how the lino cut is going. When all the cutting is complete print the washed fabric pieces and then put the prints somewhere safe to dry out thoroughly. Remember to clean the roller and the other equipment properly.

Trim round the printed design and sew the patches on to clothing using buttonhole stitch or closely worked machine zigzagging. Use badge patches to brighten up jeans, a jacket or the elbows of a sweater (printed suede patches would be lovely). They are a great idea for sports clubs – for participants or supporters.

Printing larger blocks
The lino block used for a badge-patch is small and can be printed by finger pressure alone. This would be too long-winded a process and unsuitable for a bigger design, so here is the procedure for large-scale work.

After you have completed the cutting it is necessary to stick the lino on to a more rigid background. Use heavy cardboard, or for rather large designs, a piece of hardboard, plywood or chipboard. From the backing material cut a rectangle which just fits around the design. Glue the lino block on to this rectangle with a strong adhesive such as woodworking glue. To prevent its warping, place the mounted block between newspapers and under a heavy weight while the glue is drying. Allow the adhesive time to dry out thoroughly.

To print a mounted block you will need something heavy with
which to hit the back of the block. You can buy a mallet
specifically intended for block printing, but an ordinary mallet or
a hammer (even a rolling pin) will do.

Pin out the fabric on to the blanket base in the usual way,
marking the repeat divisions if necessary (see page 98). Pin down a
scrap piece of the same cloth to make some trial prints on first.

As mentioned before, it is essential to know which way up the
design is when the block is face down – the back of a lino block
can be a very blank-looking rectangle. Either stick a paper print
on to the back, positioned to correspond precisely with the
printing surface, or mark with a felt pen which is the top edge.
The first is clearly the most informative method.

Roll the block up with ink. Place it face down on the test piece
of cloth and strike the back of the block with the mallet or
improvised mallet. The technique for printing with a proper
printing mallet, which is held seemingly upside down, is shown in
fig. 66. Hit the block once if it is fairly small or several times
around a larger block. The backing spreads the effect of the blow,
or blows, over the entire block. Lift the block away from the
fabric.

Several practice prints will enable you to establish how much
ink and how many blows are required. Different fabrics, because

66 *When printing a large block, hit it on
the back with a mallet to ensure a good
printed impression.*

67 *Small blocks can be printed with
finger pressure.*

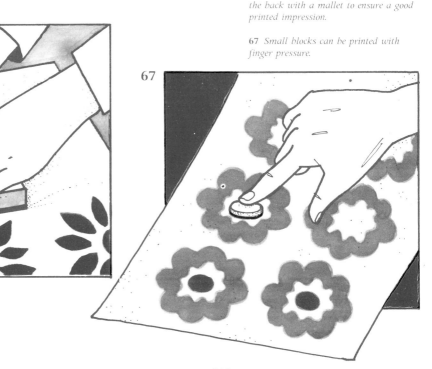

66

67

of their fibre content and the texture of the weave or knit, will absorb ink at different rates.

Designs in more than one colour

So far the lino-cut designs have been printed in one colour only, but you can get a rich variety of colour effects by printing in different coloured inks on different coloured backgrounds. For example, in some types of design where there is a small accent of a colour other than the main one, which could be printed with a tiny block using finger pressure as shown in fig. 67, the second colour can be positioned simply by eye. However, colour registration can be more complex than this and demands another approach.

First of all make a fairly complete coloured drawing on paper of your design. Use crayons, watercolour paint or felt pens for this, and don't waste time endeavouring to produce a masterpiece. This is a working drawing and its purpose is to sort out how the elements of the design are distributed and what colours they are. You'll need to cut and print a separate block for each colour so try to make the maximum use of just a few colours. Remember that a new colour results when you print one colour over another. You can get great variety out of this sort of combination by varying the textures of the two different colours too. A solid red area over a solid blue area gives a purple area. Combine a solid red with variously patterned blue areas and you introduce new colours and weights. Naturally this also works the other way round with solid blue and broken red. Textured red over textured blue gives

68 *When printing in two colours you can add a great deal of interest by varying the cut textures of each block.*

69 *The key block is the first one printed. In the case of fig. 68 it is the blue block.*

68

further possibilities. Fig. 68 shows an example of this.

Decide which is the most dominant colour in the design – the one which gives most visual information. Say the colour is blue as in fig. 69. This will be your key block. Draw directly or transfer the design with carbon paper on to a suitably sized piece of lino. Cut this block so that only the blue parts of the design are left standing in relief. Mount the cut block on to a backing board. Also, for each separate colour, mount a piece of plain lino on an identically sized backing board. It is very important to cut all the backing boards to exactly the same size, because correct registration of the colours depends upon accuracy at this stage.

Now you need to know where to position the areas that are to be printed on the second and subsequent coloured blocks. To do this you make offset prints of the first (blue) key block. Have ready a sheet of paper – plain, unprinted newsprint is best – slightly larger than the design. Ink up the key block rather more generously than usual in black or a dark colour. Place it face down on to the paper and apply hand pressure. The ink will stick the paper to the block. While the block is in this position trace in pencil accurately round the edge of the backing board on to the paper. With care lift up the block and the paper together and turn them over. Now, with the bowl of a tablespoon, burnish all over the back of the paper to get a good, strong print.

When you've rubbed it all over peel off the paper. This, incidentally, is how you can print a lino cut on paper without the use of a press – as a picture or for stationery, Christmas cards, etc.

Next, with the ink still wet and sticky, lay one of the new

69

Left. Spray printed designs have a lovely light quality, and so are ideally suited to window blinds or curtains. Because the colours are not opaque they take on an iridescent appearance when sunlight beams through them.

This window blind is made up in a lightweight cotton that has been coloured with fabric dye paste applied with an airbrush (see page 137). The tartan effect was achieved using lengths of masking tape as stencils as explained on page 135.

Above. Stencils can also be used with acrylic paints on heavy fabrics for a sharply defined image. The fabric shown here was designed to serve as a hanging in an Elizabethan room setting, for an amateur theatrical production.

Information on making your own stencils begins on page 125.

uncut, mounted blocks face down on the print. Make sure the edges of the block fit exactly inside the drawn outlines. Press the block down so that the paper adheres to it and then carefully turn it and the paper over together and burnish all over with the spoon as before. This will transfer the printed image on to the new blank lino block so that it corresponds precisely with the position of the design on the key block. Fig. 70 shows this offset method.

Pull the paper away and leave the ink on this new block to dry. Take offsets in this way with a fresh print for each colour block.

Clean up the roller, the ink slab and the key block. If you particularly want to get on with cutting the second colour block you can dry the ink off by sprinkling some french chalk or talcum powder on it and giving it a shake. You will still be able to see the image but the ink won't smudge as your hand does the cutting. If you need to, outline the areas which are to be printed in the second colour on this second block before cutting. Some more complex types of design may also need an offset of the second colour on the uncut third block. If so, print it in a different colour

70 *Using the offset method to cut the second colour block.*

from the first offset, lining it up with the outlines of the edges in the same way to register the colours.

To print a design that is in more than one colour pin out the fabric plus a trial piece. If it is a repeating pattern, rather than a single image, measure and mark the repeat lines. If you have used tailor's chalk rather than threads for this you will need some more tailor's chalk in another colour to draw the registration marks. The chalk should have a sharp point – you can buy pencil-shaped tailor's chalk. As you make every print of the first colour remember to draw lightly around each corner of the block on to the fabric while the block is still in its printing position.

Print all the impressions that you require of the first colour. Clean up all the equipment that has wet ink on it. Leave the fabric pinned out even if you have to stop printing at this point. It's impossible to repin a flexible thing like a length of cloth into exactly the same position. Dry the roller and ink slab well so that no lingering white spirit or diluted ink will affect the next colour.

Roll out and print the second colour (and any further colours) by aligning the block with the chalked corners on the fabric at each print.

Lino block printing with fabric dye paste

As mentioned earlier in this chapter it is necessary to specially prepare the surface of a lino cut so that you can print it with fabric dye paste; it has to have an absorbent coating. Flocking powder and flocking mordant (which is the adhesive) are used to produce a velvety, felt-like surface, and can be bought from a craft supplier. At the same time, buy the solvent which is appropriate to the mordant (check what it is when you buy the mordant). This process does take some time – it is no good trying to cut corners and speed it up – but a properly flocked block should last and print well for a considerable time.

First cut the design on the lino in the usual way and mount it on a backing board. Roll out some of the mordant – you can use your printing roller and inking slab. Put the block in the centre of a large piece of newspaper. Any excess flocking powder can then be easily gathered up afterwards. Roll a thin even layer of mordant on to the block. Now sprinkle a generous amount of flocking powder through a sieve on to the block. The powder will adhere to the sticky surface. Place a sheet of card which is a little larger than the block on top of the flocked surface, then, on top of that a book. The whole thing must now be left to dry out for about twenty-four hours. Clean up the roller and slab.

After twenty-four hours have elapsed shake off any surplus powder and brush the flocked surface with a dry nail brush. Then you have to repeat the process, rolling up and sprinkling again to

Both the curtains and the cushions in the photograph overleaf were printed with a design of daffodils using a stencil cut from stiff paper. This technique, explained on page 125, could be used for making fabric to co-ordinate with existing curtains or upholstery, by picking out one motif and using it for the stencil design.

The little girl's apron has been printed using the Profilm silk screen method described on pages 152-155.

be sure the velvety layer is dense enough.

To apply fabric dye paste to a small flocked lino block you can use a felt or thin plastic sponge stamping pad as shown on page 120. However, to ensure that a larger flocked block picks up the dye paste evenly all over, a slightly more elaborate pad is recommended. To make this you need a piece of wood, blockboard or chipboard that is a little larger than your printing block.

Cut out three pieces of thick felt (carpet underlay is fine) or thick blanket the same size as the wood. Lay these on the piece of wood and stretch a piece of stout plastic over it all, securing it with drawing pins or staples on the underside of the wood. This gives a good resilient base which will last for ages. Then place another piece of felt blanket (the same size) on top of the pad. This is to be the dye reservoir. Paint an even, liberal layer of the dye paste on to this felt with a small decorator's brush. Fig. 71 shows how to make the stamping pad. The flocked block is then pressed face down on to the dye-soaked pad to pick up the colour. At first you may need to press it on to the pad several times to charge it fully.

Print the block using the mallet technique (page 111). When all the printing is finished you discard the dye-drenched piece of felt and wipe the plastic covering. Wash the block and the brush clean with water. Use a new piece of felt for the next printing session; adjust the size to be economical – a small piece of felt for a small block. Don't forget to heat-fix the dye when it's completely dry.

71 *A stamping pad is made of layers of felt laid over a board and wrapped in stout polythene. Another piece of felt is put on top to serve as the dye reservoir.*

71

Chapter 5
Stencil Printing

New ways of using ready-made stencils

Stencilling on fabric is an excellent way of getting professional looking results. The ready-made stencils available commercially from a stationers or a craft supply shop, can be used very ingeniously. You can stencil print a design on its own as an individual motif on, for example, a pocket, the ends of a long scarf or on table linen like napkins or a tea cosy. Or, by using the stencilled motif in repeat you can make an attractive border on sheets, pillow cases or garment hems: use an all-over repeat for a dress length. Good, clear lettering can be produced quickly using a bought stencil alphabet sheet.

For the best results on cloth use fabric dye paste and small pieces of synthetic sponge – one piece for each colour (you can just cut up a large sponge). Using a piece of sponge rather than a stencil brush makes it easier to control the amount of colour you apply. This you do by pressure; the harder you press, the stronger the colour. The table layout for stencil printing is as explained previously on page 82. You will also need some masking or freezer tape.

Doing the printing

Pin out the washed and ironed fabric together with a piece for trial printing. Slide a piece of paper inside any double-sided article to prevent the colour printing through. With short lengths of masking tape stick the stencil down in place on the cloth. Put a little dye paste into a saucer and dip the scrap of sponge into it. Dab it off on the edge of the saucer – if it is too heavily laden the dye will creep under the stencil. Gently but firmly press the sponge repeatedly all over the open sections of the stencil. Then carefully remove the stencil; the masking tape can be re-used for positioning the next print.

MARKING REPEATS. To print a stencil motif in repeat, mark with tailor's chalk the repeat divisions on the fabric (see page 98). With a sharp craft knife cut little x-shaped, double triangular holes in the solid background area of the stencil card to link up correctly with the repeat lines. Extend this background area with taped-on card if it is too narrow.

Bleach may be used to dye a pattern out of a coloured background. The jacket in the photograph overleaf was first dyed with a commercial dye. Then, following the instructions on page 164, the decorative borders and trim were painted on. Bleach craft works best on fabric that has been home-dyed.

In the same photograph, the T-shirt has been decorated with the picture of a pop-star using the method for transfer rubbing explained on page 162. This is an excellent fabric craft for children to practise; they can decorate their clothing with pictures of their favourite comic strip character or film hero.

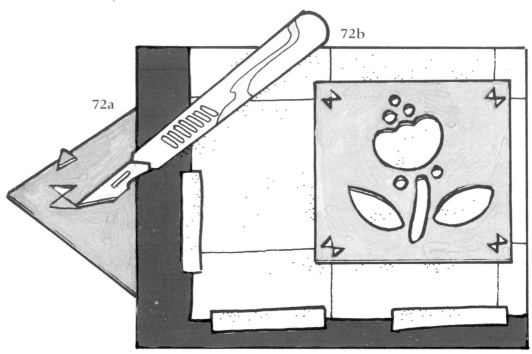

72a

72b

72a *Cut small triangles in the corners of a stencil to aid correct positioning.*

72b *Position the holes where the repeat lines intersect.*

To position the holes, find the points at which the repeat lines intersect and mark them on the stencil. Make two tiny cross cuts with a craft knife at each of these four corners and, with the point of the knife, lift out the little triangles of card (see fig. 72A). The fabric is marked out into the repeat divisions with lines of thread or tailor's chalk. As you lower the stencil on to the fabric you'll be able to look through the little holes and see the corner crosses on the cloth. You line the holes in the stencil up with them as shown in fig. 72B. Make sure you don't stencil through these holes by mistake.

If the motifs are placed quite close to one another it is advisable to print alternate ones, coming back to fill in the spaces when these first prints are dry. If you were to put the stencil down so that its surrounding border overlapped on to part of an existing still wet print, the dye could offset (print itself) on to the underside of the stencil. This dye impression could then easily be transferred to another part of the fabric without you realising it was happening. If, as with some bought stencils, there is a narrow border, it's a good idea to extend the border by taping on some extra paper edges. Then you can not sponge dye over the edges unintentionally.

In order to ensure that any letters or motifs are stencilled properly along a straight line, use the following method. Stick a length of masking tape on to the fabric, its upper edge representing the line along which you want the letters, etc. to be.

Now rule a pencil line on the stencil card exactly along the bottom of all the rows of letters, or at the base of a motif design, and continue it right out on either side to the edges of the card. Position each letter or motif for printing so that this ruled line links up on each side with the top edge of the masking tape. Either judge by eye the lateral spaces between the letters or motifs or delicately mark them in tailor's chalk before you start printing.

Often the letters on a stencil alphabet sheet are quite close to one another, so there is a danger of accidentally splodging some dye through, for example, both the A and the C spaces while you are stencilling a B. To avoid this, temporarily cover over the A and the C with pieces of masking tape as shown in fig. 73.

Similarly by masking out some areas, you can print a design in two colours. Stick the stencil down on to the fabric in the usual manner. Now mask out with sticky tape the parts of the design which are to be in the second colour. Sponge dye through the remaining open sections in the first colour. Let this dry, leaving the stencil fixed down on the material. Then peel off the bits of masking tape. Mask out all the areas already printed and proceed to sponge on the second colour. Then remove all the tape and the stencil to reveal a completed two colour design. Fig. 74 shows two-colour stencil printing.

After printing, sponge any dye off the stencil with water.

Making your own stencils

There is no need to confine fabric stencil decoration solely to

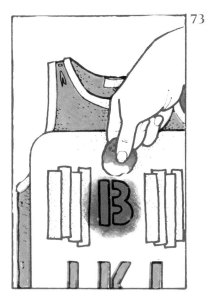

73 Cover adjacent letters on a stencil sheet with masking tape so that you print only the letter you want.

74 Use tape to mask out first and second colour areas when doing a two-colour stencil.

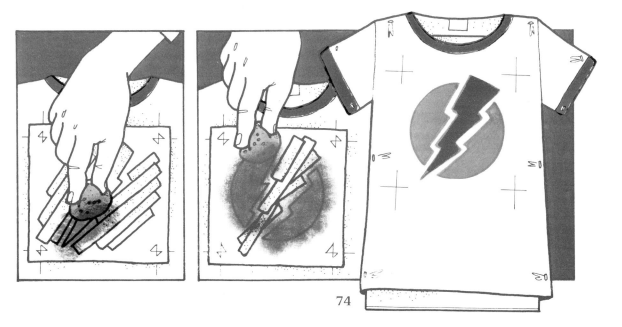

74

Left. *Fabric dye pastes are also known as fabric dye paints because they can be used for painting designs straight on to fabric.*

This is a good way to decorate ready-made soft furnishings for a co-ordinated decor. The design is first sketched on to the fabric in tailor's chalk and then painted. Alternatively, patterned fabrics can be picked out in a predominant colour.

For more on this technique turn to page 162.

Above. *A cheerful rainbow turned to a grey sky is sure to dispel any rain clouds on the horizon.*

You can make a similar design using a toothbrush, fabric dye paste, a piece of newspaper as a stencil to shape out the curves and the instructions on page 136 for spatter printing.

ready-made designs. Making your own stencils is a simple matter. You can organise and tailor a design to precisely suit a specific project.

The craft of stencilling on cloth has been practised in many different countries over the centuries. The Japanese developed it to a high degree of sophistication. In India stencilling was combined with hand-painting on fabric and several cultures used (and still do use) the stencil for resist-printed designs. In the nineteenth century, and particularly in the United States where at that time luxuries like costly patterned fabrics or carpets were not readily available, stencil designs were used extensively – not only on cloth but directly on to walls, furniture and floorboards. Stencil decorators would travel from house to house carrying out their craft.

THE MATERIAL AND EQUIPMENT. The stencil is cut in a special sort of thin card, or something similar, which will stand up to wet dye paste and washing without going soggy. There are several suitable materials on the market. An art shop will sell stencil paper (which is a heavy, brown, oiled paper) or thick acetate film. The latter has the advantage of being transparent and so it obviates the need for tracing.

You can prepare your own stencil material by giving some lightweight card or thick cartridge paper several coats of varnish. A liberal application of linseed oil followed by varnish makes a really long-lasting stencil. Recycled detergent or cereal packets are fine for this. Another method of making such card waterproof is, after you have cut out the design, to rub the edges of the holes with a candle, taking care not to tear the stencil.

Cut out the stencil shapes with either a very sharp scalpel type of craft knife or proper stencil cutters. These are little blades in different shapes made like pen nibs (see fig. 75). They will fit into a lino-cutter handle or an old-fashioned dip pen holder. (Straight lines should be cut against a steel ruler – a wooden or plastic one can very easily be cut by accident.) Also necessary is a suitable surface on which to cut – a piece of heavy card or a sheet of glass. Glass helps to achieve a good clean-edged cut, but it does tend to blunt the blades rather quickly.

Younger children should not use scalpels or stencil cutters as these tools are so sharp – they can cut out their stencil designs with small scissors. Remember when using scissors not to cut across the areas of card surrounding the shape to be stencilled. Rather, start off by pushing the scissors through the card in the centre of what will be an open space and then cut outwards towards the edges of that space.

75 *Stencil cutters and holder.*

75

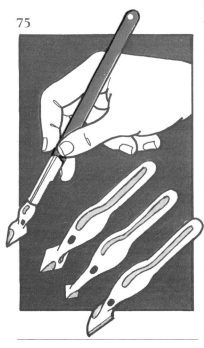

Working out your design

First make a rough drawing of your design idea. This could be
based on a geometric pattern, flower or leaf shapes, any sort of
pattern – but do not allow it to become fiddly because it will be
impossible to cut out successfully. Aim for a bold, chunky sort of
design. Study the rough drawing you have made to see if there are
any sections of the design which, when cut out as open shapes,
will become completely detached from the background. As an
example of this, look at fig. 76. The letter A cannot be cut out

simply as it stands; the whole of the upper triangular area will just
fall out. So some solution must be devised as to how to cut out an
instantly recognisable A shape, keeping the stencil still intact.
Strategically placed cardboard *ties* must be left in the design. This,
by the way, is what gives stencil lettering its own distinctive
style. Without the ties, which leave gaps when printed, it would
be quite ordinary lettering. Similarly a flower centre can't survive
on its own; it must be linked to the background by ties which can
conveniently define the petals, as in fig. 77.

The ties should not be too narrow because they may break
during the printing or cleaning processes. This is another reason
for keeping the design bold – it must be able to take quite
substantial gaps and yet still read visually as whatever it's
supposed to represent.

Another way of designing a stencil is to use a silhouette shape.
Here, although it may at first glance look like an easier approach,
the drawing of the outline of the shape must be extremely
accurate to convey the idea convincingly. Refer to the animal
shapes in fig. 78. There are no helpful visual props and hints
within the shapes, as with the traditional cut paper silhouette
portrait, the identification relies on the solid image which must be
really exact – otherwise, when printed, it will be a meaningless

76 *When cutting your own stencils,
think carefully about where to position
ties. Without them, the centre of the
letter A would fall away, and the shape
would be meaningless.*

77 *On this flower motif the ties are used to hold the flower centre in place and also to divide the petals.*

77

blob. You can prove this very graphically to yourself by tracing round an object in a photograph: you know what it is a realistic image of but the outside shape alone is quite insufficient for you to be able to identify it. The photograph in fig. 79 illustrates this.

Cutting the stencil

When you have sorted out the design the next step is to transfer it on to the stencil card.

First make a tracing of the design and tape it to the stencil card. Leave a generous border around the design, both for stength and to avoid printing over the edges by mistake. Slip some carbon paper under the tracing and, if you need to, a sheet of thin white paper between the carbon and the tracing paper to make the tracing more clearly visible. (There is no need, as with a lino cut, to reverse the design. Things come out the same way round in stencilling.) Re-draw accurately over the lines with a hard pencil to make the carbon image on the card. Place the card on the cutting surface and carefully cut round each shape and remove it. Be especially careful each time you cut up to a tie.

If you are using transparent acetate film for your stencil material you can place it straight on top of the drawn design, secure it with tape and proceed to cut it out. This will, however, damage the drawing so you may prefer to make a tracing and use that as your cutting guide.

New ideas for printing

The printing process is basically the same as described in the

78

79a

79b

78 *The shape you choose for your stencil must be instantly recognisable, as these shapes shown here.*

79a *The photograph of a swan is easily identified as a swan because of the detail. But try to turn the silhouette into a stencil (79b) and it could be anything.*

section on ready-made stencils, but here are some new avenues to explore. Experiment with shading effects by varying the pressure on the dye-charged sponge. Some intriguing three dimensional effects are possible. Fig. 80 shows the use of this technique.

80 *Two ways of applying colour to a stencil design to give a shaded effect.*

Try heavy colour in the centre of a shape fading out towards the outer edges. Then print the reverse of this with strongly defined edges and a lighter centre. Graduate the colour from light to dark across a shape too. The colonial American stencil artists were masters of this sort of thing, especially on furniture decoration. You can also vary the textural quality of the print by using a coarser sponge or a ball of crumpled paper or cloth (try different kinds) to print with.

It is also possible to use more than one colour within stencilled shapes by gradually merging one into another. Of course, you must bear in mind what sort of colour the two will produce where they actually meet.

Use a fresh piece of sponge for each colour, keeping each to its own colour throughout the printing. Don't overwork this sort of thing, because it will lose its freshness and the colours will become turgid.

Try printing your design in two (or more) separate colours in the way described on page 125. If yours is a large scale design – this is quite feasible with stencilling – cover the gaps you are not printing with paper attached by masking tape.

More complicated multicoloured designs can be printed by separating the colours and making a stencil for each colour. Here you can introduce the over-printing technique of colour on colour. As with other forms of colour printing, when you are first working out the coloured design on paper, make as much use as you can of clever combinations of the colours. Don't forget that a shaded colour can overprint a solid colour; differently coloured

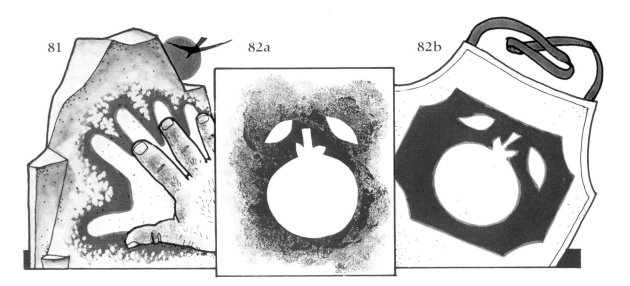

textures can be combined and so can different solid colours. The stencil for each individual colour is registered with the previous printed colour by using the X-cut technique explained on page 124. These registration holes can, where applicable, double as the guide to the placing of the stencils in a multi-coloured repeating pattern.

If your project does not have repeating pattern but requires a single print only – perhaps for a cushion cover – the registration of the colours is done by first placing the stencil for the first colour to be printed in its correct position on the fabric. Fix it to the cloth with tape as usual. Now lightly chalk through the pairs of X-cut registration holes on to the cloth. Print the first colour and lift the stencil away. Align the stencil for the next colour by eye with the chalk marks in the four corners. Print and repeat the process for any subsequent colours. Allow time between colours for the dye to dry off a little to avoid possible smudging or offsetting. There is no need to wait for it to be bone dry, just dry enough not to lift off on to your finger.

Should a stencil break (the ties are always vulnerable) it is a simple job to mend it by sticking, on the upper face, a piece of masking tape cut to the appropriate shape over the join. If you were to stick it on the underside the additional thickness would raise the stencil and colour could flow under.

Negative stencil designs

So far, only positive stencil printing (printing through a hole or a complicated set of holes) has been considered. Try out the negative stencil idea too where you apply colour around the

81 Early man used his hand as a negative stencil, spraying the colour around it.

82a The pieces cut from a positive stencil can be used as a negative stencil.
82b A frame of solid colour around a negative stencil helps to contain the design.

shape, leaving the shape itself the colour of the fabric. This is just like the prehistoric cave man's idea of painting round his hand (see fig. 81). You can use the pieces cut from a normal, positive type of stencil as templates to develop an interesting design (see fig. 82A). The dye colour can be gradually faded away from the negative image or you can enclose the template within some sort of frame as in fig. 82B. Use a weight or double-sided tape to hold the template in position when you print.

More refined ties

The Japanese, with typical exquisite dexterity, developed a technique of making very elaborate and delicate stencils in which the ties were replaced by threads of silk or human hair. Fig. 83 shows an example of this very delicate type of stencil. This meant that the negative motifs could be apparently suspended in areas of colour. The traditional technique was to cut out two identical stencils and stick one to the other with threads or hairs sandwiched inbetween. A cruder version of this, more suited to the heavy-handed Westerner, is to attach one negative shape to another, or to the surrounding frame, with thin threads stuck to the stencil by masking tape, as shown in fig. 84. With careful printing you can delicately sponge dye colour under the threads so that their presence is not visible on the finished print. Obviously you must be very careful when cleaning such a stencil.

The starch paste referred to in Chapter 3 can be used very effectively with positive or negative stencils. Apply the paste with care using a sponge, depositing as thick a layer of paste on the

83 *An example of a Japanese stencil, where the ties are replaced by hairs.*

84 *Use the Japanese idea to suspend a stencilled design in an area of solid colour.*

83   **84**

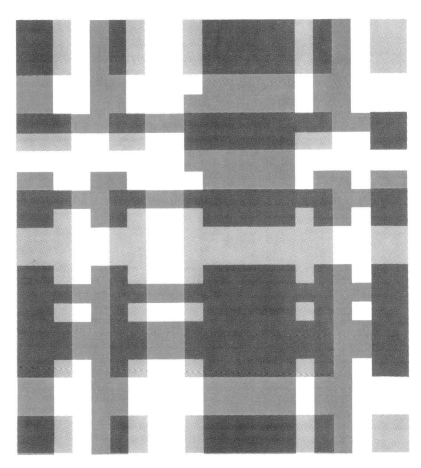

85

cloth as you can without causing splodges. Clean the stencils quickly after printing.

SOME VERY EASY STENCILLING TECHNIQUES. Consider the negative template idea. Instead of cutting out a shape, look out some objects whose shape could be used for a stencil. The object must, of course, be flat. Leaves are an ideal example – just weight down the leaf in position on the fabric and apply colour around it.

For an extremely simple stencil-type of technique, use masking tape on its own. This will confine you solely to straight lines but some interesting designs based on squares, rectangles and triangles can be developed. Pin the fabric out as usual and stick pieces of masking tape directly on to it to cover all the areas you wish to protect from the dye paste. Apply the colour and, when it is sufficiently dry, peel off the tape. More tape can be stuck down in a new arrangement and another application of dye made. Fig. 85 shows a cheerful tartan effect made in this way.

Spray printing with stencils

Spraying, as opposed to sponging, fabric dye paste through a
stencil can produce a range of effects from a crisp, clear-cut design
to a freckled look or a delicately graduated, misty image. You can
use a bought or do-it-yourself stencil, with either a positive or
negative design or a combination of the two. Over-spraying one
colour on another is particularly attractive.

There are four methods of spraying. The first, which is very
simple, employs an old toothbrush; the second a mouth-blown
diffuser. This (which you can buy from an artists' supplier) is a
small instrument used primarily for sending a spray of fixative on
to a drawing done in charcoal or some other similar medium which
would otherwise smudge. An alternative to this is the type of re-
fillable spray used for casting a fine mist of water over indoor
plants. Then there is the more professional air-brush which you
can buy from a model shop. This, providing you clean out the
container and nozzle thoroughly, can be used for spraying all sorts
of liquids – enamel paints, varnishes, water-based paints as well as
fabric dye paste. The colour is expelled through an adjustable
nozzle under pressure from a small, replaceable cylinder of
compressed air. Fig. 86 shows these four tools.

Whichever method you are using, the preparation is the
same. Pin out the fabric and a trial piece and mark out the
repeating lines if these are required for your project. Position the
stencil or stencils and, with lots of newspaper, cover the
surrounding fabric, table and any other surfaces that need to be

86 *Four tools which may be used for
spray printing stencils: from left to right,
a mouth-blown diffuser; an old
toothbrush; a plant spray; an air brush
with a cylinder of compressed air.*

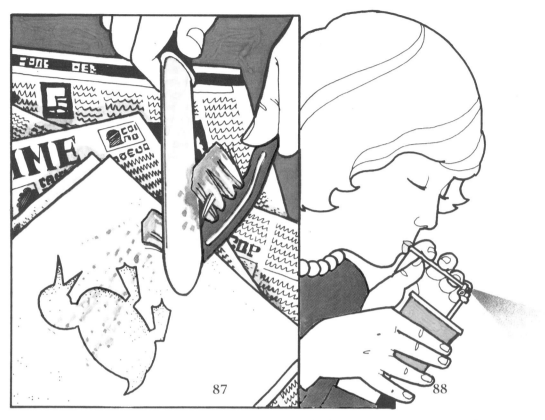

protected. Sprayed dye can travel over a surprisingly large area –
including the carpet. Either weight or tape the stencils down.

For the toothbrush approach first do a test spatter (the word
spatter eloquently describes the spotty quality of this technique)
using the dye paste as it comes straight from the jar; it may be
just the right consistency. To do the spattering, dip the
toothbrush in the dye and, holding it with the brush part facing
upwards, scrape the blade of an old dinner knife across the
bristles towards you as shown in fig. 87. A spatter of colour will
shoot on to the fabric. If the dye is too thick, put some in a small
shallow container and thin it with a little water.

For the diffuser to work successfully it will be necessary to thin
the dye paste a little more than for toothbrush spattering. This
means that the strength of the colour will be reduced, but delicate
sprayed colours look very good and lovely subtle colour
combinations are possible. Before you start, always make sure you
mix up enough of each colour to complete your project so that you
don't have to rush and mix more dye towards the end. Put the
fairly liquid dye in a small container like a yoghurt pot. Place the
upright tube of the diffuser in the liquid, the other tube in your

87 *Scrape a knife over the bristles of a toothbrush to give a spattered effect to a stencil design.*

88 *To use a mouth-blown diffuser, place one end of the tube in the dye and blow through the other end. The current of air draws up the dye and sprays it over the desired area.*

mouth – and blow (see fig. 88). The resulting sprayed effect is less freckled than that done with a toothbrush.

You will need a runny mixture in the gardening spray too. Fill the container and take aim. When you have finished, be meticulous in the washing out of both container and spray section (think of your plants).

An airbrush will be supplied with adequate instructions on how to fill the container, how to connect it to the cylinder and how to actually operate it. It is, incidentally, very easy and great fun. The manufacturers suggest that the consistency of the paint, dye, and so on, should be like milk. Extremely subtle graduating effects are obtainable with this instrument. Make sure you clean up the nozzle and dye container thoroughly after work.

All cloth stencilled with fabric dye paste will need to be fixed according to manufacturer's instructions when it has dried out completely.

Chapter 6
Screen Printing

The silk screen process

The silk screen is a direct development of the Japanese stencil (see page 134) which used linking hairs or threads in its construction: by greatly increasing the number of crisscrossing threads and arranging them closer together the result is – cloth. Fine silk mesh (hence the name silk screen) was originally used. The silk was stretched on to a rectangular wooden frame and the design, in stencil form, was attached to the taut fabric surface. Exactly the same principle applies today but some of the materials used have changed. For instance pure silk, nowadays, would be prohibitively expensive. Silk screen printing is widely used commercially on fabric, paper and many other surfaces. Despite this it is a technique that can be enjoyed by a craftsman at home or in school. The various ways of making the stencil which is attached to the silk screen enable you to create intricate designs or conversely, bold, large scale ones with big areas of solid flat colour. Most other hand printing techniques make big designs a problem to handle. So this printing method is extremely adaptable and may be used equally well on textiles for clothing or home items.

When you sponge dye on to an ordinary stencil the colour goes through the holes only. In silk screen printing you push the colour with a squeegee across the fabric surface of the screen as shown in fig. 89. This forces it through any areas of blank screen fabric (the equivalent of the holes in a stencil) on to whatever you are printing, but it cannot get through any areas which are covered or masked.

THE EQUIPMENT. The basic essentials are a silk screen frame, some suitable fine fabric with which to cover it, and a squeegee. Screens and squeegees can be bought ready-made from some art and craft shops or from a silk screen supplier. However, it is not at all difficult, and it is cheaper, to make your own. The silk screen itself can be used many times over to print designs in different sizes. One stencil is removed and replaced by another. You may be printing a single decoration, as on the child's apron shown on page 118, or repeating the print for an all-over design, so it is wise to consider carefully the size of the screen frame. Some which are sold in screen printing kits are very tiny, therefore their use is clearly limited. They are, however, quite suitable for children. It is not necessary for the design always to fill the screen completely. A portion only of the printing area need be used for a small project so, obviously, a reasonably large-size frame gives you much more scope than a little one. A useful size for printing at home is 70cm × 45cm (28in × 18in) on the *inside* measurements. The design of daffodils in the photograph (page 118) measures 50cm × 40cm (20in × 16in). The inside dimensions of the frame must be larger than the design being printed. You need an extra 10cm (4in) at both the top and the bottom end of the screen to act as a dye reservoir and an extra 2.5cm (1in) along wach side.

There may be occasions when you wish to print on paper – publicity for a local event for example. A screen the size recommended here could be used to produce posters or a large number of programme covers, greeting cards etc. You can put several repeats of a design on to one screen so that every time you make one print you get, for example, a batch of programme covers. This is a good, quick method if you're producing in quantity.

Making a silk screen

The frame is constructed out of 40mm × 40mm ($1\frac{1}{2}$in × $1\frac{1}{2}$in) planed softwood: you will need 2.5 mctres (8ft). Make sure it is free of large knots and is not warped. Experienced carpenters will no doubt have their own favourite ways of making a rectangular frame, but for novices the following method is simple and straightforward.

Saw the wood up into two 78cm (31in) lengths and two 45cm (18in) lengths. Make each corner joint by first applying woodworking glue and then hammering in corrugated fasteners as shown in fig. 90. Be sure the frame lies absolutely flat on the table when it is finished. Sandpaper the whole thing.

Several different fabrics are used in screen making but terylene is recommended, and can be purchased from a screen printing supplier. A medium gauge mesh is suitable for work such as shown in the photographs. Other fabrics, for example nylon and cotton organdie, can be used but they are not as tough and durable as terylene. Nylon has the disadvantage of going baggy when wet, as it will be when covered in dye paste, and cotton organdie tears rather too easily.

Cut out a rectangle of terylene which is 10cm (4in) longer and 10cm (4in) wider than the *outside* dimensions of the frame. For our example it will be 88cm × 55cm (36in × 22in). Lay the mesh over the frame so that an equal amount drapes over each side. Now attach the fabric to the sides of the screen, turning each edge

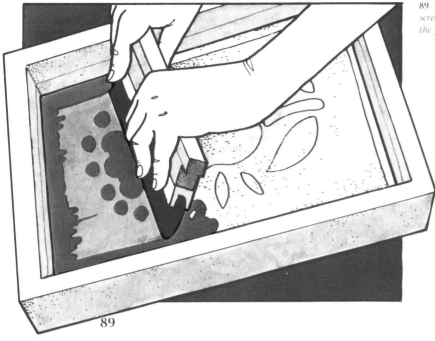

89 *When using a squeegee on a silk screen, pull the squeegee towards you on the first stroke.*

under once to make a 2.5cm (1in) turning: the double fabric is stronger when you are stretching it. You will find that a heavy-duty staple gun is best for attaching the mesh to the frame. Insert the staples vertically along the sides, not horizontally; there is greater strength this way. Drawing pins are a suitable alternative to staples.

Start by fixing the mesh to the centre of one of the long sides. Insert two or three staples (or drawing pins) about 15mm ($\frac{1}{2}$in) apart. Then, grasping the double fabric firmly between your thumb and the side of your first finger, pull it hard across to the other side and secure it in the same way at the opposite central point. Fix it similarly in the middle of each of the shorter sides. Now work your way gradually out towards the corners, alternating sides and pulling firmly each time. Leave about 5cm (2in) of loose fabric sticking out at each corner. Turn each corner under neatly as you would when wrapping a parcel. Secure the corners well, placing the staple as shown in fig. 91.

Making a squeegee
The squeegee is made to fit the screen frame, and its length should be 2.5cm (1in) less than the inside width measurement of the screen. In our example the squeegee should be 42.5cm (17in) long.

From a screen printing supplier you can buy either a ready-

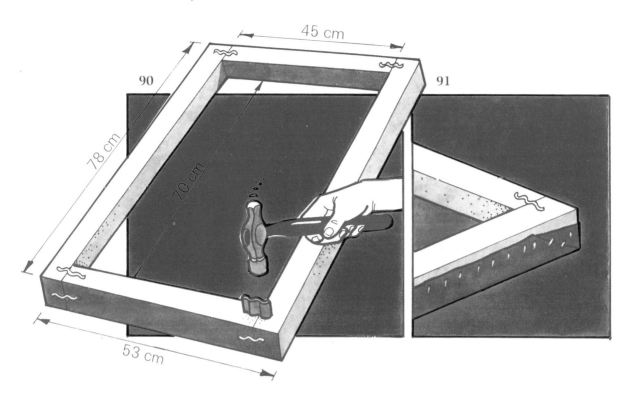

45 cm

90

91

78 cm

70 cm

53 cm

90 *Making a silk screen frame: use corrugated fasteners to fix the corner joints.*

91 *Stretch the mesh over the frame and secure it with staples placed horizontally.*

made squeegee or the appropriate length of squeegee rubber to make your own. Squeegee rubber comes in either rectangular or pointed form. The pointed type of rubber strip is best for printing on cloth. If·the rubber is sold only in set lengths and you are obliged to buy more than you need, keep the little offcut as it is useful for making a mini-squeegee – handy for very small prints.

To make a large sturdy squeegee you will require a piece of 5cm × 2cm (2in × $\frac{3}{4}$in) wood which is 10cm (4in) longer than the squeegee (piece B), and some U-section aluminium channel, also the squeegee length. You must be able to push the square end of the rubber inside the channel – and it should be a tight fit.

Screw or nail piece B to one of the narrow edges of piece A as shown in fig. 92A, so that 5cm (2in) protrudes on either side.

Now drill holes and screw the channel to the other narrow edge of piece A as shown in fig. 92B. Apply a strong glue suitable for rubber and metal to the inside of the channel and force the rubber into the channel (fig. 92C). A smear of grease or soap will make this easier.

Stand the squeegee upright on its rubber blade on a perfectly flat surface and hammer along the top edge to make sure the rubber strip slides home and that the blade edge is straight. The handle protruding on either side makes the squeegee remain upright or near vertical in the screen when it's not actually being used. Without it, it is very much inclined to keel over into the pool of dye which is messy and maddening. Some bought squeegees do not have this refinement, and it is well worth adding even just a large nail hammered into each end to serve as rudimentary handles.

For a small screen you can make a squeegee from a piece of hardboard, handles included, as shown in fig. 93. The blade of a squeegee, whether pointed or square in section, or made of hardboard or rubber, must be sharp, that is, not irregular or rounded. To achieve this nail a strip of sandpaper to the bench or to a piece of wood and repeatedly slide the blade along it. Hold a square edge squeegee upright, a pointed edge one at the appropriate angle. New rubber squeegees do not need this treatment but it is a useful tip for when they become worn. If you drill a hole through one end you can store the squeegee by

92 *Making a squeegee with a rubber blade.*

93 *A basic squeegee made simply from a piece of hardboard.*

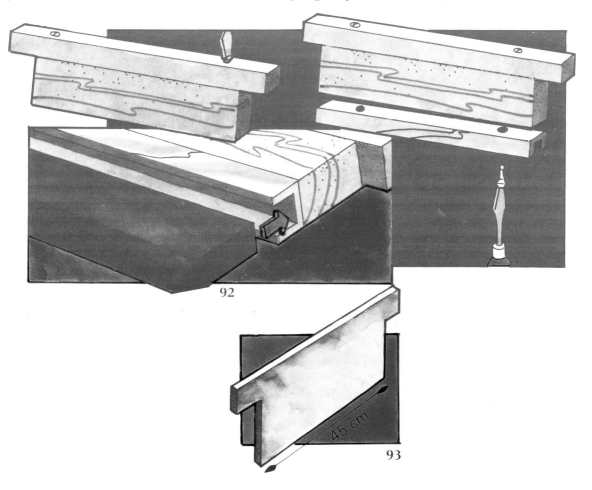

92

93

hanging it on a nail, helping to prevent possible damage to the precious blade. Varnishing a hardboard squeegee will prolong its life.

The printing table

If you intend to confine your silk screening to single prints in one colour, as, for example a one colour design on a carryall or a tea towel, you can work on a table arranged as previously outlined on page 82. Here you pin out the fabric and you can position by eye or by chalking the outside corners of the screen on to the cloth. Then you lower the screen into these chalk marks (However, the very essence of printing is the facility to repeat an image, and you will surely want to experiment both with patterns in repeat and the introduction of additional colours. For these two activities you need a sound registration system to make sure everything fits together as it should, and this is detailed later.)

Your printing table must be firm and preferably quite long. To print a screen of the size used here with outside dimensions of 78cm × 53cm (32in × 22in), the table should be at least 75cm (30in) wide. Altogether you have 28cm (11in) of non-printing depth of the screen. This is made up by the thickness of the wooden frame (40mm [2in] at each end) and 10cm (4in) at each end inside the frame which serve as the dye reservoirs. Thus, you can allow the screen frame to overlap the table a little, bearing in mind that the registration system will occupy 3cm (1¼in) or so of the width of the table.

The table should preferably be long so that you can place print alongside print as many times as possible. Having completed a table length you then move the cloth on, draping it to allow it to dry and proceed to print the next table length. If you intend to use silk screen printing extensively (this could apply to a school, for instance) it is worthwhile considering making a special tabletop out of blockboard or chipboard. Fix several wooden blocks to the underside of the new top so that when you lower it, it will fit snugly on to the original tabletop. If you are thinking of printing 90cm (36in) wide fabrics with all-over designs, the special tabletop should be 120cm (47in) wide and as long as both the supporting table and the room can accommodate. When not in use the top could be stored vertically, face to the wall. This will avoid accidental damage to the special covering.

Whether you are operating on a stout kitchen table or on a specially made printing tabletop, the table covering for silk screening is the same. First cover the table with a thick blanket or a piece of carpet underfelt. This should be stretched taut and wrinkle-free, and each edge secured to the underside of the tabletop with staples or drawing pins. Stretch a sheet of heavy plastic over the felt and fasten in the same way. For a more professional screen printing surface use rubber sheeting, for example, Neoprene, instead of plastic.

Making the first print

Having assembled the basic equipment, start by doing a design in one colour. This will give you the experience of putting the design stencil on to the screen in the simplest way and going through the printing procedure. Different forms of screen stencil, extra colours, designs in repeat and registration will be explained later, but it is important to get the feel of the medium as soon as possible.

Try a single colour square-shaped design which you could use for a headscarf, a cushion cover or a small tablecloth. Think up an interesting dye colour over coloured cloth combination. For a tablecloth arrange the print so that there is an ample border of plain unprinted cloth all round it – otherwise it will be a very small tablecloth. A screen of the size recommended will print a square design up to 40cm (16in) square.

In addition to the fabric being printed, you will need some 5cm (2in) wide brown paper gumstrip, shellac varnish (which is known as knotting, and is available from hardware stores) some thin plain paper, preferably unprinted newsprint, and a piece of scrap fabric to test print before you commit your precious material and fabric dye paste (printing a silk screen requires more dye than printing a small block). Refer to page 80 for information on the pigment and binder version of fabric dye paste.

It is a good plan to have an old sheet or a length of obsolete curtaining to use for test printing. It can be used over and over again and washed thoroughly to soften it when it becomes heavily dye-laden, and as the dye will not have been fixed, much of it will wash out. It is very important to do a test print or two before starting on your finished item, in order to check that there is nothing wrong with the screen.

The printed dye will go right through some very fine fabrics such as cotton cheesecloth or very light silk. This could cause problems on a non-absorbent plastic or rubber surfaced table, so here it is advisable to stretch a length of cheap calico along the whole length of the table. This is called the backcloth and is left in place to absorb excess dye when you print the lightweight fabric which is laid on top of it. Staple or pin it to the underside of the table. As with the test-print piece the backcloth can be laundered as required.

MASKING THE SCREEN. The elementary form of screen stencil you are going to start with is made simply out of paper. First, though,

94 *Sealing the frame and mesh with strips of gummed paper.*

95 *Building the dye reservoir on the outside of the screen.*

you must mask the edges of the screen. This has to be done whichever type of stencil you are going to use. It makes both a permanent seal around the screen (to stop any dye squidging out) and forms the dye reservoir.

Cut four lengths of gumstrip to fit the inner edges of the screen. Fold each piece lengthwise and wet the gummed side thoroughly with a damp sponge (more pleasant than licking it). Inside the

94

95

frame, position each length along the right angle between the wood and the mesh (see fig. 94). Push the gumstrip down with a soft dry rag to make sure it is sticking properly. Turn the screen over and stick lengths of gumstrip over all the inner edges of the frame, half on the wood, half on the mesh. Put further strips around the outside of these too. Build up the dye reservoir area by overlapping strips on the back of the screen at either end. These reservoirs should each measure 10cm (4in) in from the inner edge of the screen. See fig. 95.

Allow all the damp gumstrip to dry out completely, then coat it all, on both sides of the screen, with knotting. Be careful to avoid spilling or splashing any knotting on to the open mesh. Let the varnish dry with the screen laid flat but supported on pencils under each corner to prevent it sticking to the table. Clean the brush in methylated spirit.

Stretch the washed and ironed final fabric and the test piece over the table. If you are using a backcloth pin the cloth to it with the pinning technique shown on page 82. Pin into the backcloth only, NOT through the table covering. If there is no backcloth, stretch and fasten the fabric to the table top with masking tape.

MAKING A STENCIL. With the paper stencil method you create the design very much as you print it, as opposed to preparing the screen beforehand. First cut some newsprint strips and attach them to the back of the screen with short pieces of gumstrip so that the inner edges of the newsprint strips define a square of open mesh which is the size of your design.

To visualise the design, chalk a square of the same size on to the test fabric. On this make an arrangement of shapes cut and torn out of newsprint. Juggle them around until you like the look of it. The cloth background represents the printed parts of the design, the newsprint those sections which will be masked out and therefore unprinted (see fig. 96).

Play around with torn cloud shapes, squares, rectangles, stripes, some with irregular torn edges, some crisply cut; crisscross one or two to enclose new coloured (printed) shapes. Don't overlap more than two pieces, though. When you like the arrangement gently lower the screen, mesh side down, on to the paper layout. Look through the open mesh so that you can line up the edges of the square on the screen with that on the table.

GETTING READY TO PRINT. The printing process, especially if you are using a large screen, is much easier if someone else helps you. Your assistant stands on the other side of the table and holds the screen steady by its outer edges. If you have to print alone use two G-clamps to hold the screen firmly to the table. Place the

96 *For the first silk screen experiments,
make a design from paper shapes applied
directly to the screen.*

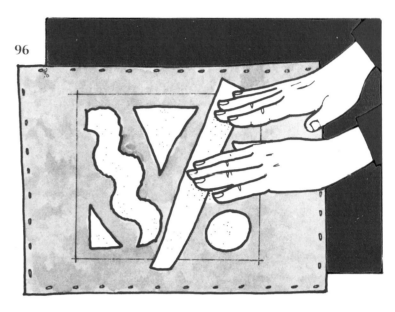

96

squeegee upright at the end of the screen furthest away from you
as shown in fig. 97. Leave a little gap between it and the screen
wall. All along this gap pour a line of well-mixed dye paste; be
generous and make the line about 5cm (2in) or so wide.

Now grasp the squeegee firmly with one hand on each end of it
and slope it slightly in your direction. Pull it firmly across the
screen. Pull carefully and steadily towards you, right up to the
end of the screen, maintaining even pressure all the time. Do not
perform this action too swiftly or with so much gusto that the
squeegee meets the end wall of the screen with a resounding
smack, covering everything, including your face and clothing
with dye.

Repeat the stroke, this time pushing the squeegee away from
you, back to the far end of the screen, at a slight slope in that
direction. Printing this way round is more difficult so, if you have
one, let your assistant print the return strokes.

Prop the squeegee upright in the screen so that it holds the dye
behind it. If you're using G-clamps, remove them now. At first,
hold the right-hand edge of the screen down on to the fabric and
gently lift from the left-hand side, peeling the screen face away
from the table as shown in fig. 98. This lifting technique avoids
smudging and displacing the fabric, which, although it is fastened
to the table, will try to come up with the screen.

Put the screen down on a convenient flat surface, supporting
the end without the squeegee on a strip of wood. Do not lay it flat
down on a table.

The paper shapes will be stuck firmly to the underside of the

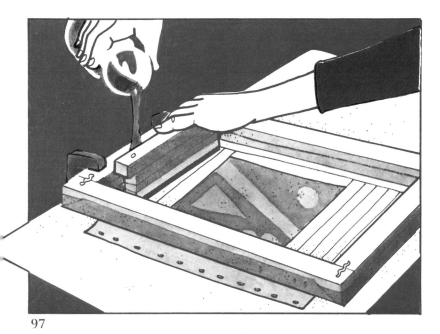

97 *Holding the squeegee upright, pour dye into the reservoir.*

97

98 *To avoid smudging the fabric lift the screen from left to right as though opening a door.*

98

screen with dye. You can reprint this design a number of times, replenishing the dye as it is used up. It now becomes evident that if you were to use more than two layers of paper in your arrangement they would not adhere properly.

Making test prints (whatever type of screen stencil is in use) on fabric rather than paper is recommended. Dye paste, being rather liquid and not viscous, is not really suitable for printing on paper, and could easily splodge under the stencil. Such errors are a bit tricky to correct on the screen (you remove them carefully with a cloth), particularly on a paper stencil. Also, fabric absorbs the dye more than paper and gives a truer test result.

If you want to print another paper stencil design in the same colour, first peel off all the bits of the old design. Preserve the outer border unless it is falling apart and needs replacing. Now make a print on to the test fabric through the plain mesh to clear away any evidence of the former design. This, by the way, is a useful way of printing a plain area of solid, flat colour. Devise a new design on the test fabric and proceed as before. Ready-made paper shapes could be employed in such a design. Look out for interesting stickers, stars, arrows, dots, etc., or sections of paper decorations and doilies. Things like leaves (real ones) can be used too. For a more complex version of paper stencil, cut a design from newsprint with a craft knife. Arrange the pieces on the test fabric and take a print to fix them all to the back of the screen. Then proceed to print as many impressions as you require.

CLEANING UP. Remove all the newsprint from the screen. The cleaning up process, which should be carried out as soon as you finish printing, is the same for all types of screen stencil. Never let the dye dry in the screen or on the squeegee as it is extremely difficult to remove. In dire cases use paint stripper but do try to avoid this.

Put the screen on some newspapers. With a palette knife or blunt dinner knife scrape as much dye as you can back into the pot. Scrape and wipe the squeegee too. Ideally use a cold water spray or hose to cleanse the screen. If circumstances do not permit this, sponge the screen and squeeze thoroughly and repeatedly with cold water. Then wash both screen and squeegee with detergent and warm water, rinse and allow to dry.

Other forms of screen stencil
DIRECT PAINTING. The direct painting method of making a screen stencil means painting the sections to be masked (unprinted) straight on to the screen mesh. You must use a coating which will not be affected by the water in the dye paste: knotting (shellac or varnish) is suitable.

To make sure the screen mesh is free of grease, so that the knotting will adhere properly, first wash it with detergent and hot water. Rinse and dry it well. (A hand-held hair dryer is often very useful in silk screen printing.) Even a new screen needs cleaning first.

If it is not done already, mask the screen edges and the dye reservoirs with gumstrip as previously explained. Varnish over the dry gumstrip with knotting.

Place the screen with the mesh lying over your design. In pencil, trace the design on to the mesh. Now turn the screen over, and on the back paint knotting over all the parts that are not to be printed. Use a watercolour brush for the finely defined sections and a small decorator's brush for broad areas.

Keep the screen horizontal as you do this to avoid dribbles of knotting running across any open mesh areas. Let the first coat dry and then go over it once again. Check the screen against the light to see if there are any pinholes – those are tiny dots left open when they should have been filled in with knotting. Touch in any pinholes, let the knotting dry completely and the screen is ready to use. Clean up your brushes with methylated spirit.

GREASE RESIST. The grease resist stencil method sounds complicated but in certain aspects it is the most straightforward way of putting an image on to a screen. With direct painting you work in a negative fashion, painting all round the shapes you want to print. With grease resist you paint or draw the image just as it will appear when printed.

You will need knotting and a lithographic drawing ink called *tusche* (lithography is another type of printing) and either a tusche crayon or an ordinary wax crayon. These lithographic materials are stocked by some artist's suppliers or screen printing or lithographic suppliers.

First clean the screen with hot water and detergent. Trace your design on to the screen or, alternatively, work freely, painting or drawing staight away with the tusche or crayon. Apply the tusche liberally. If you are using a wax crayon make sure you deposit plenty of wax on the mesh.

You can introduce drawn texturing with the crayon or a dryish brush. Try laying the screen over textured material corrugated cardboard, etc., to make a crayon rubbing (see fig. 99). Do not use anything with a sharp surface which could puncture the mesh. Remember you are creating the design as it will appear when printed.

When it is dry paint the entire screen, right across the tusche or waxed areas and the open mesh background, with two coats of knotting. The grease in the tusche will resist the knotting. When

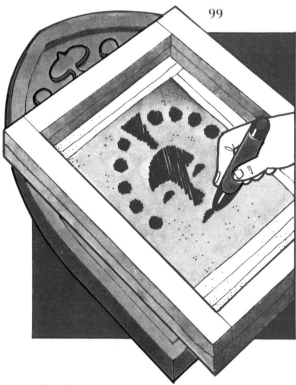

99

100

99 *Introduce drawn texturing with a wax crayon by placing the screen over a raised surface and rubbing over with the crayon.*

100 *Wash away the drawn areas with white spirit. This leaves the printing areas surrounded by non-printing areas masked out with knotting.*

the knotting has dried wash warm water over the screen. This will loosen the tusche which will start to lift off. Help it and the wax crayoning along with some white spirit. Soon you will have a clear image in open mesh with all the non-printing areas masked out with knotting as shown in fig. 100.

When you have finished printing a design where knotting has been used soak the screen in methylated spirit to loosen and remove the varnish. Do this on a pad of newspapers. The screen may then be used for a new design.

Profilm

Profilm is a material for making a long lasting screen stencil. It is a paper with a special coating over a transparent backing. With a craft knife or scalpel, the areas of the design which are to be printed are cut out of the coating film, leaving the backing intact.

This means you can cut out much more involved designs than with a paper stencil because everything is held together by the backing. You can buy Profilm from some art shops or from a screen printing supplier.

De-grease the screen first by washing it well in detergent and hot water.

Draw your design on paper and then tape it to a suitable cutting surface. Securely tape the piece of Profilm, shiny side uppermost over the drawing. The Profilm should be about 5cm (2in) larger all round than the design. You will be able to see the design through the Profilm. Carefully cut around each section that is to be printed. (See fig. 101.) You must try to cut through the coating only, not through the backing sheet. Peel the cut out pieces away from the backing and discard them. When you have cut out all the parts which are to print, remove the Profilm from the cutting surface.

The heat from an iron is used to melt the Profilm coating on to the screen mesh. Cover the table with an uncreased blanket and then an old sheet. Lay the Profilm, shiny side up, on the sheet. Place the screen, mesh side down, on the Profilm; make sure it's absolutely flat. Put a piece of thin, unprinted paper inside the screen; you iron through this. Use a cool iron, working your way carefully over the whole of the inside of the screen. Do not use a steam iron for this. The coating will gradually melt, lifting away from its paper backing and adhering to the underside of the screen. As this happens the Profilm will go darker. When it is evenly dark all over, turn the screen over and very delicately peel away the paper backing. If some areas resist, re-iron them. Stick gumstrip over any open mesh areas around the screen between the edges of the Profilm and the gumstrip masking. The screen can now be used for any printing medium that *does not* contain water, such as the silk screen ink used for printing posters.

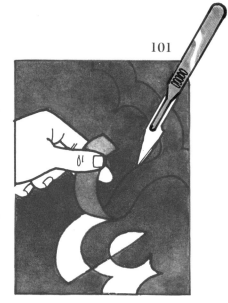

101

101 *When using Profilm carefully cut out the areas that are to print with a scalpel.*

PREPARING PROFILM FOR FABRIC DYE PASTE. If you wish to use fabric dye paste, the Profilm stencil must be specially treated to protect it from the water in the dye paste. This is done by applying varnish to the stencil and is not as difficult as it may at first sound. You will need some polyurethane varnish, knotting, white spirit, methylated spirit, a decorator's brush and a few soft clean rags. Work in a well-ventilated room away from naked flames.

Brush polyurethane varnish all over the inside of the screen – over the Profilmed parts and the open mesh. Put a little white spirit on a rag and, holding the screen upright, rub the outside of the screen. This removes the varnish from the open mesh parts as white spirit is the solvent for polyurethane varnish. Change the rags as they become impregnated with diluted varnish, using a drier cloth towards the end. Check the screen against the light to see if there is any varnish left on the open mesh. If it is all clear stand the screen upright and leave to dry.

When the application of varnish on the inside of the screen is absolutely dry you have to repeat the procedure on the other side, painting the outside and rubbing through from the inside. Use knotting for this second varnishing. Rub the open mesh parts clean with methylated spirit on a cloth. (Methylated spirit is the solvent for knotting.) Do not forget to check the screen against the light again. Leave it flat to dry. You now have a very durable silk screen, reinforced on both sides and fine for printing many times over.

Such a stencil can be removed when you have finished printing the design, though the procedure is somewhat tedious. A proprietary paint stripper which specifies that it will remove polyurethane should be applied to the polyurethane varnished side of the screen. Follow the instructions on the container. To clean off the knotting and the Profilm, methylated spirit is required (this applies also to an unvarnished Profilm, as you would use for printing on paper). Soak some newspapers in meths and lay the screen on them. Place another pad of meths-sodden newspapers inside the screen. Leave for ten minutes or so to soften the knotting and then rub the screen clean with meths and a clean rag. You may need to repeat this.

Registering several colours

As with a lino cut, where you have a block for each colour, a silk screen design in several colours requires a separate screen of the same size for each colour. (Check back to page 112 for how to sort out the key colour).

Complete the screen for the key colour. Tape (or pin) some test fabric to the table. On this take a print of the key colour. Before you lift the screen away from the print mark all round its edges on the fabric. Remove the screen and clean it up.

Place the new blank screen for the second colour exactly inside the drawn rectangle. Trace from the print of the first key colour (which you can easily see through the mesh) those areas where the second colour will come. Make the screen stencil by whichever method you wish and repeat this procedure for additional colour screens.

If you are printing a multicolour design that is not in repeat all over a fabric but is a single print, like the apron in the photograph on page 118, first attach the material to the table. Next, ascertain where you must place the screen of the key colour in relation to the piece of cloth or fabric shapes. Draw accurately around the

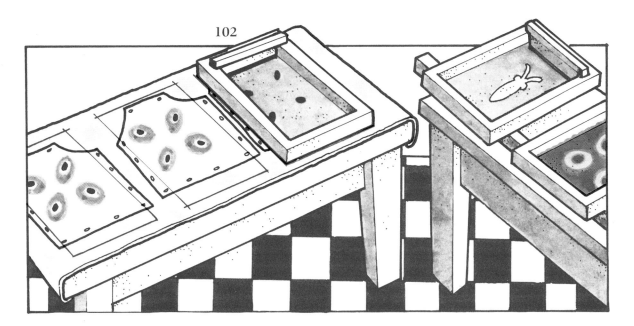

102

outer edge of the frame with tailor's chalk for each print. It does not matter if these drawn rectangles are partly on the cloth and partly on the table.

Make sure you have ample space to put the screens down in between printing them. Arrange a side table with a suitable length of wood on which to prop up all the different colour screens. Decide in which order the colours are to be printed – it does not necessarily follow that the key screen is printed first. Sometimes the order of printing is governed by deliberate overprinting. A yellow may have to follow a red so that a good orange is produced, or you may need to use the screen which prints an outline around the design last of all. This kind of thing should be sorted out in experimental test prints rather than taking chances with your final material. Fig. 102 shows a working arrangement for printing a three-colour design.

Take all the prints of the first colour placing the screen frame carefully inside the chalked rectangle each time. Lay that screen on the side table. Allow the printed dye a minute or two to soak into the fabric. You don't want it to offset on the underside of the next screen. Accurately position the second colour screen inside each of the drawn rectangles for each print. Other colours follow on in the same way. Clean up all the screens and squeegees as soon as the printing is completed.

Registering a repeating pattern
The same principles as outlined in Chapter 3 apply to a screen

102 This is the ideal working arrangement for printing a three-colour design; fabric in place on one table and the screens in readiness on another.

printed all-over fabric design. With a screen of the suggested size (the maximum design area is 50cm × 40cm [20in × 16in]) you can print a length of 90cm (36in) wide fabric by printing two rows of the repeat, one row lined up along the bottom edge of the cloth, the other along the top edge. Each repeat can be as wide as 40cm (16in) and should be 32.5cm (17in) deep. Thus, two prints across the width of the fabric will produce an all-over pattern of 87cm (34in), leaving 15mm ($\frac{1}{2}$in) unprinted at each selvedge. A single repeat print of this size may contain a number of motifs, flowers, for instance, themselves arranged in a repeating pattern (see fig. 103).

First tape the cloth to the table or pin it out on the backcloth. A piece of cloth the same length as the table should be attached to the tabletop on all four sides as usual. If you want to print a piece of cloth that is longer than the printing table use a backcloth and the pinning method described earlier. (The backcloth should be wider than the fabric.) After you have pressed it, you must roll the fabric to be printed round a cardboard tube. This roll is placed on a chair or small table at the right-hand end of the printing table; a block of wood will prevent it rolling off by accident.

At the other end of the table fix up a clothes horse or a system of chair backs over which you can drape the printed portion of the fabric. Think carefully about this arrangement because the fabric will be wet with dye at this stage, and could so easily smear.

Unroll a complete table length of the material and pin it to the

103 *A repeating arrangement of flowers on the screen is used in repeat for an all-over fabric design.*

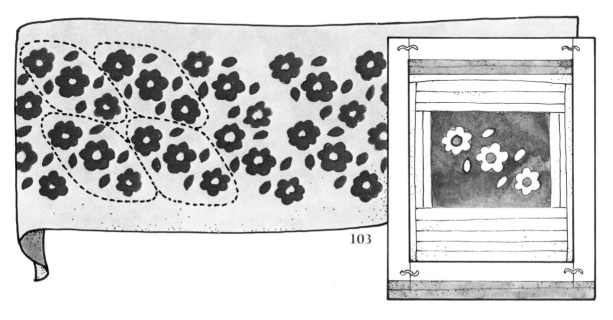

103

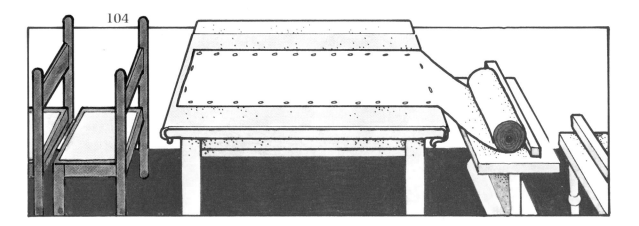

backcloth. Pin securely across the width of the fabric at the righthand end of the table too. Position the fabric 15cm (6in) in from the bottom edge of the table. On a table 120cm (48in) wide this will leave another 15cm along the top edge. Fig. 104 shows the ideal arrangement for printing table and chairs to carry the printed fabric.

At the extreme left-hand end of the table lay your paper design on the fabric so that the bottom edge of the repeat runs parallel to, but 15mm ($\frac{1}{2}$in) from, the fabric selvedge. Fix the design to the fabric with sticky tape to hold it in place temporarily. Place the screen, without any dye in it, aligning the stencil on top of the paper design. In the case of a design in two or more colours use the key screen for this.

Stick a short length of masking tape on the table, its upper edge lining up with the bottom outside edge of the screen frame. Measure the distance from the edge of the table to the upper edge of this piece of tape. (It is all right to move the screen.) Mark this distance at points all along the table. Now stick down a long piece of tape so that its lower edge runs along the marked distance.

Remove the first short piece of tape. Reposition the screen exactly over the design. The frame will now cover the masking tape. On the tape mark with a felt pen the outside edges of the sides of the screen. If the repeats are immediately adjacent, these screen edge markers on the masking tape will overlap. If the repeats are spaced out and there is unprinted fabric between them, they may not. However, to make things clearer, measure out and mark alternate screen positions in a different colour all along the tape. For a border, as on the daffodil curtain, that is all the marking needed as only half the width of the cloth is printed. Before each print (this applies to each colour too) the screen frame is carefully lined up between the appropriate two markers with

104 *Arrange the printing table, chairs to carry the fabric and the roll of cloth as shown here when printing a fabric length.*

the outside lower edge of the frame lying along the bottom edge of the tape.

For an all-over pattern as opposed to a border, mark the screen placings in the same way along the top edge of the table using the top end of the screen frame. You may like to develop a design in which the screen is turned round after printing the bottom line of repeats and printed 'upside down' along the top edge of the fabric creating new shapes. Here the bottom edge of the screen frame sets out the registration system at either side of the table.

The method for marking repeats is illustrated in fig. 105.

Print alternate repeats along the table; let the dye dry off for a minute or two and return to print in the gaps. This avoids prints offsetting on the back of the screen. Should there be persistent trouble with offsetting – perhaps a certain fabric takes a long time to absorb the dye – try using a hair dryer. Alternatively, cover the still damp, printed repeats with clean newspaper as you take the next print.

For a length of fabric which is longer than the table you must make an additional reference marker. When you take the last extreme right-hand print (or prints, if you're doing an all-over pattern) do not lift the screen away from the fabric as usual. Whilst it is still in the printing position, lightly chalk lines on to the cloth along either side of the frame. Do this also on either side of a screen being printed along the top edge of the table. Then remove the screen, unpin the printed cloth and pull it on carefully to drape over the chair backs. The chalked lines which show where the screen lays are lined up to coincide exactly with the

105 *When using a screen 'upside down' to print an all-over design, mark the registration as shown here.*

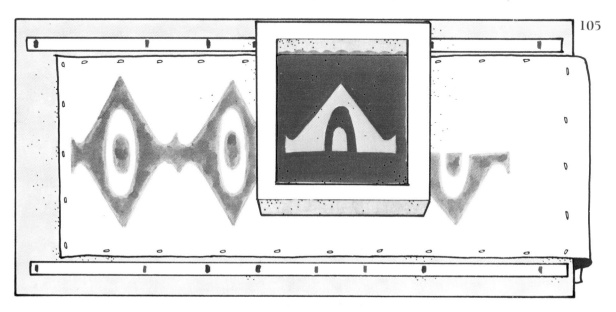

105

corresponding lines of the first left-hand screen position as the
new length of cloth is pinned out (see fig. 106). Thus you can
continue printing an uninterrupted repeating pattern.

It is easier to print an all-over pattern with a large screen than
with a small one. Commerical printers use big screens which cover
the entire width of the fabric. The fewer joins there are between
repeats the less chance there is of error. However, it is possible, if
somewhat laborious, to print an all-over pattern using a small
screen. First you must establish a grid for positioning each print so
that the all-over pattern flows freely.

106

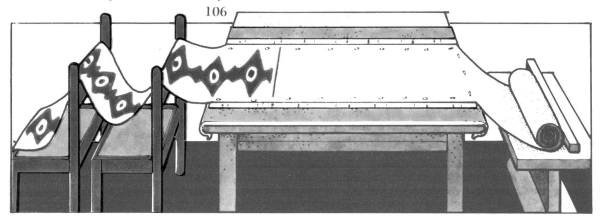

Draw out the motif and enclose it in a rectangle. Your final
printed pattern can be composed of a single motif per repeat or a
group of smaller motifs, themselves in repeat, filling the screen.
The drawn rectangle represents the size of the repeat, so if you
want a densely printed effect the lines of the rectangle will be
very close to the motif; if you want the motifs more spread out,
surrounded by blank, unprinted areas, draw the rectangle further
away from the motif.

The depth of the repeat rectangle should divide evenly into the
width of the cloth. Make some tracings of the motif and the
rectangle and, as shown in fig. 107, butt them up against one
another to see the all-over effect. Extending each of the sides of
the surrounding rectangle makes this much easier to do accurately.
(Refer to pages 91-92 for repeat pattern ideas.) Having settled on
the repeating arrangement make the screen stencil.

Mark out the fabric with the repeat grid (page 156). Fasten the
paper design (or a tracing) on the fabric in the correct position
inside a rectangle of the grid. Line up the screen stencil over the
paper design, and on the sides of the screen frame mark in felt pen
where the grid lines come (see fig. 108). To make each print you
must always align these drawn lines with the grid lines on the
cloth.

*106 Mark the fabric also when printing
a length of fabric longer than the table.*

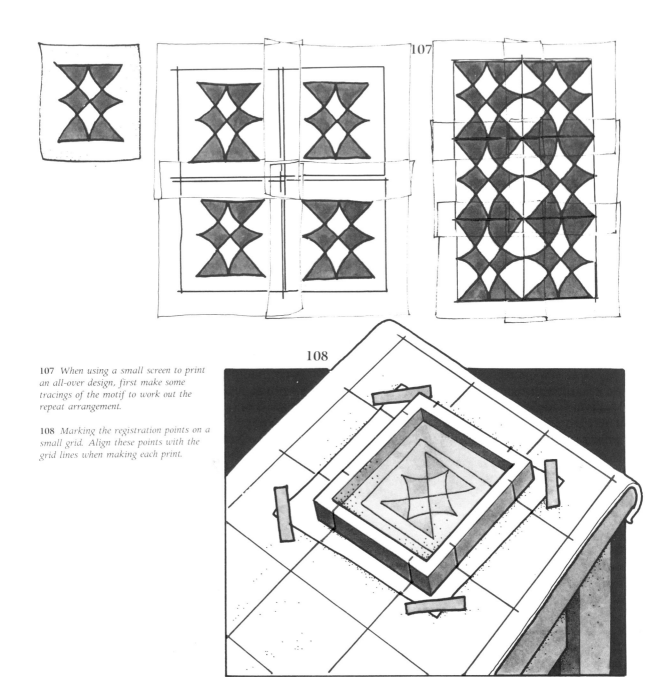

107 *When using a small screen to print an all-over design, first make some tracings of the motif to work out the repeat arrangement.*

108 *Marking the registration points on a small grid. Align these points with the grid lines when making each print.*

Rather annoyingly, the dye paste which doggedly refuses to dry when printed on the fabric shows a tendency to dry up in the screen, especially in warm conditions. To prevent this stretch a cloth, dampened with cold water (not dripping), over the entire screen when the screen is not in use between prints.

Never forget to heat-fix the dye to make it fast.

Chapter 7
Simple and Fun

Simple and fun

These unusual methods of decorating fabrics are quick to do and very entertaining. None of them requires special equipment so they are well suited to children, although adult supervision is recommended.

Transfer rubbings

Here is an intriguing technique – you can actually transfer a photograph or a drawing from a magazine on to cloth. Use it on clothing – it is especially good for decorating plain T-shirts – or things like shoe bags, but whatever you choose, it should be light coloured or white as the transferred image will be delicate. A transfer rubbing will withstand gentle hand washing. All you need is a modicum of patience, some white spirit and your chosen picture, preferably one taken from an inexpensive colour magazine rather than better quality 'glossy' publications.

First do a small test on a piece of the fabric – perhaps inside the hem or along the seam allowance – to see if your type of picture will work. On a board with a smooth, flat surface, tack or staple the cloth flat. Cut roughly round another picture in the same magazine and place it on some newspaper. Thoroughly drench it with white spirit and leave it to soak for about three minutes. This softens the ink with which the picture is printed.

Now lay the test picture, face down, on the test fabric and pin it in place along the top edge. With the handle of a spoon or a knife, rub firmly and persistently all over part of the back of the picture. Peel a corner back to see how it is coming along; being pinned it will return to its correct position. If the image is being transferred continue rubbing over the entire picture. If no image at all is being deposited on the cloth try either an alternative solvent – methylated spirit or lighter fuel – or a different magazine. If you still have no luck choose another fabric.

When you are satisfied with the results, start on your finished item. If you want part of an image, say only the face out of a full figure, try fading it out round the edges by rubbing less hard.

Painting on fabric

You can paint straight on to cloth with fabric dye paste (like Dylon Colorfun Fabric Paint). Ordinary cold water dye – the type in which you immerse an article – is far too liquid to control as a painting medium on cloth; it will seep in all directions. Artists' acrylic paints may be used but, because they make the cloth rather stiff they are best used on materials like canvas or thick denim.

Stretch the washed garment or piece of cloth out and pin it on a flat board. Slide a piece of card inside things like socks or the legs of jeans to stop the colour going through on to the other side. Stuff sneakers or other fabric shoes with newspaper.

Draw the design on to the fabric using ordinary chalk or tailor's chalk, and then paint in each section. As when painting with watercolour or poster paints, you wash the brush well and dry it off on a rag between different colours. The nature of the design really dictates the kind of brush to use – a small watercolour brush is best for detailed work on clothing, larger oil painting brushes or even a sponge for bigger areas as on a wall hanging.

Fabric dye paste colours are transparent, excluding white, so the colour of the fabric will clearly influence the painted colours. If you want to paint a light, bright colour like yellow on a navy blue background it is necessary first to apply a coat of white. Let this dry before painting over the yellow. When you have finished your design wash the brushes well in water. Let the painted fabric hang up to dry and then heat fix it for washability (see the instructions on the dye paste jar). Acrylic paint needs no such fixing. It will stand up to careful hand washing. You can't iron shoes to heat fix the dye – but then you're not likely to wash them.

Try adding painted decoration to patterned fabric. Pick out, in new dye colours, certain flowers on a floral patterned dress or blouse; amuse yourself by colouring in just some of the spaces on a striped or gingham curtain or the cuffs and collar of a checked shirt.

Marbled patterns

For a technique as simple as this one, the results are quite dramatic. You have probably seen marble patterning on the endpapers and page edges of the old books and ledgers. The same method of decorating can also be employed on fabric as well as paper. Try it out first on some sheets of paper and then with some smallish cloth articles like ribbons or handkerchieves. The size of the piece of paper or fabric you can marble successfully is governed by the size of the container you have to use. You want a large, shallow area of water, so utilise something like a

photographic developing tray or a big bowl. You could, providing
there are no objections, use the bath.

You will require some fabric printing ink (this must be oil-
based, see page 76), some white spirit, small jars and spoons or
sticks for colour mixing. Make sure too that there is a good,
uncluttered flat space, covered with clean, unprinted newsprint or
shelf paper, on which you can lay the paper and fabric to dry as
soon as you have finished marbling each piece.

Fill the receptacle with cold water. Put a small amount of
printing ink into one of the jars and mix it with a little white
spirit until it is a creamy consistency. In one of the other small
containers similarly dilute a different colour. Now, using a
mixing spoon or stick, drip a little of the first colour on to the
water. It should float, spreading out over the surface. This is
because the oil in the printing ink and the water in the bowl will
not amalgamate. If the colour spreads immediately over the
water's surface, more or less disappearing, the ink mixture is too
liquid and you must add more printing ink. On the other hand, if
the blob of colour sinks instantly the mixture is too thick, so add
some more white spirit.

When you have achieved the right consistancy drop in some of
the second colour too and stir the water around very gently. This
will cause wierd, swirling patterns to appear. Don't keep messing
them about because the patterns will then tend to disintegrate.
Carefully place a sheet of paper on to the surface of the water, not
pushing it under but letting it float for a second. Then peel the
paper away from the water. The paper will have lifted the marbled
pattern intact off the surface of the water. Lay it down in the
drying area.

You will have to keep topping up the amount of diluted
printing ink on the water. Try out some new combinations of
colours. After you have experimented with pieces of paper, have a
go at marble-patterning a handkerchief. Be careful when placing it
on the surface of the water to let go completely, just for a second,
before you lift it off. If you neglect doing this you will get a blank
patch where your fingers were holding on.

Ribbons can be marbled in sections. Let the first part of the
length down on to the water. gradually lift away the end that is
done, letting a new piece flop gently down on to the surface. (See
fig. 109.) Use marbled ribbon as an attractive trimming or binding
on a garment or as an edging for curtains, bedspreads, etc.
Children may like to make short pieces into hairbands. This type
of patterning is very much suited to floaty silk scarves. Try
joining several together to make an evening top or a shawl.

Always leave the marbled pieces flat to dry out completely. The
ink requires no fixing process. Clean up bowls with white spirit

109 *Coloured printing inks floating on water produce lovely marbled patterns. Let the fabric drop gently on to the water so that the ink is not disturbed too greatly.*

followed by a good wash with hot water and scouring powder.

Wash marbled patterned fabrics carefully by hand in mild soap and lukewarm water.

Bleach craft

A design is usually created by adding coloured shapes or patterns to a white or light coloured background. With bleach you work the other way round – you remove shapes and patterns from a coloured background, producing a design in white or a light colour. Many of the techniques already discussed can be used for this reversal process, and ordinary household bleach is suitable.

Before you start, however, there are three important points to remember. First, neat bleach is dangerous so children should be well supervised. You must take care to avoid getting it on the skin, particularly the eyes and face. Should this happen wash it off immediately with lots of cold water. The second point is that strong, undiluted bleach is harmful to many fabrics because it rots the fibres, so use a mixture of water and bleach. You want it to be as mild as possible but still, of course, effective. The proportion of five parts of water to one part of household bleach is recommended, but it is impossible to state a precise ratio because the various makes of bleach are of differing strength. Thirdly, do not mix bleach with other cleaning agents such as powders as sometimes dangerous fumes result. Bear this in mind when you are clearing up after a dyeing and bleaching session.

Cotton is the best cloth to use for bleach techniques. Dygon colour and stain remover may be used as an alternative to bleach. It is suitable for cotton and for fabrics made with lots of other fibres – see the details on the container.

Test the material first to see if it will, in fact, bleach. Some dyes cannot be removed; some will bleach out only partially, leaving not white but a paler version of the original colour. Most home-dyed fabrics will bleach successfully. On a bought, ready-coloured piece of cloth or a garment try out the technique on a small area where it willl not show to check the effect of the bleach.

Apply a spot or two of dilute bleach and leave it for five minutes or so. You will be able to see if it is going to work or not. If the area is turning lighter wash or sponge off the bleach with water. This is the procedure whichever method of application you now adopt.

It is a good idea to cover the table first with a sheet of plastic to protect it. (Cover yourslef with an overall too.) Lay some clean, unprinted paper on the plastic and then place the washed and ironed fabric on that. Any double-sided article should have a piece of card placed inside it to save the underside from the bleach.

Try drawing and painting with the dilute bleach first. As bleach is inclined to rot bristles use only old or cheap brushes. A dip pen or a stick are also very suitable; you can both draw and write with them. The bleach is extremely liquid so it will creep along the threads of the fabric, spreading each applied mark. The amount of spreading that takes place depends upon the thickness of the threads and the closeness of the weave. Draw, write or paint the bleach on to the cloth, leave it and wash off as explained above.

Try out a reverse form of tie-dye. First you dye the fabric, select a strong colour so that you will get a good contrast. Tie, knot or peg it in any of the ways suggested in Chapter 2. Immerse the piece either in a mixture of five parts of water to one part of bleach or use Dygon. With Dygon it is necessary to soak and then simmer the fabric so do follow the instructions given with the product. Rinse the piece of cloth and undo it to find a dark-coloured tie-dye pattern on a light-coloured cloth. The colour has been stripped from the background but retained in the tied sections.

Several of the block printing methods discussed in Chapter 4 will work to give a reverse design using liquid bleach. The material from which the block is made must be capable of absorbing the bleach to some extent. Pipecleaner and felt blocks, vegetables and corks may be used.

However, you can mix the bleach into a paste, making it much more versatile. Then it can be used with a variety of relief printing blocks, with stencils and silk screen. You may also prefer to paint with the thickened version too. You will need some Manutex, which is a dye thickening substance that you can buy from a craft supplier. Mix some with a little water into a stiff paste. Leave it to stand for at least a half-hour and then add to it a slightly more concentrated dilution (four parts of water to one of bleach). Stir it thoroughly. This mixture should be applied quite liberally to the cloth, using whichever method you choose. Leave it for awhile to loosen the dye colour and then rinse it off.

This sort of technique is known commercially as the discharge process. When it was first used only a lighter coloured or white design could be obtained, as with home bleach craft. Nowadays printers can add certain dyes to the discharge paste which are not themselves affected by the discharging substance. Consequently as one colour is stripped another colour is simultaneously applied.

Mistakes – and how to remedy them

When you are using any liquid colouring agent, do take the precaution of holding a rag under your brush, or whatever implement you're working with, to catch any stray drips. But what do you do if you do get an accidental blob of colour on your work? Often it is quite feasible to alter the design so that you can rearrange the motifs in a new way and the mistake is concealed or even turned to your advantage. Alternatively, you can sometimes deliberately make it into something like a passing bird or butterfly or let it become part of a general textured background by adding lots more similar blobs.

If all that is out of the question consider the following suggestions:

Splashes of liquid dye can be removed from a white fabric with Dygon (follow the manufacturer's instructions) or diluted household bleach. Don't use concentrated bleach as it may rot the fabric.

An unwanted mark of fabric dye paste can be removed if you act fast. Sponge the area first with cold water, follow that by washing it well with detergent powder and a little hot water and then rinse it. An old toothbrush may be handy here, used as shown in fig. 110. Don't attempt to print or paint the place while it is still damp.

Accidental spots or finger marks in fabric printing ink can be removed by the swift application of some white spirit on a clean rag. Keep replacing the rag, or else you will spread a diluted version of the colour over the cloth. When removing printing ink or fabric dye paste errors, cover the adjacent design area with a piece of card so that it is not affected.

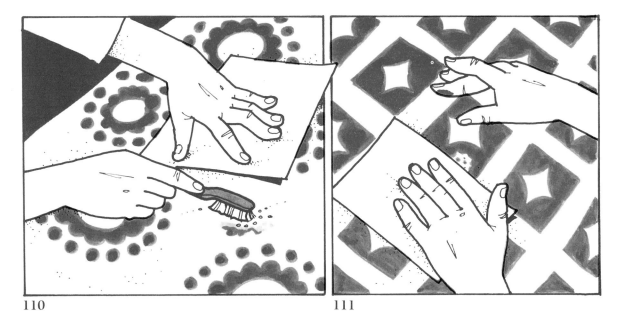

110   111

To do the reverse, that is, to fill in with colour an unwanted
blank spot on a print do not use a brush. This will deposit a
thicker layer of dye paste or printing ink thus making the repair
look a darker colour. Instead, pick up a little ink on the end of
your finger and lightly dab it over the unprinted part. If, for
example, you are patching up what should be a straight edge of a
shape, mask the unprinted cloth where necessary, see fig. 111.

110 *Removing an unwanted spot of dye
paste with an old toothbrush.*

111 *Masking the unprinted cloth with
paper when touching up a straight
printed edge.*

Useful Addresses

Dryad Ltd., P.O. Box 38, Northgates, Leicester, LE1 9BU, can supply many exciting craft materials. They have a comprehensive catalogue and mail order service.

Dylon Ltd., manufacture a wide range of dyes and fabric paints available from most department and chain stores. Contact their Consumer Advice Bureau, Dylon International Ltd., Lower Sydenham, London SE26 5HD, for stockists nearest you and if you have any questions concerning the use of their products.

Yately Industries, Mill Lane, Yately, nr. Camberley, Surrey, produce and sell a wide range of excellent hand block printed articles, such as those shown on page 79, from their shop at the preceding address. Write to them at that address to arrange guided tours of the workshops (Tuesday, Wednesday and Thursday only). Illustrated talks for classes and interested groups may also be arranged by letter.

Acknowledgements

The author would like to thank the following people for their help in printing, dyeing and making the projects in this book: Susan Bader, Jane Callender, Ethne Clarke, Frances Diplock, Nicky Marsh and Dylon Ltd.

Line artwork by Terry Burton.

Endpapers in New England design by Juliet Glynn Smith.
© 1976 Hunkydory Designs Limited

Pictures
Mike Cooper: p. 23.
Di Lewis: all other colour photographs.
Victoria and Albert Museum: pp. 14, 54, 65, 69, 76, 106.

Index